What Will I Be

What Will I Be

American Music and Cold War Identity

PHILIP M. GENTRY

OXFORD
UNIVERSITY PRESS

Oxford University Press is a department of the University of Oxford. It furthers
the University's objective of excellence in research, scholarship, and education
by publishing worldwide. Oxford is a registered trade mark of Oxford University
Press in the UK and certain other countries.

Published in the United States of America by Oxford University Press
198 Madison Avenue, New York, NY 10016, United States of America.

Library of Congress Cataloging-in-Publication Data
Names: Gentry, Philip M., author.
Title: What will I be : American music and Cold War identity / Philip M. Gentry.
Description: New York : Oxford University Press, 2017.
Identifiers: LCCN 2017005803 | ISBN 9780190299590 (hardcover) |
ISBN 9780190299606 (updf) | ISBN 9780190299613 (epub)
Subjects: LCSH: Music—Political aspects—United States—History—20th century. |
Music—Social aspects—United States—History—20th century. |
Cold War—Social aspects—United States. | Music and identity politics.
Classification: LCC ML3917.U6 G46 2017 | DDC 306.4/84240973—dc23
LC record available at https://lccn.loc.gov/2017005803

This volume is published with the generous support of the AMS 75 PAYS Endowment of the
American Musicological Society, funded in part by the National Endowment for the Humanities
and the Andrew W. Mellon Foundation.

9 8 7 6 5 4 3 2 1

Printed by Sheridan Books, Inc., United States of America

CONTENTS

ACKNOWLEDGMENTS

Major research for this book was accomplished thanks to the institutional support and library holdings of the University of California, Los Angeles; the College of William and Mary; and the University of Delaware. Further archival research was performed at the Library of Congress's Manuscript and Music and Performing Arts divisions, Northwestern University's McCormick Library of Special Collections, the Getty Research Institute, and the University of Pennsylvania's Van Pelt Library. A small portion of chapter 3 was published in a special issue of *American Music Review* edited by Elizabeth Keenan, and a portion of chapter 5 was published in the French journal *Tacet*. Suzanne Ryan and several anonymous reviewers for Oxford University Press provided generous and invaluable feedback for the present manuscript.

I first wrote about John Cage under the guidance of Henry Abelove, and in a more musicological context with Jane Alden, both of whom are inspiring role models and key members of the special intellectual climate of Wesleyan University. A seminar with Georgiary McElveen inspired my first work on R&B vocal music during my short time at Brandeis. At UCLA, Robert Fink advised the dissertation that is the source of some material in this book, and since then I have more or less done my best to live my musicological life by his intellectual example. Timothy Taylor's suggestion at my dissertation defense that I think more historically about identity proved key in shaping the new direction of my research. Sue-Ellen Case, Tamara Levitz, Raymond Knapp, and Mitchell Morris all contributed in substantive ways to this project, and with the dream team of Susan McClary, Robert Walser, Elizabeth Le Guin, and the late Philip Brett created an inspiring and unique graduate program. Elizabeth Morgan, Marcie Ray, Des Harmon, Eric Wang, and Ross Fenimore were an exemplary graduate cohort, and I learned so much from them and all of my classmates—too many and amazing to name here. The interdisciplinary Center for Performance Studies at UCLA provided a crucial environment to me, especially with chances to study with Marta Savigliano, Sue-Ellen Case, and Susan Leigh Foster, and I'm particularly thankful to Nicole Eschen for her interdisciplinary friendship and advice.

Many individual parts of this book began their lives as conference papers at the Society for American Music, my primary disciplinary home and a wonderful source of scholarly camaraderie. Kariann Goldschmitt, Ryan Banagale, Drew Massey, Ryan Dohoney, Marianna Ritchey, Stephan Pennington, Ben Piekut, and Elizabeth Morgan all read parts of this project during the year and provided very helpful feedback. I should also thank generally the many people whose contributions to my research have occurred through the medium of Twitter and in reading my blog.

The University of Delaware has been a wonderful place to work during much of the writing of this book, particularly thanks to my partners in musicological crime, Russell Murray and Maria Purciello. For the last decade, Philadelphia has been my adopted home, and has been a thriving intellectual environment for myself and my family. It's hard to properly acknowledge how my family has shaped this project beyond a simple list: my mother, who taught me how to write; my late father, who would have dearly loved to see this finished project; my sister Katy and my sister-in-law Anne; my two children who are very much the center of my life, Wilfred and Amelia. And most of all, my wife Mary Peacock, with whom I have shared the entirety of adult life, and to whom I owe everything.

What Will I Be

Introduction — Music and Identity

A Postwar Genealogy

The biggest hit of 1949 was a languid country waltz. A contemporary reviewer described it as "without frill or furbelow, the plaintive cry of a girl who at a mountain dance introduces her best beau to her best friend and promptly loses him."[1]

I was dancing with my darling to the Tennessee Waltz
When an old friend I happened to see
I introduced her to my loved one and while they were dancing
My friend stole my sweetheart from me

I remember the night and the Tennessee Waltz
Now I know just how much I have lost
Yes, I lost my little darling on the night they were playing

Patti Page's "The Tennessee Waltz," a pop cover of Pee Wee King's 1948 country release, wears its simplicity on its sleeve. Introduced by a muted trumpet, the song gently rocks in triple meter. The accompanying vocal harmony is unadorned, and Page downplays both her native Oklahoman accent and her background in big band jazz singing. Despite the regional specificity of its country origin and title, the performance aspires to be as unmarked as possible, hoping that the widest possible audience might identify with its small story of love and loss.

The enormous success of Page's "Tennessee Waltz" in prompting a feeling of listener identification was the product not just of the abilities of its creators but also of a multitude of larger forces. For one, the song is an aural portrait of a simpler time, but is also indelibly marked by technological modernism. In addition to being one of the first hit songs released in the seven-inch 45 r.p.m. monaural format, "The Tennessee Waltz" was one of the first hit records to make systematic use of overdubbing. Page did not sing alone, or rather, she sang along with herself several times over. The three-part close harmony of the song is all provided by Page in multiple takes. Although not the first recording to use this trick, earlier examples had never been widely popular, and for many listeners, the sound of all-Page harmony was quite a novelty.[2] And yet, this novelty was not produced as seamlessly as it eventually sounded on record. The record industry was only just beginning to adopt magnetic tape and with it the ability to easily record and edit multiple takes, and the studio where Page recorded this song did not yet have this equipment. The multi-tracking, therefore, was produced in a manner both old-fashioned and also recklessly experimental: having already recorded the main melody, Page then shared a microphone with a record player, singing the accompaniment while the machine beside her sang the melody. The resulting song might have sounded like it was produced without "frill or furbelow," but in reality it was a tense mixture of nostalgic conservatism and technological bricolage.

In one of the few scholarly treatments of Patti Page, James Manheim compares her version of the "Tennessee Waltz" with the original country recording by Pee Wee King in 1948. Pointing out that King was extending the country-and-western idiom by utilizing the Tin Pan Alley AABA form, Manheim argues that this brought an unusual amount of dramatic tension to the original version, heightening the sense of loss and nostalgia implied in the lyrics. In the B section, the narrator turns from past-tense description to direct address: "now *you* know how much *you* have lost." In the latter version by Page, on the other hand, the tension of the B section is lessened by its familiarity in the pop idiom, and the direct address of the lyrics is rewritten in the first person: "Now *I* know how much *I* have lost." Manheim is blunt in his assessment: "Page's handlers eviscerated King's song musically, largely replacing experience with image. Page's 'Tennessee Waltz' was a family-album snapshot, an ideal offering in the new music industry that merchandised recorded images instead of recorded concerts."[3]

What exactly does it mean for a song to produce an "image"? It's hard not to miss the gendered nature of Manheim's critique, but it does tell us something about the changing nature of popular music and its relationship with listeners. In any case, clearly Page's version of "Tennessee Waltz" hit much harder with the listening public than Pee Wee King's, and while popular approval does not grant aesthetic legitimacy, it also should not negate it. "Tennessee Waltz" became something of an anthem over the next few years, and if it is difficult to precisely label the object of its nostalgia—former lovers? Old homes? Simpler times?—a sense of communal feeling is palpable. This is one of the odd attractions of its primitive multitracking. With a chorus of like-sounding Patti Pages singing the simple melody together, there is a certain sense of timelessness evoked, perhaps even of solidarity not unlike the "mass songs" of the 1930s, or the popularity of Mitch Miller's *Sing Along with Mitch* television specials a decade later. Even, perhaps, the singing of hymns, many of which, at least in the Baptist and Methodist traditions of Page's childhood, would have been in a slow three-quarter or six-eight time. If the "Tennessee Waltz" was an image—perhaps more specifically, a portrait—it seems to have been a portrait in which many Americans saw themselves. Their sense of identification with the song, we might say, was on an individual level, but also on a group level.

The tension contained within "The Tennessee Waltz" stages some of the great cultural transformations that occurred in the United States after

World War II. The social dislocations and migrations of the two previous decades, through famine and war, had created a situation in which the question of who one's self ought to be in relation to others was at the forefront of the popular imagination. The simplicity of the song belies its anxiety, and the immense resonance of "now I know how much I have lost." And seemingly in contradiction to the experimental modernism of the recording process, the simplicity speaks to a newfound sense of what one might later call "authenticity."

Authentic to what? Page was one of a generation of "girl singers" whose careers had begun in midwestern dance bands. Thrust now into the Tin Pan Alley commercial song tradition, she and her cohort spoke especially to the experience of assimilation and naturalization. As we will see, the rise of white middle-class suburbia was, on the one hand, an accumulation of power, but on the other, it was a process also imbued with loss, as long-standing social ties were severed. The seeming simplicity, even blandness, of Page's song, and the hundreds of other hits like it, was necessary precisely so as to include more citizens under the rubric of "white" than ever before, and it was a blandness that required an extraordinary amount of effort.

At the same time, elsewhere on the popular music charts, different kinds of selves were being articulated. The historian Michael T. Bertrand quotes Carl Perkins:

> There was an integration problem in this part of America, a pretty severe problem back then. But there was no [segregation] in music. When you walked up to an old '54 or '55 model Wurlitzer jukebox, it [didn't say] "Blue Suede Shoes," Carl Perkins, white, "Blueberry Hill," Fats Domino, black. No. There was no difference. Kids dance to Little Richard, Chuck Berry, Elvis. . . . Chuck Berry said to me one time, he said, "You know Carl, we might be doing as much with our music as our leaders are in Washington to bring down the barriers." He was right.[4]

As Perkins and Berry indicate, their musical performances, and those of Patti Page, were taking place alongside historic political movements that focused on questions of the self in relation to society. The postwar African American civil rights movement is the most famous, but alongside it came a series of legal challenges to combat discrimination on the basis of ancestry, leading to important Supreme Court victories in *Mendez v. Westminster School District* (1947) and *Hernandez v. Texas* (1954); the first modern gay rights organizations, Harry Hay and Rudi Gernreich's Mattachine Society, founded in 1949, and the Daughters of Bilitis founded in 1955; the stirrings of what would become known as second-wave feminism, conventionally thought to have begun with Betty Friedan's reporting on her own college reunion in 1957.

What is the relationship between these waves of new postwar political movements and the musical revolutions that seem to dovetail so neatly? The central argument of this book is that the cultural transformation at work here is more fundamentally the project of self-making called "identity." It is a project that is at once both psychological and sociological, a process by which an individual knows him or herself in relation to others in a specific historic moment.

Despite the widespread currency of this term, "identity" is a new phenomenon in the postwar era. As Timothy Taylor has pointed out, the very term was an innovation popularized by social scientists in the early 1950s, and was connected with new forms of consumer culture.[5] As such, it makes an important break with earlier notions of selfhood, be they more biological and nationalist notions of race, or moral notions of "character." As Taylor writes, imbricating identity in postwar capitalism, it is a "process of recognition and construction. It is not a natural condition."[6]

"Identity" gives rise to what we later have come to call "identity politics," the collective action on behalf of these newly articulated subjectivities. Similarly, music—performing, composing, organizing, listening, and so on—became a space, and perhaps the most important one, for collective articulations of self. From the mass-cultural pronouncements of Patti Page, to the subcultural stirrings of rhythm & blues, from the Broadway stage to the most obscure avant-garde provocations, musical performances took center stage in the new project of identity.

■

The term "identity" is perhaps the most challenging and politically fraught concept of the late twentieth century. Contained within such a simple and everyday word is a world of cultural work. In using it we lay contemporary claim to age-old philosophical speculation: Who am I? We similarly invoke the question of social allegiance: With whom do I share my lot? While these questions might be ages old, their answers are rooted in specific historic moments and in particular communities. The recent lineage of the term "identity" is surprising to many, but indeed, a simple graph courtesy of Google makes the point (figure 1.1).

Google tracks the appearance of words or phrases in the entirety of the Google Books database, about 5 million books published between 1800 and 2008.[7] The limitations of this particular data set and the tools provided by Google are duly noted, but the comparatively recent common usage of the term is quite clear.[8]

I will return in a moment to asking how this new rubric came about, but it is important at the outset to make the point that political and cultural organizing around a psychologized concept of identity tends to be structurally different from earlier ideas of race and self. This is not to say

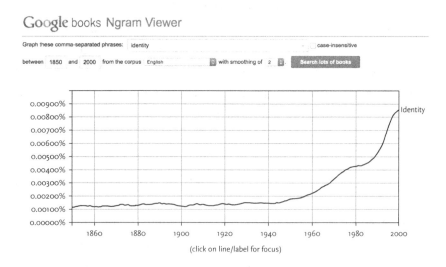

Figure 1.1 History of the term "Identity," 1860–2000.
Courtesy of Google.

there is no similarity in organizing around affinity groups before and after 1950; the National Association for the Advancement of Colored People (NAACP) was founded in 1909, after all, and remains an important force today. However, the conceptual shift is important, and in fact might help to explain why the NAACP was not at the forefront of some of the most important postwar political movements. The organization's legal department under Thurgood Marshall, largely a separate entity, was famously responsible for the landmark victory of *Brown v. Board of Education*, but the NAACP itself spent the late 1940s and early 1950s largely embroiled in protecting both the institution and the larger civil rights struggle from the persecutions of McCarthyism. A great deal of energy was spent in making sure that the various investigatory apparatuses of McCarthyism did not view membership in the NAACP as a red flag, and in disavowing relationships with more leftist activists such as Paul Robeson and the group's founder, W. E. B. DuBois. None of this was the fault of the organization, of course, and it is to the credit of its director, Walter White, that the NAACP managed to emerge from McCarthyism in better shape than many other liberal groups.

However, there did emerge a disjuncture between the older leadership of the NAACP and the new postwar generation. As is so often the case, musical taste reveals the gap. Walter White had been the director of the group since 1931, cutting his teeth on anti-lynching activism during the Great Depression. His own personal taste in music laid largely in the realm of classical music, and the organization promoted the careers of African American classical musicians. He particularly championed the career of African American conductor Dean Dixon, pushing for orchestras to consider him as a guest conductor, raising money for European tours, and even mailing notices of his concerts to Virgil Thomson.[9] In addition to supporting classical musicians such as Dixon, the organization promoted spirituals in the concertized tradition of the Fisk Jubilee Singers. In 1949, for example, they sponsored a recording of "Lift Every Voice and Sing" to be sold as a benefit. Roy Wilkins, then White's assistant, wrote to the musicians agreeing that "the rendition should be one of dignity and thankfulness. It is not a protest hymn and cannot be made such no matter what a recording group does to it."

Thus if the musical taste of the national NAACP could be generalized, it would be as an interest in an aesthetic of dignity and uplift. Popular music was treated with a great deal of suspicion. In 1949, the manager of the legendary vocal group the Ink Spots got in touch with the organization asking if the singers could be given some sort of formal citation for having broken color barriers in performance venues. Not knowing the group and worried about the moral standing of popular music, White was concerned that it was not an appropriate association for the NAACP. After some research he did agree to write a letter commending their successes, but did not make a public citation. In retrospect, of course, the smooth, urbane, and wildly successful music of the Ink Spots seems a no-brainer to us as a model of desegregationist sentiment, but for an older generation in the 1940s their music did not fit within a mold of racial uplift. The difference, I would argue, is the cultural work performed by the notion of identity.

To take another and more explicit example of this political and cultural shift, this time from the domain of intellectual history, the rise of identity is often seen to track the demise of the Old Left, with its emphasis on class-based labor organizing. McCarthyism is the political context of this moment, of course, and indeed we might think of McCarthyism as not just triggering a shift away from class-based politics but also embodying the earliest forms of identity politics. This was, at least, the argument of many intellectuals in the 1950s. As early as 1954, a group of left-leaning scholars assembled a faculty seminar at Columbia University on the subject of "political behavior," with a focus on McCarthyism in particular. Led by Daniel Bell, the distinguished group included such figures as Richard Hofstadter, David Riesman, Nathan Glazer, and Seymour Lipset. Contributions to this seminar were eventually published in 1955 as an essay collection titled *The New American Right*.[10] Bell saw the volume as an attempt to add a psychological element to more conventional political analysis, which he saw as overly rooted in eighteenth- and nineteenth-century historical issues. McCarthyism, Bell argued, could not be adequately explained in traditional terms, given that it was in some respects an "irrational" social movement: whatever danger organized communism might have once posed to the United States, the movement had largely been stamped out of existence by the time of McCarthy's infamous 1949 speech claiming communist subversion in the State Department. Why, then, the "intense emotional heat" of McCarthyism?[11]

The answer for Bell came in the collection's central essay, Richard Hofstadter's "The Pseudo-Conservative Revolt." Hofstadter argued that one of the salient features of the new right-wing movement was that pervasive status anxiety characterized not just an elite group clinging on to power but also formerly marginalized groups now moving up in society. Case in point were the former Coughlinites and ethnic Catholics who were thought to make up the base of McCarthy's support, and who were turning away from previous allegiance to radical populist movements. Chapter 3 will discuss (and critique) this movement in more detail, but suffice it to say that these third-generation immigrants had long been marginalized along religious and ethnic lines. Now that they themselves had entered the middle-class establishment, their politics melded seemingly contradictory elements: a simultaneous desire for, and a suspicion of, authority. Thus the label "pseudo-conservative," which Hofstadter drew from Theodor Adorno's *The Authoritarian Personality* (1950), implying that although this new force in American politics aligned itself with traditional conservatism, some of its positions were in fact quite radical, such as abolishing the income tax or withdrawing from the United Nations. Hofstadter's argument, however, is striking in both its tone and its use of psychoanalytic language:

> Pseudo-conservatism is among other things a disorder in relation to authority, characterized by an inability to find other modes for human relationship than those of more or less complete domination or submission. The pseudo-conservative always imagines himself to be dominated and imposed upon because he feels that he is not dominant, and knows of no other way of interpreting his position.[12]

Ironically, the *New American Right* authors, caught up in their assumption of basic irrationality, barely mention foreign policy or even a general

fear of communism as a rationale for McCarthyism. In an important critique of these arguments, the political scientist Michael Rogin framed
his own project as an attempt to understand this and other absences in
the social scientists' research, referring to it as the "myopia of a trauma-
tized intelligentsia."[13] Indeed, the *New American Right* was the product
of a liberal intellectual set that had suffered greatly during McCarthyism.
Unfortunately for the left, this trauma had far-reaching consequences. As
Rogin noted, at its heart the *New American Right* reads as anxious and
fearful, especially when it came to mass-based movements. If a dema-
gogue such as McCarthy could turn old-fashioned populism into a force
for conservatism, one reads between the lines, then perhaps populism
itself was suspect. Ironically, some of the greatest damage McCarthyism
caused the left was not the actual blacklisting but, rather, this fear of radical populism.

Generational gaps are nothing new in politics, but these show the
impact of three trends, all worth noting as they will resurface throughout
this book. Perhaps foremost, the examples given thus far all operate in the
larger international political context of the Cold War or, rather, perhaps
a tension between that context and a more hermetic, domestic sensibility.
For the past decade or so, there has been an ongoing trend in cultural history that reads a great deal of cultural work in the postwar era as indicative of a Cold War sensibility.[14] The historian Ann Douglas has put this
argument forward in a particularly cogent manner, arguing that rather
than adopting the terminology of literary analytical schools to periodize
the twentieth century—postmodernism, postcolonialism, and so on—we
ought to take as our starting point the major geopolitical conflict of the
century's second half.[15]

Her argument is not one of causality, but of synchronicity: the shape
and structure of the series of smaller "hot" military conflicts and larger
"cold" diplomatic struggles that made up the Cold War match neatly with
the shapes and structures of a large array of cultural works. The more
typical periodizations of literary theorists are easily subsumed within
the larger Cold War narrative: postmodernity is not only chronologi-
cally coterminous with the Cold War, but in its rejection of fixed truth it

formally aligns with Cold War espionage, with its "Pynchonesque, hyper-fictive scenario of agents, double agents, secret strategic weapons, forged document, and operational feints."[16] Postcolonialism, on the other hand, is "less comprehensively and less satisfactorily" aligned with the Cold War, but nevertheless aligns with the Cold War's geographical conception of a "Third World"—that is, those countries not specifically aligned with either American or Soviet interests—and marked by the often devastating military interventions by both superpowers. While acknowledging the U.S.–centric nature of a Cold War analysis, Douglas makes a powerful argument for putting the late twentieth century's largest military-political conflict at the center of our understanding of its culture.

For reasons both ideological and practical, musicologists have been swift to adopt the Cold War periodization.[17] Some early examples of a Cold War aesthetic were hard to miss: Martin Brody's diagnosis of Milton Babbitt's "Cold War Music Theory" long predated Ann Douglas's call to arms, perhaps because in addition to certain aesthetic qualities Brody elegantly formulates, Babbitt was quite clearly a literal member of the military-industrial complex, having served in secret government operations during World War II and collaborated in early developments of computer technologies in the 1950s and '60s.[18] Very little metaphorical reading is necessary in Babbitt's case to ally his music with the Cold War. More practically, the transformation of the Soviet Union and its satellite states in the late 1980s and early 1990s made it much easier for United States–based scholars to gain access to archival materials, resulting in such important projects as Peter Schmelz's work on late Soviet music critics, Andrea Bohlman's history of music and activism in Poland in the 1980s, and Danielle Fosler-Lussier's reappraisal of Bartok's legacy.[19] Furthermore, the declassification of documents in the United States has meant that as historical events gradually pass through the typical twenty-five-year waiting period, archival work on subjects such as cultural diplomacy has become more possible.[20] Similarly, Freedom of Information Act requests on historical figures such as Leonard Bernstein have been more easily granted in the post–Cold War era, lending new insights into the impact of domestic surveillance programs.[21]

Taken individually, these Cold War projects are enormously useful. However, as much as I respect these projects, and value some heuristics of a Cold War analysis, I begin to wonder if that search for global cultural coherence can sometimes erase important local particularities. Writing after, not during, the Cold War, I hope that our perspective on the borders enacted by that war can become somewhat more distanced and critical. In an important recent critique, Tamara Levitz has pointed out the ongoing borders created by the Cold War, even after their demise.[22] A historical study such as this one needs to pay tribute to the conceptual power of Cold War borders, but it needs to do so critically, and with awareness of their fragility.

McCarthyism is an excellent example of how the Cold War analysis can become overdetermined. Peter Schmelz, for example, speaks of McCarthyism as merely a "frequent metonym" of the American aspect of the Cold War.[23] He is not wrong that this usage is often the case, but I push back from that practice. It seems obvious that there is a relationship between McCarthyism and the Cold War, but how useful is it to emphasize that relationship? To be sure, the early Cold War provided Senator McCarthy with the tools he needed for political success, and it is not hard to find cultural work that resonates with larger geopolitical conflict. However, those resonances are in fact quite hazy and nonspecific in important ways. I would argue, for example, that Senator McCarthy was distinctly unconcerned with the realities of the Cold War in an international sense, as evidenced by his attacks on the State Department and the U.S. Army. Despite all evidence, communism was for McCarthy and his followers a particularly *domestic* threat. In many respects, this was the downfall of the Democratic Party in the 1952 elections—the party wrongly assumed that its toughness on foreign policy, especially in Korea, would assuage voters concerned with communism. Instead, the Republican Party's emphasis on domestic security, as fictional as threats to it were, resonated more successfully at the polls. For many individuals in the United States, it was local media representations of Cold War theater that mattered, not the war itself. And of course, to many other individuals, even those representations mattered little. Was the Cold

War narrative so all-powerful that it filtered down to every single act of cultural work?

This is not to say that isolationism is therefore an appropriate analysis. The early fifties are the beginning of modern globalization, as projects both imperial and corporate hastened the circulation of commodities around the globe, and as patterns of consumption reflected the transformation of many borders. The Cold War between the United States and the Soviet Union was certainly part of these transformations, but only one aspect of those stories. The somewhat hermetic domestic sensibility of McCarthyism is best understood not as actually isolationist but, within the larger framework of globalization, an example of culturalism that, as Arjun Appadurai writes, involved "the conscious mobilization of cultural differences in the service of a larger national or transational politics." [24]

Another conceptual change in racial formation went from biological to cultural, under the paradigm of "ethnicity." Michael Omi and Howard Winant have pointed out that the use of "ethnicity," which is to say the privileging of culture over biology, has passed through three paradigmatic phases in the twentieth century: in the 1920s and 1930s it was an insurgent, antiracist gesture; in the 1940s and 1950s it was part of a general liberal consensus; and then, after the mid-1960s, it became a neoconservative reaction against the civil rights movement.[25] This middle phase, when the ethnicity model had become the mainstream in social science but had not yet undergone a socially conservative transformation in the hands of writers like Daniel Moynihan, characterizes the historical moment under question. As Karen Brodkin describes it, "the word 'ethnicity' became a cornerstone of a new liberal consensus about the United States as a pluralist and democratic society."[26] As Omi and Winant later describe it, this cultural ideal helped create a situation in which the "rearticulation of collective black subjectivity" could give rise to a new form of politics.[27]

Another related trend was the psychologization of this cultural ideal. As I have argued elsewhere, the 1950s can generally be characterized by a widespread interest in popularized psychology.[28] Here, as in so much of the postwar era, there were important links to the war effort: as Nathan Hale has pointed out, during the war the U.S. military had adopted psychoanalysis on a wide scale as an administrative tool; returning home from the war, millions of Americans had experienced some form of psychoanalysis.[29] As Taylor and others, including the ethnomusicologist Timothy Rice, point out, it was at this moment that the psychologist Erik Erikson published his classic treatise *Childhood and Society* (1950).[30] Erikson is an intriguing figure to place at the center of this particular genealogy. Danish-born and of part-Jewish heritage, he ended up being raised in Germany and trained in Vienna with Anna Freud. Sigmund's youngest child, Anna Freud, was an expert in child psychology, and Erikson's attention was drawn to the development of children from earlier days.[31] As he wrote in *Childhood and Society*, "all peoples begin in their nurseries."[32]

Childhood and Society does not depart unduly from Freudian precepts, but Erikson does pay an interesting amount of attention to social processes. The book begins with a case study of a young Jewish boy whose parents have moved to a predominantly Gentile neighborhood. Forced to adjust to new surroundings, he must transform physical aggressiveness into intellectual temerity; after a series of misfortunes he develops severe epilepsy. Erikson draws from the introductory study his initial definition and theory of identity: "of being one's self, of being all right, and of being on the way to becoming what other people, at their kindest, take one to be."[33] He elaborates a system of "processes which govern us": those of the body, of the individual ego, and of social organization:

> The human being, at all times, from the first kick *in utero* to the last breath, is organized into groups of geographic and historical coherence: family, class community, nation. A human being, thus, is at all times an organism, an ego, and a member of a society and is involved in all three processes of organization. His body is exposed to pain and tension; his ego, to anxiety; and as a member of a society, he is susceptible to the panic emanating from his group.[34]

The book draws interestingly on postwar liberal anthropology in the Boasian tradition, especially the work of Margaret Mead, and several key sections draw upon the fieldwork of anthropologists working with Native

American communities. As Timothy Rice points out, a crucial division emerges over the course of Erikson's theories, a divide between a sense of self-identity on its own terms and a sense of identity as in one's relationship with a larger group that shares certain characteristics of self-identity, such as race or gender. In this respect, Erikson is in alignment with other social scientists of the day, even if the term "identity" was not yet widely deployed. In David Riesman's *The Lonely Crowd* (1950), for example, this division famously meant a tension between the "inner-direction" of steering according to your own values and the "outer-direction" that finds its highest value in getting along with others.[35]

The historian Christopher Shannon is one of the few scholars to have engaged in detail with Erikson's work and its implications for politics. From Shannon's perspective the identity concept "provided a model of selfhood appropriate to the midcentury triumph of the cultural revision of classical liberalism."[36] Shannon is, in fact, a pointed critic of the concept. For him, the creation of identity masks a deeper and unmarked consensus on what he terms "the instrumentalism of nature and society in the service of human liberation."[37] Liberation, here, is a condition of relentless experimentation, connected to a specifically American context figured by Erikson as rootless and transient. Whereas more tradition-bound societies experience specific "fears," the modern subject instead deals with nameless "anxiety." With traditional authority no longer a possibility in the wake of fascism, the only possible response to this anxiety is constant self-examination performed in the context of a medical-therapeutic relationship. This, Shannon argues, is not liberation, but merely the internalization of authority. It's crucial to note that Shannon's perspective is one of Roman Catholic conservatism, and he sees in this foundational moment of the identity concept a crisis that will erupt in the identity-politics movements of the 1960s. For him, countercultural movements organized around race, ethnicity, gender, and sexuality are structured along "micro fault lines" that inevitably lead to separatism and a much larger historical shift from tradition to modernity. I do not share Shannon's political viewpoints, but writing from outside the liberal tradition makes this critique particularly salient. Even if his ultimate solutions differ, his critique echoes, in fact, many critiques of identity politics from the left that worry about the abandonment of class-based politics.

Drawing upon Shannon, the historian Immanuel Wallerstein, and the ethnomusicologist Elizabeth Keenan, Timothy Taylor takes up the call to historicize identity. As part of a much larger study of difference and global-ization across several centuries, he is particularly concerned to tie identity to changing consumption practices after World War II. As Taylor points out, identity making is a "project" rooted in very specific social practices, rejecting any claims to universalized human nature: "Self-fashioning can thus be seen as a modern project in which selves are made out of one's relationship to one's Others, from one's identification with one's profes-sion, from one's relationship to production."[38] The concept of choice is crucial here, with many of these practices involving conscious agency on the part of actors, often in the realm of consumption. How we dress, what music we listen to, what food we eat—these are the conscious choices that have in recent decades, in particular social groups, become inextricably wound up with identity.

In several of these discussions, the concept of identity begins to bleed into the related world of identity politics, a term bearing a great deal of weight and anxiety. The *Oxford English Dictionary* (*OED*) only traces the phrase to 1979; it often seems to be a term owing its existence to its critics, as with "baroque" or "impressionism."[39] During debates on multicultural-ism in the 1980s and 1990s, it became a scorned target of conservative activists, while also often targeted from the left. This left critique could be important, as in the case of women-of-color critiques that offered up "intersectionality" as a more useful rubric; or less useful, as in the endless Marxist readings of identity politics as insufficiently committed to more supposedly broad-based class struggle. Either way, as Judith Halberstam has ruefully noted, by the turn of the millennium "identity politics has become the new 'essentialism,' a marker, in other words of some combina-tion of naiveté and narrowness that supposedly blocks more expansive and sophisticated projects."[40] Today, the discourse concerning "identity" and "identity politics" is perhaps more visible than ever before. Mainstream political debate made much of a "post-identity" moment in the election of Barack Obama in 2008, even as a short eight years later Hillary Clinton's 2016 presidential campaign was widely seen as mobilizing a more old-fashioned sense of identity politics, and her electoral loss has heightened a sense that the question of identity politics, wherever one may stand, is at the center of American political life.

The concept of identity politics certainly traces its roots especially to postwar social movements. Although the *OED* finds its aforementioned earliest use in a 1979 scholarly article on disability studies, most give credit to the famous and oft-anthologized Combahee River Collective Statement of 1977. A group of African American feminists organizing in the Boston area since 1974, the collective argued powerfully for rooting political struggle in the individual experience of structural oppression: "This focusing upon our own oppression is embodied in the concept of identity politics. We believe that the most profound and potentially most radical politics come directly out of our own identity, as opposed to working to end somebody else's oppression." [41] Reading the statement almost three decades after its authorship, it is hard not to notice that "identity politics" here reflects a thoroughly intersectional impulse, representing individualized experiences of race, gender, sexuality, and class. Nowhere to be found is an articulation of a politics in which rigid boundaries of one aspect of identity are pushed forward at the expense of others.

Recent work on identity politics, such as that being conducted by the Future of Minority Studies Research Project, has attempted to reclaim this liberatory heritage, and to take the conceptual space of identity as a uniquely powerful social location for social change.[42] Or, as Sarah Ahmed has put it more elegantly, "to rally around our particulars is to refuse to be led by those whose will has already been given general expression."[43] Academic discourse has also been revived by contemporary social movements, from Black Lives Matter to the so-called social justice warriors of the social media, who despite the condescending name bestowed upon them by critics both right and left, have brought unflinching protest politics to the fray.

This book hopes to join this conversation concerning the future of identity politics. My goal is that it will enrich the conversation and activism in two ways: by emphasizing both the historicization of identity and the performative nature of politics. To take the first, I refer to the fact that both scholarship and activism around identity show a persistent failure to not only acknowledge the recent nature of the term but also to examine how its particular formulation provides contour to its politics. Even the most developed and nuanced theories of identities have tended to ignore the question of history, even in explicitly political and cultural contexts.

For example, a recent collection on the subject of "music and identity politics" edited by Ian Biddle offers a comprehensive overview of several decade's worth of scholarship.[44] Organized in groups based on larger themes—"Gender and Sexuality," "Race," and "Social Identities"—the collection stretches back to include early modern Europe, and around the world from contemporary Indonesian pop music, to postwar Yiddish song, to Bartok, and much more. The essays, many of them quite well-known, were all previously published elsewhere, and so Biddle's act of curation is all the more striking. Biddle's introduction attempts to impose order by positing identity as a seemingly universal, or at least widespread, category of self-fashioning. He traces the emergence of the word to its Latin and middle French roots, and in the style of Raymond Williams, excavates its various transformations over time, from a medieval term denoting "sameness" to a post-Reformation ideal of "identity" as indicative of individual characteristics. Drawing upon Gilles Deleuze, he argues that "the logical complexity of 'identity' as political category already at work in its earliest deployment is brought into full view."[45]

This reading of "identity" as teleological, seemingly born centuries ago in the exact state that we find it today, is not the most historical reading, and I don't think it is the most politically useful valence, either. Later in the same introductory essay, Biddle more fully describes our recent inheritance of the term:

> On its own, the term identity, then, particularly in its theoretical or
> philosophical articulation, comes to us, at least for the most part,

via the German Idealists and their reading of Immanuel Kant and, before him, Gottfried Wilhelm Leibniz. Put simply, the German philosophical tradition makes its own claims to thinking uniquely about identity. . . . And yet, even here, the apparent "certainties" of the notion of identity are always already under constant attack from within: in the work of Friedrich Schelling for example . . . later thinkers such as Nietzsche, Bergson, and even Deleuze, Guattari and others . . . have found a countervailing tendency to critique the overreliance on dualistic thinking. . . . Nonetheless, the dominance of universalist notions of identity in the nineteenth-century German tradition has had a tangible influence on identity politics in the late twentieth-century, especially for those groups who sought to articulate something inalienable or "essential" in their identity.[46]

I present this genealogy not so much for its actual argument—and I don't wish to unduly criticize one work, as it is representative of a great deal of similar scholarship—as it brings me to the other area of emphasis in which this book hopes to intervene. In addition to the lack of historicity, there is the other problem: suddenly this vital political work of the post-war era, largely accomplished by people of color and others working from a space of oppression, is being traced not to their own work but to that of nineteenth-century European philosophers. This is a common problem in academic discourse, of course. We are by our nature accustomed to deal-ing with certain kinds of texts, and texts by fellow academics, even histor-ical ones, are much easier to engage with. Christopher Shannon's work, while otherwise strongly informing this book, is an excellent example of this tendency. As he states from the very beginning, his historicization of identity is rooted in a desire to "shift the debate from the social to the intel-lectual level through a close reading of a few key texts."[47] True to his prom-ise, each chapter focuses on a few prominent intellectuals from the 1950s and 1960s: Erik Erikson, Ruth Benedict, David Riesman, Ralph Ellison, Alfred Kinsey, and so on. I don't begrudge Shannon his choices, especially given how transparently he states his methodology, and I appreciate his attempts to include women and people of color among his authors. And certainly, the written intellectual tradition plays an important role in the story that will follow.

However, this genre of intellectual history severely limits our possibilities. For one, I am reminded of Sarah Ahmed's critique of academic citationality, our practices by which even the most critical work revolves in an orbit around key texts by white men. As she writes,

> To be influenced by a tradition is to be citing white men. Citing; reciting; an endless retrospective. White men as a well-trodden path; the more we tread *that way* the more we go *that way*. To move forward you follow the traces left behind of those who came before. But in following these traces, in participating in their becoming brighter, becoming lighter, other traces fade out, becoming shadows, places unlit; eventually they disappear. Women too, people of colour too, might cite white men: to be you have to be in relation to white men (to twist a Fanonian point). Not to cite white men is not to exist; or at least not to exist within this or that field. When you exercise these logics, you might come to exist, by writing out another history, another way of explaining your existence. If to cite is to wipe out your history, what then?[48]

To be sure, Biddle's genealogy is to some extent a result of his robust engagement with theory and philosophy, and I do not want to suggest that theory itself is the problem. There are many kinds of theory, though, and the specific tradition of Western philosophy is mobilized all too often simply by default, or to lay claim to the most prestigious and authorized forms of academic discourse. Furthermore, the downfall in restricting oneself to written intellectual history, as Shannon does, is that the work of identity often takes place outside written texts. Shannon's chapter on sexuality politics, for example, closely reads the work of Alfred Kinsey and its critique by Lionel Trilling, together with the 1964 collection of essays entitled *Sex in America*, Frances FitzGerald's reporting on San Francisco's Castro quarter in the 1970s, and Adrienne Rich's famous essay on compulsory heterosexuality. Through these texts he traces a "discourse of conformity" in which the purest form of liberation is to achieve true agency, even if, he argues, this supposedly liberatory ability to make one's own choices is in reality constrained and enabled by the usual forces of modernity.

However, the actual people engaged in this cultural work are missing in Shannon's accounts. It is telling, I think, that many of the intellectuals he engages with tend to themselves be journalists and scholars, often outsiders to the practices of identity they write about. When it comes to the Castro in the 1970s, however, is it fair to draw conclusions about sexual practices based on a journalist's outsider account? As an alternative, one might offer, for example, the anthropology of Gayle Rubin, based on her study and participation in San Francisco's BDSM scene in the same era, with its sensitive accounts of the radical exchange of power.[49]

Furthermore, any text can go only so far. One of the important theoretical contexts informing this project is the discipline of performance studies, or as Barbara Kirshenblatt-Gimblett calls it, "the postdiscipline of inclusions."[50] The basic strategy of performance studies is deceptively simple: rather than treat different forms of performance separately, according to the logic of text, it considers them together, as instances of a fundamental human practice. Accordingly, when considering "performance," that term is taken to mean as wide a range of human behavior as possible. The relationship between music and politics is often analyzed in simplistic terms, with music simply "expressing" the creator's political views, or at most acting as a kind of cheerleader to a social movement.[51] Analyzing a range of performances in a moment in time shows a web of interactions between people, movements, styles, and actions.

Not only can more connections be made, but we also become aware of historical and cultural information found outside of written texts. This has been a longstanding concern of performance studies, which often deals with repertoires where notation is impossible, or at least beside the point. If we direct our gaze slightly to the side of "the music itself," we can examine the space of performance for meanings not present in the score, or even in the recording. What kinds of bodies are present, producing and consuming the music? How does the music and its context privilege certain bodies above others, and what changes might it thus effect in structures of privilege? These are questions that a number of musicologists have begun to ask. [52]

But many such debates do seem to occur at cross-purposes. Closer musicological attention to and participation in similar debates within performance studies would be extremely valuable for both disciplines. The performance theorist Peggy Phelan, for instance, has argued for decades that the category of performance is in some respects fundamentally irrecoverable.[53] Once a performance is finished, it is ontologically lost. Performance leaves traces, of course—descriptions, transcriptions, films, records, and memories—but mediations immediately inflect performance, infusing it with ideological interpellations impossible to separate from the original. A chapter of this book focuses on a legendary work of the American postwar avant-garde composer John Cage, his 4′33″—a work analyzed (perhaps) to death as a text of philosophy, a brilliant but totally abstract conceptual stroke. I will attempt to refocus attention on 4′33″ as *performance,* seeking a thick description of the famous first performance by David Tudor at the Maverick Concert Hall in Woodstock, New York, in the summer of 1952. Peggy Phelan would remind us that this performance *qua* performance is nearly irretrievable. There are historical accounts of the performance, and members of the audience are still alive to replay their memories. One can still visit that concert hall, which stands in more or less the same condition. The original score Tudor used is lost, but we do have a good idea of what it looked like and how it functioned. We even know what the weather was like that evening—it was raining, a not unimportant detail given the parameters of this piece. However, this original performance is still fundamentally unavailable to us, and attempts to fix such performances in time succeed only in the multiplication of texts, robbing performance of its disruptive power. As Phelan notes, performance "becomes itself through disappearance."[54]

More recent approaches in performance studies, however, such as the influential work of Joseph Roach and Diana Taylor, have attempted to interrogate the traces of meanings, tactics, strategies, and information still transmitted by performance, even if as an ontological matter the object of performance study is lost. In effect, we might view performance not as a thing to be analyzed but, rather, what Taylor describes as "an episteme, a way of knowing."[55] Taylor asks us to make a provocative choice between an archive of dead objects and a repertoire of living meanings. Similarly, Susan Foster, a dance historian, has proposed that rather than "reading" a performance as a text—as, for instance, Judith Butler does with the performance of gender—we might inscribe our analysis under the rubric of "choreography." Not only does the notion of choreography "encompass corporeal as well as verbal articulateness,"[56] the process of choreography in a modern dance context is both social and individual: the choreographer chooses movements from a socially grounded and historically contextualized repertoire of possibilities, which are also tied to anatomical possibilities in a perhaps dialectical relationship. For Foster, this analysis is liberating; actions "defy strategies of containment and move us toward new theorizations of corporeal existence and resistance."[57,58]

Music, however, is something of a special case of performance. This is especially so because for a large number of genres of music, memory and transmission of musical knowledge is mediated by a text, broadly defined. Phelan, after all, in analyzing the immediate disappearance of performance after the fact, was actually speaking of one particular mode of performance: late 1980s performance art. Much music of the early fifties, however, had an important existence as text, perhaps in the form of a score, perhaps as a set of chord changes, perhaps as a recording. This is not to say that those texts were the same as performance; as an endless succession of aestheticians have pointed out, a performance of a symphony is in no philosophical sense identical to the printed score. However, our analytical knowledge of the work—indeed, our sense of it as a work at all, not to mention the composer's vision of it and the performers' encounters with it—are unavoidably mediated by the presence of that score. And although not perfect or complete, the score does nevertheless provide a transcription of some critical aspects of the movement of bodies on the stage of a symphony hall at a certain moment in time. As it happens, in the case of Cage's 4′33″, archival research shows us that, indeed, the original score of the work was crucial for understanding the politics of its original performance.[59]

To summarize, the focus of this book is thus on the political work of identity as found in the realm of music. The outcome hopes to be more descriptive than prescriptive, focusing on small details of specific individuals rather than on grander theories of social behavior. For example, chapter 2 looks at the early R&B vocal group the Orioles, often credited with launching the musical style later known as doo-wop, especially with their 1949 crossover hit "It's Too Soon to Know" and their last charting number, "Crying in the Chapel" (1953). Their smooth romantic ballads—featuring the hugely popular Sonny Til as the lead vocalist—turned the members of the Orioles into some of the first crossover stars of the postwar era. In a historical moment when the newly invented category of "rhythm & blues" had yet to coalesce into a coherent musical style, the Orioles helped create an alternative to the more aggressive masculinities emerging out of jump blues.

Chapter 2 illustrates this "choreography of gender," to use Foster's term, through multiple modes of performance: live stage shows, recordings, interviews, and period reviews in the African American press. Selections from the short-lived postwar periodical *Tan Confessions* add particular nuance to the discussion, with interviews of stars like Sonny Til alongside fan fiction and housewares targeted aimed at African American women. There, I argue that this alternative masculinity should be understood as a strategy linked with Cold War discourses of consensus and consumption, and the anxieties over masculinity famously expressed in Franklin Frasier's *Black Bourgeoisie* in the historical moment of *Brown v. Board of Education* in 1954.

Chapter 3 illuminates some of the most popular music of the postwar period that is today much less appreciated, the music of the post-swing-era girl singers such as Patti Page and Rosemary Clooney. It was this music that many critics then and now have positioned as the staid, conformist popular music against which the countercultural trend of rock and roll rebelled. This chapter takes its cue from critical race studies to show how the whiteness of the genre was an ideological product of a larger story of ethnic assimilation and the emergence of a universalized American identity, whose middle-class, white, suburban ethos has become a metonym for "the fifties" ever since.

In chapter 3, the focus is on the most iconic of the girl singers, the singer and actress Doris Day. I trace how her performance of whiteness emerged over the course of her early musical film career, beginning in *Romance on the High Seas* (1949), continuing in *Calamity Jane* (1953), and finally in Alfred Hitchcock's *The Man Who Knew Too Much* (1957). Engaging especially with the work of Richard Dyer, I explain how it was precisely Doris Day's performance of whiteness, mixing a tightly wound inward focus with occasional eruptions of violence (and singing) that became so particularly famous and influential. By focusing on these three films, the chapter also provides further context for the development of white identities, including her earliest film's travels through the Caribbean and South America, *Calamity Jane*'s spoof of the classic Western, and *The Man Who Knew Too Much*'s tale of anxiety and terrorism in a particularly explicit thematization of Cold War drama.

Much of this book is self-consciously domestic, focusing on a somewhat hermetic and inward-focused United States. However, as the Cold War framing of the project implies, this domestic focus was, of course, part of a larger process of globalization transformed by World War II. In chapter 4, I consider the intersection of white engagement with representations of Asian culture, and something of its opposite: a nightclub in San Francisco known as Forbidden City, in which Asian American musicians and dancers put on a kind of whiteface show in which, for example, singer Larry Ching performed as the "Chinese Frank Sinatra." These dueling representations—white performing Asian, Asian performing white— illuminate two larger and intersecting trends. One was the experience of white American service members returning home from the Pacific Front, bringing home with them a newly globalized sense of racial identity. The other was the experience of Asian American in California, especially in the Bay Area where many Chinese Americans were joining the suburban middle class. Globalization was nothing new in the 1940s, but in the context of the Cold War, the development of these new styles of representation took on particularly fraught meanings.

Chapter 5 takes a look at one of the most notorious moments of music-making during the early Cold War, considered against the backdrop of the "lavender menace" and McCarthyist persecution of gay men: the premiere of John Cage's *4′33″* in 1952. A prominent thread of criticism has found in Cage and his circle an "aesthetic of indifference," a stance that by its conspicuous refusal to communicate nevertheless reveals powerfully oppositional politics. I complicate this analysis by situating Cage's work within the still-nascent postwar development of gay male identity, contrasting Cage with philosophical rivals such as his old friend Harry Hay and the queer anarchist writer Paul Goodman.

Chapter 5 also looks in detail at the origins of the premiere and the sense of panic it engendered in the audience. I make the case that later versions of *4′33″*, especially those taught in today's textbooks and music appreciation contexts, miss out on the work's historical presence, especially its first, now-lost score, in which the silence was strictly notated rather than left as an abstract context. Together, this historical context of an emergent gay cultural identity alongside a carefully crafted musical experience provides an excellent closing example of the possibilities of these new postwar tools of self-fashioning. As Cage's example shows, identity was an imperfect and in some ways restricting concept, but ultimately was too potent to ignore.

Singing Smoothly

Masculinity in Early Doo-Wop

n the summer of 1949, the representation of African American masculinity became a preoccupation of many in the United States. It began in
April, with a speech by Paul Robeson in which he claimed that it was
"unthinkable that American Negroes would ever go to war on behalf of
those who have oppressed us for generations."[1] This touched off a firestorm
of discussion in the American media, and soon played a central role in an
ongoing series of congressional hearings on "Communist infiltration of
minority groups." In the hands of the House Committee on Un-American
Activities (HUAC), the question was not so much whether civil rights
organizations such as the National Association for the Advancement of
Colored People were being infiltrated by communists—their own investigator found no evidence of such—but whether the "Negro people" themselves were more susceptible to communist influence, a question of racial
character more than political affiliation.

As so often happens in politics, the hearings became a play of synecdo-
che: personal experiences and anecdotes were extrapolated to represent
the larger forces at work. General Dwight D. Eisenhower testified by letter
that he had never known a disloyal Negro in the Armed Forces during
World War II. Most symbolically, in order to provide a visible representation of an alternative to Paul Robeson, the baseball player Jackie Robinson
was subpoenaed, an African American man who began his testimony not
with a political statement but with a joking aside about his salary: "It isn't
very pleasant for me to find myself in the middle of a public argument
that has nothing to do with the standing of the Brooklyn Dodgers in the
pennant race—or even the pay raise I am going to ask Mr. Branch Rickey
for next year!"[2]

The symbolic juxtaposition of Jackie Robinson the capitalist and Paul
Robeson the communist was the celebrity highlight of the hearings. The
fact that these icons were men was no accident. The lead investigator,
Alvin W. Stokes, testified that the question of communist infiltration was
limited to men:

> I think it should be reported, to the honor and the glory of the Negro
> woman, that her rejection of communism is a strong and formidable
> factor in limiting Communist political and civic influence among
> Negro men specifically, and the Negro population generally.[3]

Pointing to a broader fear of African American masculinity, Stokes constructs the African American male as impotent twice over: he can be over-
powered either by communists or by women. And to the evident relief of
the committee, he poses no threat either way.

African American masculinity in the postwar period was a location of
tremendous discussion and anxiety for both black and white critics. The
immediate source of this discourse was the process of intense racial desegregation that occurred during World War II. Almost half a million black
men had served in the military during the war, and although participation was still highly segregated—at several American military bases during the war, German prisoners were allowed to eat with white American

soldiers while African American men were relegated to separate mess halls—integration had begun to seem inevitable to many Americans outside the Deep South. Add in the millions of men and women who had migrated to urban areas in the North and West, and we find white and black Americans living and working in closer quarters than ever before.

But a specifically gendered anxiety over integration echoed across the country in newspaper editorials, employment restrictions, and of course, lynchings and castrations. Steve Estes writes that for black men after World War II, "the ever present threat of lynching for supposed sexual improprieties meant that their survival could depend on their ability to mask their masculinity."[4] The construction of African American masculinity as a "problem" to be solved became the sociological consensus of the era, epitomized by the infamous Moynihan Report of 1965. The report, known formally as *The Negro Family: The Case for National Action*, argued that black inequality could be traced to a matriarchal system of familial power. The report, commissioned by the Johnson administration and written by a sociologist who would later become a senator from New York, has been rightfully criticized for its patronizing and racist conclusions.[5] It is here noted not as truth but as evidence of just how contested black masculinity had come to be.

Indeed, anxiety regarding black masculinity was not limited to white political discourse. With integration and economic success came worries about the changing character of black men. In 1955, the African American sociologist E. Franklin Frazier published his controversial study *The Black Bourgeoisie*, a polemic that criticized, in the words of the title of one chapter, the transition "from the making of men to the making of money-makers."[6] Although *The Black Bourgeoisie* echoed similar critiques by white authors, such as David Riesman's *The Lonely Crowd* (1950), the polemic was written by a black intellectual for the black community. Drawing upon his long career as a sociologist, Frazier argued that class aspiration was eroding traditional African American social structure, and thus sapping its political strength. Black men, in particular, suffered from an "inferiority complex," according to Frazier: "These discriminations cause frustrations in Negro men because they are not allowed to play the 'masculine role' as defined by American culture."[7] The African American male, Frazier argued, is squeezed between a "tradition of female dominance," on one hand, and racist subordinations to white society, on the other.

We thus can begin to see why the question of masculinity is so crucial to this historical moment, and why the performance of gender has been an important focus of scholarship on African American music in this period. This is especially true for doo-wop, a genre often seen as straddling multiple worlds: it was secular but influenced by gospel quartets; it featured "white" songs sung by black singers; most important, it was sung by men, but presented a very "unmasculine" sensibility. The last of these has proven particularly interesting to many writers, drawn to the genre's use of youthful musicians, falsetto voices, and a generally clean-cut lyrical sensibility at odds with the bulk of early 1950s R&B. Jeffrey Melnick's essay "The Black Men and White Sounds of Doo-Wop," one of the first to bring critical scholarly attention to this music, focused on what he termed doo-wop's "surprising expansiveness for men with regard to gender and sex roles."[8] Arguing for a more nuanced history of black masculinity in the 1950s, Melnick portrayed a musical genre uniquely able to draw upon multiple sources of gendered performances, unconstrained by either the color line or the *Billboard* charts.

Brian Ward similarly focuses on the music "alternate vision" to the "black macho" politics of R&B.[9] Adding more historical nuance to our understanding the genre, he convincingly shows how R&B of the era reflected "a new vision of black sexual politics," with the raw blues shouters reifying a "powerful, resolutely masculine, compensatory male identity."[10] Ward's example of the compensatory male identity comes in the form of Wynonie Harris, in his extraordinary self-reflective essay on "Why Women Won't Leave Me Alone." "I play to create impressions," wrote Harris. "The women who really know me also know part of my secret. We can laugh about it together for they know how women can get stirred up by a man who seems cruel, ornery, vulgar, and arrogant." The essay was accompanied by pictures of Harris posed with multiple admirers, with the caption "On stage, he can become a snarling, insulting character who makes women patrons sizzle."[11] By contrast, vocal groups tended toward a romantic idealism that by the mid-1950s, in Ward's words, "concentrated almost exclusively on evoking a juvenile world of specifically teen trauma and romantic delight."[12]

We also see why the question of this masculinity can't be considered solely within the context of one musical genre, or indeed solely within the context of music. In other words, we need an analysis of how doo-wop's alternative vision of masculinity more specifically operated within the larger discourse of masculinity in its period. Thus, rather than consider the wider question of genre, I take a close look at just one group, and one of their hits: the Orioles, and their pioneering crossover hit "It's Too Soon to Know," which in addition to topping the R&B charts, made it to #13 on the *Billboard* Pop charts. The Orioles were led by the charismatic tenor Sonny Til, a man whose voice was described by one bemused contemporary in the black press as combining "the fervor of a pre-bellum Baptist minister and the sincerity of an insurance salesman."[13] Against recordings and accounts of their live performances, I will juxtapose fiction, advertisements, poetry, and record reviews in black periodicals, especially in the little-known magazine *Tan Confessions*. Although not a long-lasting success, this publication was a uniquely important forum for public discourse on black masculinity. Embedded in postwar discourses on consumption and consensus, the music and performances of the Orioles provides a sharp reflection of one black masculinity just as the civil rights movement and the birth of identity politics were beginning to take shape.

■

The HUAC hearings were not the only public location where representations of African American masculinity were being reevaluated. Just a month earlier, on June 25, 1949, the music industry had quietly transformed perhaps the most crucial national forum for representing blackness, the *Billboard* "Rhythm & Blues" sales chart. For over forty years, the sales charts that covered music by and sold to African Americans had been known as the "Race" charts. From 1942 to 1945, there had been a brief attempt to relabel the charts the "Harlem Hit Parade," but this unwieldy moniker had not stuck. The phrase "rhythm & blues," however, coined by

Jerry Wexler in his early days as a staff writer for *Billboard*, did stick, and is still an important sales-tracking category today.[14] Although the term "rhythm & blues" was, in theory, a description of musical style rather than racial type, the genre was a social, not a musical construction. According to *Billboard*'s own tautological description, these charts consisted of "rhythm and blues records that sold best in stores according to *Billboard*'s special weekly survey among a selected group of retail stores, the majority of whose customers purchase rhythm and blues records."

Chart position was the result of complex mediations among market forces; internal and external politics; geography; aesthetics; and the efforts of musicians, songwriters, managers, DJs, label executives, jukebox manufacturers, television bookers, journalists, and—once in a while—record buyers. The final product was a play of synecdochal representations. Unlike the relatively cohesive style of today's R&B, the first chart in 1949 covered a jumble of genres, musical techniques, and social contexts: a smooth "club" blues, raw shouting numbers, a crooning ballad by the Orioles, several jump blues tunes, one woman—Ella Fitzgerald with Louis Jordan's Tympany Five—and two versions of the ribald "Drinkin' Wine Spo-dee-Oh-Dee," sung by both Wynonie Harris and its author, Granville "Stick" McGhee (see table 2.1).

In 1949, the *Billboard* R&B charts were less a parade of national hits (who really knew how many records sold in all those regional markets?) than a set of possibilities—ten different possibilities every two weeks for what it could mean to be African American in the United States. These models showed the diversity and utter intersectionality of African American culture after World War II, each reflecting a constellation of class, gender, geographical origin, and religious belief, as much as they evoked race. To read the R&B charts in the early fifties is not just to read the history of musical performances; it is also to encounter a hidden history of social and political performances.

On this first chart, one performance stands out. There is only one vocal harmony record on this first R&B chart, "Tell Me So," an unpolished, emotive-to-the-point-of-histrionic ballad sung by the Orioles, a group of young black men from Baltimore, and written by their nineteen-year-old

TABLE 2.1   FIRST *BILLBOARD* RHYTHM & BLUES CHART, JUNE 1949

1. Charlie Brown, "Trouble Blues"
2. Paul Williams, "Hucklebuck"
3. Bull Moose Jackson and His Buffalo Bearcats, "Little Girl, Don't Cry"
4. Amos Milburn, "Hold Me, Baby"
5. "Stick" McGee, "Drinkin' Wine, Spo-Dee-O-Dee"
6. The Orioles, "Tell Me So"
7. Jimmy Witherspoon, "Ain't Nobody's Business"
8. Roy Milton, "Hucklebuck"
9. Wynonie Harris, "Drinkin' Wine, Spo-Dee-O-Dee"
10. Herb Lance, "Close Your Eyes"
11. Louis Jordan's Tympany Five, "Cole Slaw"
12. Ella Fitzgerald and Louis Jordan, "Baby, It's Cold Outside"
13. Lucky Millender Orchestra, "D' Natural Blues"
14. Todd "Rhodes, Pot Likker"
15. Amos Milburn, "In the Middle of the Night"

white manager, Deborah Chessler. A piano introduces and gently accompanies the track, but the focus is on singing: the mellifluous voice of twenty-one-year-old lead singer Sonny Til, baritone George Nelson's throaty take on the bridge, and Alex Sharp's meandering obbligato countertenor.

"Tell Me So" was a popular song, but its success was dwarfed by the Orioles' first hit, "It's Too Soon to Know." This 1948 release, also written by Chessler, quickly climbed to number one on the "Race" charts, and made it to an unprecedented #14 on the pop charts. Those few critics who today remember "It's Too Soon to Know" speak of it in awestruck, almost mystical terms. Albin Zak refers to its signaling "unexplained disturbances."[15] No less an authority than Greil Marcus has called it the first rock and roll record:

Suddenly, everything around it, on the radio, on the jukeboxes, sounded stale. In the voices you could hear—and you can hear today—a quality of contingency, a setting of everything in doubt, the echo of an event, happening now. The feeling is, had things been just slightly different—the weather, the circumstances of the singer's birth, the news—this event could have turned out differently, or never happened at all. It's a sense of open possibilities; it is also a sense of danger, a fear of everything closing up. For as long as the record keeps its life, the singer escapes genre and the music has no style.[16]

This is quite an existential burden for a song that, Marcus's claim for its transhistorical appeal notwithstanding, is rarely heard today. At first listen, it can be hard to see how a slow romantic ballad with none of the supposed markers of subcultural African American musical authenticity—no blue notes, no driving rhythms, no sexually knowing lyrics—could possibly be the spark for the postwar R&B explosion. The standard story of R&B tends to privilege those musical and social aspects that most clearly prefigure the rock and roll of the mid-1950s and beyond: electric guitars, boogie-woogie bass lines, fast tempos. On that first R&B chart in 1949, this position was taken by Wynonie Harris, Stick McGhee, Bull Moose Jackson, and other refugees of the great postwar exodus from swing bands. The performances of these men created a sound image of rural, working-class, heterosexual masculinity. This picture was not necessarily a simple mirror image of reality (most of them were sophisticated urban professional musicians), but it was the performance they succeeded in bringing before the public eye. The Orioles, on the other hand, despite occupying similar subject positions themselves, carefully performed a specifically bourgeois, urbane black masculinity, one no less heterosexual, no less black, but designed and performed for very different effect.

The Oriole's musical style was rooted in the longstanding African American vocal harmony tradition of groups such as the Mills Brothers, the Ink Spots, and, most proximately, the Baltimore-based vocal quartet, the Ravens. Musically, the Orioles partook of an established, if subtly articulated, system of signifying musical gestures; socially, they were following in the footsteps of the small number of African American performers able to make a good living by carving out a spot in the white popular musical world. Gage Averill and others have usefully described the racial dynamics of vocal harmony, the complex interplay between black and white sounds and bodies. As Averill puts it, "close harmony, like so much American vernacular and popular music, has provided an expansive terrain for both blacks and whites to experiment with racial identity in sound."[17] Without losing the obvious intersectionality inherent in this music, or neglecting the role of race, I direct our focus toward the "choreography of gender" in vocal harmony, to use Susan-Leigh Foster's term.[18]

I am drawn to Foster's framework here, like many scholars attempting to productively analyze the social content of performance traditions, because she helps broaden the somewhat limited notion of gender as "performance." Judith Butler's famous analysis paradoxically ignores the actual "performing" arts (music, dance, theater) in favor of philosophy and literature.[19] Her examples are largely taken from literary texts, and performativity itself functions in her work as a technical term from linguistics. Theater scholar Sue-Ellen Case has pointed out the irony that there is very little performance involved in performativity: "One might argue," she writes, that "the project of performativity is to recuperate writing at the end of print culture."[20]

Thus, when music is under discussion, we must be careful about the ways we construe "gender as performance." Foster, herself a choreographer and dance critic, proposes "choreography of gender" as an alternative framework. To choreograph is to use our bodies, to draw upon repertoires of knowledge that are only rarely notated but fundamentally constitutive of selfhood. "Only by assessing the articulateness of bodies' motions as well as speech," Foster argues, "can the interconnectedness of racial, gendered, and sexual differences within and among these bodies matter."[21] Notational systems in Western music allow easy recourse to linguistic models of analysis—models made even more useful by the fact that much of this music comes with words. R&B vocal harmony is no different in this respect, and its texts are important reservoirs of meaning. But thinking carefully about what role the performers' bodies play in articulating those meanings allows us access to other modes of knowledge, many of which point toward the crucial intersectionality of difference Foster references.

By way of illustration, consider two musical gestures popularized by the African American vocal group tradition: the deep talking bass and the soaring high tenor. The former dates at least to the 1920s, as illustrated in some early recordings of groups like the Norfolk Jazz Quartet and popularized in the 1940s by the Ink Spots. The high-tenor vocal type is, of course, not unique to African American vocal harmony, but by the 1950s the sound of a light countertenor voice, often in falsetto, floating over the percussive vocal syllabification known from gospel singing as the "clanka-lanka," was inextricably intertwined with the sound of R&B— which is to say, the sound of blackness. The talking bass and the floating tenor are today nearly impossible to separate from racial identification. One need only think of smooth-talking *bassi profundi* like Isaac Hayes and Barry White, or the falsetto employed by Prince and Michael Jackson to acknowledge the inescapable influence of the black–white color line in the perception of these two vocal types. At the same time, their dichotomy reinscribes the binary organization of gender in our culture. Governed by the cultural contingency of vocal technique, but also the physiological reality of vocal folds, the talking bass and the wordless falsetto demarcate the corporeal and aural outer boundaries of masculinity, even as they imbue those boundaries with social meaning.

The Orioles did not generally use a talking bass, perhaps because their immediate predecessors in the Baltimore vocal group scene, the Ravens, had just transformed the bass role. In the capable voice of the Ravens' Jimmy Ricks, the bass was increasingly assigned melodic prominence, as in their popular and insouciant cover of "Ol' Man River." Few other groups adopted this model exactly, but Ricks did succeed in liberating the bass voice from rhythmically static accompaniment to partake of the doo-wopping bass lines favored by countless mid-1950s vocal groups.[22] On the other hand, with the exception perhaps of "Deacon Jones" (1949), the Orioles kept their harmony close and high, and rarely separated the accompanying voices in any meaningful way. Their vocal aesthetic emphasized smoothness and blend to an extreme degree. As many vocal groups sought the novelty found at the outer boundaries of vocal capability, the Orioles, and the groups who followed in their lead, looked for the vague, ambiguous, "blended" middle. Stanley Goosman, whose book *Group Harmony* is one of the few extended treatments of postwar African American vocal harmony, has difficulty articulating what singers meant by the term *blend:*

> blend is a desirable consequence of singing well together, but the manner in which these vocalists seem to have internalized and socialized "blend"—and then talk about it years later—was distinctive. There was no standard for blending. It was not simply singing in tune. . . . The singers themselves spoke of something that to them sounded or felt good, or right. Blend was something emotional as much as musical. When singers spoke of blend, they as much meant getting along, falling in with each other, participating and anticipating, as they did a purely musical blend. Clearly, this was a process, and not something you could measure.[23]

Goosman is undoubtedly correct to zero in on blend as a social ideal, not simply a musical one. However, if we are to take the vocal choreography of group harmony as a repertoire of physical gestures, it seems overhasty to skip ahead to the social significance of those gestures without understanding their actuality as performance.

Many, if not all, participants in the vocal group scenes of Baltimore, New York, Washington, and other cities of the Northeast had formal musical training. This was largely thanks to big-city public school systems that, although segregated, offered musical training to their students at a level unusual today. Some well-known performers even pursued musical training advanced by any standards; most famously, Billy Ward of the Dominoes studied theory and composition at Juilliard.[24] The Orioles, however, were not trained musicians, and neither they nor their manager/songwriter could read music. Chessler confirms that she invented melodies more or less in her head, and would find a friend to notate a lead sheet.[25] She would then sing the melody for Sonny Till, and guitarist Tommy Gaither would provide a grounding for the other singers to feel their way through the chords.

This intuitive "feeling through" chords, as Goosman and others have described it, largely resulted in simple triads.[26] Most of the chords in "It's Too Soon to Know" feature the performers singing in thirds with one another. The individual singers sound as if they know well only their own line; it sometimes takes an extra moment or two for each chord to come into focus, as the slow harmonic rhythm grants the group time to listen to one another and adjust accordingly. This gives rise to a distinctive wavering sound, a sound further enhanced by the way the backing singers occasionally add very slight embellishments to their lines. It is almost an exaggeration to call them "embellishments," as these minute gestures are barely pitched—more of a slight sigh or groan than a melodic gesture. Bass Johnny Reed, for example, just arches his line upward from time to time, as toward the end of "A one-sided love will break my heart" (0:44). His very slight bend up from G does not even reach G sharp; if anything, it sounds like he simply pushed a little harder on the G, and in so doing opened his mouth just a bit more, allowing the accumulation of a few more upper partials. These tiny moments of harmonic confusion—we can think of them as an instance of Charles Keil's participatory discrepancies— give the song a slightly out-of-focus quality.[27] Ironically, the Orioles' ideal blend, at least in these early tracks, is a little grittier and somewhat more heterogeneous than one might expect.

The heterogeneity comes more explicitly to the fore when the entire group bends notes. Each singer seems to have picked his own tempo at which to slide, and sometimes the final goal is not entirely audible. Some bends follow the established conventions of "swiping," whereby one or two voices carefully retain their pitch while others change to a new harmonic configuration. The clearest example of this occurs at 1:17, on the words "I won't die." Til retains his high D, while the others bend their D major into a somewhat ambiguous G chord over A in the bass. Much more hetero-phonic, however, is the bend at the climactic moment of the song, near the end, after the full stop at 2:18. As Til again croons "I Won't Die," the others again support him with a D-major chord and then bend it. Here, however, the gesture is simply to move up by increment, while attempting to fade out. The result is a scattering of pitches that briefly touches on a very odd-sounding E major before faltering into silence. It is an affecting moment of Marcus's "setting everything in doubt" that wears its strangeness on its sleeve.

Practically speaking, some of the vagaries can be chalked up to amateurism. The Orioles were young and inexperienced. They were recorded by a small, obscure independent label on amateur equipment, and despite Deborah Chessler's obvious talent, they had no experienced mentors. By 1953, when they charted their final hit with "Crying in the Chapel," they had buffed their harmonizing to a professional sheen, leading one to suspect that their initial tentativeness was not necessarily a conscious choice.

However, what does it mean that this strange, contingent, heterogeneous ideal of "blending" struck such a chord with thousands of young African American teenagers? Just months after the release of "It's Too Soon to Know," the Orioles had become a phenomenon in the emerging black youth market across the country. The black press ran dozens of Sinatra-style stories detailing riots at shows, clothes being ripped off the singers, sometimes mid-performance. A 1952 profile in *Ebony* magazine told the story of a thirteen-year-old being dragged off by police after she "attacked" the Orioles as they left a theater: "Go ahead. Put me in jail," the girl cried. "But give me a record-player and some of the Orioles' records. I just want to hear them sing 'It's Too Soon to Know.'" Accompanying the story were several photographs of the scene, showing a bewildered looking Sonny Til being bundled by police through a throng of young women.[28]

The original Orioles never appeared on television, nor were their club performances ever filmed, as far as I know. Many fans saw them perform, of course, and their memories and a few photographs are our only record of these events. We can reconstruct that the singers followed the standard practice of employing two microphones, one for the lead, the other for the accompaniment. In an interview, Harold Winley of the Clovers described their typical arrangement:

Did you ever see them work? O.K. Sonny was like so, on a mic by himself. Alex Sharp, George Nelson, and Tommy Gaither over here. George is in here; this is George in the middle. When Sonny changed, sang his part, George would spin around, man, from here, and go over there and tear the house down. . . .

The Orioles, their thing was a little more active than the groups that you had seen before. A little more active, you understand what I'm saying? Because I'm saying now this man is pleading now, he's down on his knees, he's begging, he's sweating profusely. Sonny, you know. And he's beggin', you know.[29]

Most accounts of the Orioles confirm this basic blocking, which created a strong physical separation between lead and accompaniment. And rather than creating a contrasting B section through a different melody or instrumental break, most of their hits songs would create contrast through a shift in the lead—George Nelson would step up to the solo microphone and Til would retreat into the background. As Winley notes, thanks to this kind of trading off, and also thanks to Til's emotional performance style, the Orioles were considered more "active" than many of their contemporaries. Prior to World War II, most secular vocal groups, such as the Mills Brothers or the Ink Spots, had appeared in contexts that privileged flamboyant showmanship: vaudeville, song and dance revues, club venues alongside swing bands. Though the Mills Brothers and Ink Spots both remained stationary as they sang, they were frequently accompanied by actual dancers—there was no sense in developing elaborate choreography if you were going to have the Nicholas Brothers tap dancing next to you! The relative "activity" of the Orioles has more to do with the small nightclubs in which they were appearing, often as the sole performers. This context reflected a postwar scarcity of money and manpower, and was reflected in other genres of music as well, as in the transition in New York City from large dancehalls to small "modern jazz" clubs.[30] And just as in bebop, there was also a new relationship with the audience: concertgoers listened to, rather than danced with, the music. Within the world of R&B, the Orioles seem to have been pioneers in this regard: an article at the time noticed with awe that "fans give the Orioles rapt attention. Characteristically, dancing ceases when the group goes into action."[31]

And at the head of all this attention was the meticulously dressed and groomed Sonny Til. "A performer," he told an interviewer in 1952, "is always on stage."[32] Supposed to carry over 300 ties with him on the road, Til took his role as teenage idol very seriously. Like many other African American performers of the era, he straightened his hair in the process known as a conk, in which periodic treatments of lye were applied.[33] Til's conk was especially luxuriant, grown out to a considerable length, straightened, and piled on top as a pompadour. The other members of the group styled their hair similarly, although not to the same flamboyant extent.

The choice of conk was not a simple one, especially for a man who was, like Til, extremely conscious of self-presentation. Maxine Craig notes that in the 1940s "members of the black middle class or those who accepted middle-class values generally granted that the style was appropriate for celebrities but assumed that ordinary men who wore conks were either of a lower class or criminals."[34] The exception for celebrities obviously applies to Til, but not completely. Part of the charm of the Orioles, and what differentiated them from earlier vocal harmony groups, was the very amateurish quality that comes across so clearly in their early recordings. The Orioles were ordinary young men who had lived normal lives in middle-class black Baltimore. Their public persona was as a bunch of regular guys next door who just happened to have lovely voices—the writer for *Ebony* described them as a "happy-go-lucky group of fellows who had hit the jackpot in life."[35] Indeed, it could be argued that the tremendous influence the Orioles had on the next generation of vocal harmony groups was due not so much to their music as to their myth of origin. The romantic story of young black teenagers discovered singing on the urban street corner formed the core narrative of the mid-1950s vocal harmony scene later called doo-wop.

Thus, in their everyday tonsorial performance, these "lucky fellows" could not just adopt the slick showbiz panache of their fellow performers. For the Orioles to flaunt their success with what Thorstein Veblen famously dubbed the "invidious display" of the (white) leisure class was a risky commercial strategy.[36] On the one hand, it affirmed new postwar middle-class values regarding consumption, a topic to be discussed shortly. But on the other hand, it could work against those values, establishing the bearer of a conk as either a criminally inclined lowlife or (at best) a flamboyant preener, like the equally pompadoured Little Richard would soon be.

The reason Til was able to style his hair so exotically, I believe, was another much-remarked upon quality of his performances: the sense of effort. Every single contemporary account of an Orioles performance noted that Sonny Til was a strenuous performer, dancing and sweating and singing hard. This choreography is more common today, especially in the wake of James Brown's carefully crafted persona as "the hardest working man in show business." But prior to World War II and up until the late 1940s, an aesthetic of effortless performance was much more dominant, at least in secular venues. More sedate vocal groups such as the Ravens would never have broken a sweat on stage. And even more dance-oriented and blues-indebted R&B performers similarly shunned Til's practice of embodying struggle on stage. Louis Jordan certainly worked hard, and the many filmed performances we have of his act show him to be an extremely physical performer. Nevertheless, it was always clear that Jordan was performing, in total physical control, on a stage he understood to be a stage. While Jordan and African American performers as diverse as Cab Calloway and Dizzy Gillespie deployed their off-stage identities as part of the general entertainment, it was nevertheless entertainment. Til, on the other hand, had created a style that foregrounded an intense, physicalized sincerity. The flamboyance of his hair was belied by the constant perspiration—chemical hair straightening in this period was almost immediately undone by any moisture. As his elaborate hairdo unraveled, audiences saw direct evidence not just that Til was working hard but also that he was *feeling* hard.

■

For all the frenzy accompanying the Orioles' live performances, judging from the music, the sexuality on display was not particularly aggressive. The songs were slow, the themes sentimental, many of the tunes still out of the Tin Pan Alley tradition. And it was not just the Orioles' live theatrics that drove their fans into a frenzy. Note the young girl quoted in the *Ebony* piece earlier: she doesn't mind being put in jail, because a recording of an Orioles song will suffice. There is undoubtedly conceptual slippage here between the live and the recorded, but nevertheless the calm, sedate recording of "It's Too Soon to Know" itself maintains the ability to inspire intense devotion. Recall the words of the anonymous writer for *Ebony* who described Til's voice as part "pre-bellum Baptist minister" and part "insurance salesman." It is easy enough to hear the preacher in Til; what of the insurance salesman?

The idea of Sonny Til as an "insurance salesman" might not actually be the best business metaphor in the context of the 1950s, and particularly in the context of "blending" described earlier. There were no shortage of convincing, suave African American balladeers at the time; the unusual aspect of the Orioles was not just Til's sincerity and personal charms but also their ability to produce that romantic sensibility with a group of men, rather than a solo singer. Sonny Til himself—or perhaps his publicist—addressed this issue forthrightly in an essay titled "Why Women Go For Me."

The subject of his article is the phenomenon of teenage fans, who as he says, "take the love songs I sing seriously and want to do something about it."[37] While expressing some bemusement at the reaction to his singing—the story is packed with anecdotes of women harassing his dates, their jilted boyfriends attacking him, and a daily plague of frenzied fans—Til keeps the focus on his fellow Orioles:

> I don't want to be the *boss*. I don't want to be a dictator. I want to see decisions made by all of us. I want us to argue and fight—not physically of course. I want us to be unselfish at all times and to stand up only for the things that are good for the Orioles, not for our individual selves. . . . A lot of people don't realize that without the teamwork of the other fellows; without the harmony and rhythm they keep moving behind and around me; without the background and atmosphere they create, Sonny Til wouldn't be anything but just another singer.[38]

Til rejects the metaphor of the solitary salesman or the corporate boss. In its place he substitutes an athletic metaphor, a team "moving behind and around me." This ideology of teamwork is embedded in discourse of the 1950s that goes far beyond the world of music. The desire to work together as a team, and to blend smoothly together, was an aesthetic act intertwined both with the postwar economy's emphasis on consumption and with the political mainstream's emphasis on consensus. Both of these features of postwar cultural politics—consumption and consensus—were impossible to separate from the choreography of gender.

Both Til and Harris's self-reflective musings were published in the same magazine, *Tan Confessions*, providing us with a chance to dive into these ideologies as they were reproduced at the smallest level. The magazine was created by Chicago publishing magnate John H. Johnson, who had also founded *Ebony* and *Jet*. Like those publications, *Tan Confessions* attempted to be a specifically black version of established genres of white periodicals—in this case, the longstanding tradition of "confessional" magazines. This genre, which dated to the late nineteenth century, was generally aimed at working-class women and tended to contain a blend of domestic advice and semi-fictional first-person stories about the various dangers of modernity: abortions, drug abuse, adultery, and so on. Although they were moralistic in tone and dire in depicted consequences, it was generally understood that most read such stories for titillation.[39]

From the beginning, *Tan Confessions* was met with suspicion from the black community. Despite Johnson's later claim that he hoped "we could dignify even a confessions magazine"—and the "we" in his sentence should be read as both his publishing company and the inherent dignity of middle-class black culture—few agreed with him about *Tan Confessions*.[40] Even the first issue published a series of letters written preemptively against a magazine that imported what was seen as the worst of white culture into the black community:

Dear Editor: A friend of mine told me some weeks ago that you people were planning to put out a magazine called *Tan Confessions*. Let me say now—even before I see your rag in print—that I object to seeing this kind of publication aimed at the Negro market. Confession magazines exist merely to titillate the sense of unreality common to uneducated people.[41]

The author of this letter puts an aspirational notion of class at the center of her criticism: confessional magazines are for "uneducated people." The positive letters to the editor Johnson chose to publish in this inaugural issue similarly foregrounded class. One writer assured the editor that she knew *Tan Confessions* would be "high class and not too trashy," and another lauded Johnson himself for his financial success: "It is indeed gratifying to see our people with ability to become financially successful in legitimate business."[42] Reviews of *Tan Confessions* in white periodicals similarly positioned Johnson at the vanguard of a new black middle class. *Time* announced the creation of the magazine with a short profile of Johnson's material success:

At 31, John Harold Johnson has made the most of his opportunities. A hard worker from the day he left the University of Chicago, he puts in 10 1/2 hours a day on the job, skims through some 30 newspapers and magazines each morning ("All I'm looking for is the word 'Negro' "). He long ago moved out of the shabby two-by-four office in which he started publishing, now occupies brightly decorated quarters in a remodeled mortuary. His own 29 by 24 office has 1-in.-deep buff carpets, rust and green drapes, a huge bay window, and a massive white oak desk flanked by a bronze nude and a gold-painted Dictaphone.

Says pudgy Publisher Johnson: "We can do more good for the Negro by being successful than anything else. . . . A strong, solid publication, run by Negroes, can wipe out all this prejudice. That's what we want to do."[43]

The imagery here is more than a little condescending, no doubt an attempt by *Time* to exoticize a wealthy black man and his *parvenu* taste. However, we would be remiss to read this description solely in racial terms, or to read *Tan Confessions* itself as indicative solely of African American upward mobility. Consumption of material goods was, in the late 1940s, a national concern. The wartime economy had revitalized a massive industrial machine that churned out both military hardware and something close to full employment. The prospect of converting this economy into a peacetime one while maintaining the economic momentum gained during the war was a daunting one for postwar policymakers.

In her important study *A Consumer's Republic*, historian Lizbeth Cohen argues that increasing material consumption was the consensus in postwar politics. The key measure was consumer purchasing power. On the right, groups like the National Association of Manufacturers and the U.S. Chamber of Commerce fought vigorously against Keynesian attempts by the government to moderate the flow of production with the Full Employment Act of 1945 or hold over the wartime price controls such as occurred in the United Kingdom; ultimately, they hoped to roll back Roosevelt's New Deal programs altogether. Crucial to this strategy was finding a new private-sector market to replace the government and military spending that had previously fueled growth. As Cohen puts it, "for them, more private investment leading to increased productivity was the route to economic growth and postwar prosperity, but the profits they sought from more efficiently produced and cheaply priced goods still depended on a dynamic mass consumer market."[44]

Cohen argues that labor unions and other liberal groups also embraced mass consumption after World War II, even as they disagreed on the details of how the new market should be created. For them, "purchasing power," not private control of investment capital, was key. Cohen quotes a Congress of Industrial Organizations (CIO) document from 1944: "Our economy feeds and grows on purchasing power as a baby does on milk."[45] Right and left harmonized, the former advocating an expanded consumer market because it drove private investment and the latter looking for full employment for those doing the purchasing. Together, they agreed that that the U.S. economy should be heavily dependent upon private consumption, an ideological consensus that reigned unchallenged for over a decade, until the shock of Soviet technical advances fueled a revulsion from the materialism of the "affluent society."[46] Through the end of the 1950s, the act of consuming material goods was figured as a patriotic duty to create a strong national economy, and by extension, a strong nation. As William Whyte famously proclaimed in 1956, "thrift is now un-American."[47] The plush carpet and bronze nude in John Johnson's office might not have been exactly what Whyte and the U.S. Chamber of Commerce had in mind, but they fulfilled the consumerist ideology all the same.

As Cohen and a number of critics have pointed out, the reliance on mass consumption to prop up the postwar economy had crucial implications for the choreography of gender.[48] Consumption was intrinsically linked with domesticity, a concept that was under tense renegotiation in the late 1940s. Certainly middle-class married women had long been established as homemakers, unlike their men, who worked for income outside the home. That World War II caused considerable disruption to this binary domestic model is well known: millions of men were stationed overseas away from families, and in turn, millions of women began earning independent incomes in their place. After the war, women were forced to leave their jobs so they could be given back to returning veterans, and the tax code was substantially rewritten to make it more difficult for women to inherit money and obtain mortgages or other credit. Thanks to landmark legislation such as the Servicemen Readjustment Act of 1944, popularly known as the G.I. Bill, the U.S. government funneled massive amounts of financial subsidy to male citizens in this period: women who had served in the Armed Services were rarely classified as veterans, and were thus not eligible for benefits.

Consumption of goods in the domestic economy—food, household appliances, furnishings, and so on—became one of the few means of agency for women. Although African American male veterans were often excluded from benefits as well, the dynamic was repeated across racial and class lines. *Tan Confessions*, for instance, was not only devoted to lurid fiction and celebrity gossip. The other half of the magazine, of which Johnson and the editors were more proud, contained domestic advice columns and consumer buying guides. In the first issue, for example, several pages were devoted to "This Month's Best Buys in New Products," featuring waffle irons, hairbrushes, a transparent door kick plate, and washable lamp shades.[49] There were also recipes for Thanksgiving puddings, advice on getting young children to eat and for stopping tooth decay, and a guide to "Modern Lamps." When *Tan Confessions* later dropped the confessional half and became simply *Tan*, it was this home service section that remained.

Fifties "domesticity" was obviously gendered, and in a self-conscious, arguably reactionary way. However, it seems to me slightly too facile to abandon an analysis of gender at the doorstep of "domesticity." Though larger ideologies of material consumption shaped the black middle class, there was surely more to the choreography of gender than the division of labor and consumption. As Rod Ferguson has argued, "the study of African American sexual and gender formations suggests that class differences represent negotiations with gender and sexual normativity."[50] *Tan Confessions* gives us a chance to take a remarkably unguarded look at exactly those negotiations—the lines men and women drew between themselves.

One of the most remarkable features in the magazine was a monthly column called "If You Married. . . ." The goal of this column was to provide a bit of fodder for presumptively feminine daydreams. Each month an anonymous author penned a fictional direct-address account of what married life would be like with, say, Jimmy Edwards, an actor and activist most famous for his role as Private Peter Moss in the 1949 film *Home of the Brave*. Interspersed with uplifting biographical details ("You'd share with Jimmy the responsibility he feels towards his people . . .") were the details of what married life could be like:

> You feel those hard, long arms go around your shoulders. You look up at that clean-cut, smooth face with the proud eyes and firm lips. Your husband is smiling at you with the even laughter he always has for you. Then you see his eyes warm up and his voice whispers softly to you. He's not the tall, tough, cool movie star anymore. He's just your man.[51]

The aesthetic at work here is worth exploring in detail, since it is reproduced in many other aspects of the magazine and resonates deeply with lyrics of the Orioles. In the case of these columns, the details were strikingly libidinal in a very specific mixture of strength and serenity. Compare this description with a poem published in the same issue, by the otherwise unknown "Binga Dismond."

This thing I know: I never feared
But some day would come kind fate
To turn around those dearest steps
Which left me broken, desolate.
A childish whim had torn my heart
And lost for me those million years
I missed her eyelash on my cheek
And moaned the sweetness of her tears.

That wind which blew her jet black hair
Across my lips and in my eyes,
Those stars that smiled down on the sea
Beneath the azure of those skies.
Were treasures through the countless years
When fled was hope, and gone was song;
They gave me the will to live
Through wretched days and nights too long.

This thing I know: I never feared
The book was closed. 'Twere false alarms
To dream that she would e'er remain
In any place but in my arms.

Written in a presumptively male first person, this poem constructs its narrator as a somewhat more Victorian version of Jimmy Edwards, a Sonny Til without the doo-wop harmonies. This black man is sensitive, he is attentive to the woman he loves . . . or at least *now* he is. Some mysterious "childish whim" in the near past is a source of regret. Unlike the similar pain holding back the protagonist of "It's Too Soon to Know," this transgression seems to have been perpetrated by the man, and unlike the anxiety expressed in the song, the narrator here seems convinced of the truth of his emotions as they now stand. In both texts, the strong arms of a man feature prominently, providing symbolic security to the presumptively female reader. Racial signifiers are subtly used to play into a desire for physical features that read as phenotypically white, or at least "tan": the "firm lips" of Jimmy Edwards seem a barely coded rejection of more visibly black facial features, and the "jet black hair" of the beloved in the poem is not only straight but fine enough to flow loosely in the wind.

Almost all men in *Tan Confessions* express a similar sensitivity toward their imaginary female partners. Other men who found themselves in a fictional marriage with the readership included Sidney Poitier, Errol Garner, Johnny Hartman, and William Warfield. Another regular feature was a column titled "How He Proposed," and written each month by the wife of a celebrity. Proposals recounted included those of Sugar Ray Robinson, Louis Armstrong, Nat King Cole, the saxophonist Willie Smith, pianist Eddie Heywood, and band leader Count Basie, and—the sole female celebrity—Sarah Vaughn. Factual or not, all these stories portray relationships where strong, faithful *Tan* men provided physical and emotional security. The cover of the inaugural issue set the tone: Billy Eckstine and his wife June in an embrace, his arms clasped around her not unlike those of the fictionalized Jimmy Edwards. Inside, Mrs. Eckstine contributed an essay about her husband titled, "My Prince Charming."

The ideal masculinity being choreographed in *Tan Confessions* relies upon a pervasive discourse of smoothness. Jimmy Edwards's face was literally smooth, but smoothness was also an aesthetic of performance. To be smooth meant to avoid extremes. Edwards's smoothness is also reflected in his "even laughter" and his "soft whispers." In the advice columns and letters to the editor, both men and women are counseled to avoid extreme emotions, to remain level-headed, and above all to avoid causing any kind of public disruption.

Even the music criticism of the magazine reflects these values. For the entire four-year run of *Tan Confessions*, through several different music critics, there is a near-uniformity of opinion that the best popular music is that which remains gentle and smooth. Nat King Cole's recording of "Jet" was "unusually smooth." Billy Ekstine's "vocals . . . virtually glow with smoothness and pretty tones." A new release by Duke Ellington features a "subtle but pulsating" solo on "Solitude." In a review of Chris Powell and his Blue Fames, the reviewer wrote that "the unique singing bandsmen stress unusual blendings and shadings of their voices that have a soothing, pleasing effect on records they have made thus far." Musicians not typically known for their smoothness are lauded when they accomplish it: apropos of the LP *Charlie Parker With Strings*, the reviewer notes that it "demonstrates effectively that the alto sax can adapt beautifully to the fluid melodic strains of string backing."[52] Examples of this discourse of musical smoothness abound in nearly every issue of the magazine, far outnumbering any positive mention of energetic, loud, or otherwise disjunctive music.

What does this discourse of smoothness signify? Hazel Carby has argued that middle-class black women's culture of the period reacted strongly against the working-class black southern women who recently migrated to the north.[53] But we need not read *Tan Confessions* as uniquely the product of women's culture. This would be to take the magazine at face value, to assume that it reflected without distortion the desires of its ideal readership, which is to say middle-class African American women. Noliwe M. Rooks has indeed shown how such magazines, beginning with *Ringwood's Afro American Journal of Fashion* in 1891, provided a rare and crucial public forum for these women.[54] At the same time, however, the idealized vision of masculinity being presented in *Tan Confessions* is not necessarily the creation of women. The publisher and the entire editorial board, with the exception of the editor of the home services section, were men. We do not know much about the operation of the magazine beyond that, but Johnson was known to keep tight editorial control and to hire mostly male writers. The result, then, was a middle-class black magazine that was written by men, mostly about men, but figured as they imagined women wanted them to be. The elaborately choreographed masculinity betrays both a drive to police female desire and an insecurity about the ability to do so. Smoothness, then, was an attempt to create a masculinity that did not draw excessive attention to itself, or traduce the narrow boundaries of black bourgeois propriety, but nevertheless maintained a certain power and control over women's minds and bodies.

Smoothness was a musically, socially, and physically gendered value deeply embedded in middle-class black culture of the late 1940s and early 1950s.[55] It was also a politically gendered value. For mainstream African American activists in this period, there were two pressing, but occasionally contradictory, imperatives. One was to turn the civil rights movement into a respectable issue untainted by association with other left-wing organizations, most notably the Communist Party, one of the oldest and staunchest allies of civil rights. Conservative activists and segregationists had long attempted to link civil rights with communist subversion; if the link had survived into the postwar Red Scare, organizations such the National Association for the Advancement of Colored Persons (NAACP) would not have, and the civil rights movement would have been irreparably damaged. As the historian Manfred Berg summarizes it, "the price for survival [was] the detachment of black civil rights from a more comprehensive concept of social reform and a self-imposed limitation to the narrow goals of desegregation and voting rights."[56] Civil rights activists maintained a fairly low profile, worked primarily within established legal channels, and rushed to criticize those, like Robeson or DuBois, who championed more radical reform. In effect, the strategy of the NAACP, by necessity, emphasized smoothness. The disruptive acts for which the civil rights movement later became famous—sit-ins, marches, and acts of civil disobedience—were not possible under McCarthyism, especially within a black middle-class value system that privileged order and control.

However much as the Orioles and their audience seem emblematic of a general postwar move toward David Riesman's "other-directed personality," we cannot forget that self and other take on quite a different aspect on the other side of the color line. A concept like "teamwork" will always mean something different to a marginalized group. This is especially true

with Til's choreography of gender, as always a location of heightened anxiety for the color line. As music by African American musicians became
more and more popular in the United States, the Orioles found themselves
in an increasingly difficult position. Partly this was the result of unavoidable circumstances. Til's essay was published in the aftermath of tragedy: a
car accident on tour in November of 1950 killed guitarist Tommy Gaither
and severely injured George Nelson and Johnny Reed. In the wake of the
accident, Nelson, whose gravelly voice had so effectively counterpointed
Til's on the contrasting bridges, developed a drinking problem, and was
asked to leave the group early in 1953. By 1954, they had broken up, just as
R&B vocal group music was starting to cross over in earnest.

The demise of the Orioles was also, however, to the shifting line of
respectability when it came to black musicians in the United States. The
Orioles managed one last hit that illuminates their difficult situation.
"Crying in the Chapel," a cover of a country tune, was released late in 1953
and spent eighteen weeks on the R&B charts, five of them at #1. The cover
was not unusual; "It's Too Soon to Know" and "Tell Me So" were anom-
alies in that they had been written expressly for the Orioles. Like most
"smooth" R&B vocal groups, the Orioles developed most of their material in the same manner as white pop singers, covering successful songs
in the hope that their own rendition might strike a receptive chord with
the record-buying public. Although popularly imagined to work only one
way—white pop labels covering black R&B songs for financial gain—the
reality of the practice was more complex and spanned nearly every genre.
Hits by white pop titans like Doris Day and Rosemary Clooney were particularly popular with the R&B vocal groups, and it was an old Tin Pan
Alley standard—"Blue Moon," written in 1934 by Richard Rodgers—that
provided the circulating I-vi-ii7-V chord progression that was becoming
near-obligatory for the genre.

"Crying in the Chapel" bears the unmistakable trace of its multi-generic
history. Its origins were in country swing, having been penned by a fairly
obscure Texas songwriter named Artie Glenn, guitarist of the Light Crust
Doughboys, who had written some numbers for Bob Wills. According to
Glenn family lore, "Crying in the Chapel" was written after Glenn suffered

through a painful but successful medical operation. Needing spiritual redemption, he walked across the street to the nearest church, the Loving Avenue Baptist Church, in Fort Worth, Texas.[57] The resulting song was given to his teenage son Darrell, who recorded it for the independent country label Valley.

The song was lifted from obscurity by the pop singer June Valli, one of the hosts of the radio program *Your Hit Parade*. Her version peaked at #4 in April of 1953. This lead to renewed interest in Glenn's original version, which entered the pop charts in July to peak at #6. Another country version of the song, by Rex Allen, made the charts at #8 in August, and the Orioles followed suit with their version the same month, which peaked at #11 on the pop charts.[58] Even as the mainstream of the genre of R&B was beginning to pull away into a more raucous direction, it is still easy to hear crucial differences between the Orioles and their white counterparts' versions of the song. Whereas Glenn, Valli, and Allen all articulated the text setting in a fairly straightforward manner, Til elongated most vowels into syncopated melismas. Another difference has more to do with recording technique: similar to Patti Page's reimagining of "The Tennessee Waltz," Sonny Til's lead vocal is significantly enhanced with reverb, whereas Glenn sings with a remarkably dry mix. As Peter Doyle has argued, part of this difference has to do with generic differences between the swiftly coalescing R&B and country industries. R&B producers tended toward a more reverberant mix—read by Doyle as therefore more emotionally exuberant—whereas country producers tended toward a dry mix driven by an ideology of natural authenticity.[59] The Orioles echoing mix, however, is not just an index of generic difference. Obviously, the reverberation of Sonny Til's voice is intended to portray the aural soundscape of a church. The sound world of Til's "Crying in the Chapel" tells us that the singer is not merely telling a story; he is *literally* in the chapel at the moment of our listening:

> You saw me crying in the chapel,
> the tears I shed were tears of joy.
> I know the meaning of contentment
> I am happy with the Lord.

Just a plain and simple chapel
Where all good people go to pray.
I pray the Lord that I'll go stronger,
As I live from day to day.
I search, and I searched.
But I couldn't find
No where on earth
To find peace of mind.
Now I'm happy in the chapel
Where people are of one accord.
Yes we gather in the chapel
Just to sing and praise the Lord.

The churchy effect is further enhanced by the cascade of tubular bells that open the song. Many other versions, including the original, but also those by Valli, Elvis Presley, and even Italian pop singer Bobby Solo, accompany the song with bell-like sounds, but most use a simple xylophone for the effect and none use real bells. The Orioles and their producers were attempting to create a song that made heavy, even theatrical gestures toward the eponymous chapel. In so doing, they kicked off a moment in the mid-1950s that saw religious-themed songs released by several R&B vocal groups, some inspired directly by the Orioles' version of "Crying in the Chapel." The Cadillacs, for instance, famous for their flashy stage show choreographed by Cholly Atkins, scored a major hit with "Gloria," in 1954, which began with lead singer Earl "Speedo" Caroll doing his best to imitate plainchant. The Drifters had a similar hit with their cover of Bing Crosby's "The Bells of St. Mary" in 1956, and other groups had smaller hits in a spiritual vein.

What is interesting about this mini-fad for religious subject matter is that it was not about gospel. It was *not*, for the most part, related to one of the most famous stories in popular music history: the migration of musical styles from African American ecstatic religious traditions into the genre later known as "soul." Ray Charles is often cited as the inventor of soul, with his sophisticated reworkings of gospel standards into R&B

singles. He was accompanied by singers who began in sweet groups on the gospel music circuit but later "crossed over" to R&B, such as Sam Cooke; and Pentecostal "street preachers" like Sister Rosetta Tharpe whose blues-based gospel numbers wavered back and forth across an increasingly blurry line. As the work of Gayle Wald has outlined, the conceptual line between sacred "gospel" and secular "rhythm & blues" was a crucial structuring factor in the social arrangements of the black musical world.[60] Even if styles and techniques crossed freely from one to the other, there were real social risks and rewards for those who "switched sides." Tharpe was the target of considerable opprobrium when she appeared on the same bill with jazz singers, despite her often-stated commitment to religious music. A figure like Mahalia Jackson, who resisted the allure of commercial success in the pop market in favor of a (still lucrative, of course) career in the gospel market, was widely lauded in the community for her commitment.

R&B vocal groups, however, are not so easy to place in this gospel/R&B dialectic. In fact, very little of the conventional wisdom with regard to the origins of "soul" applies to them. Very few were from the South, or at least any farther south than Washington, D.C. Those few who attended church were largely members of mainline denominations whose relationship with ecstatic worship traditions of Pentecostal or Sanctified churches was ambivalent at best. Many received a traditional musical education, thanks to the segregated but nevertheless comprehensive public education system in the northeast. And almost without exception, these musicians were admitted fans of the postwar pop world dominated by white singers. All of this is not to say that the R&B vocal groups such as the Orioles were somehow "less black" than their counterparts in other sectors of the charts. They simply represent a different aspect of African American life than that which is often privileged in popular music histories.

This is why the "religious" music of the Orioles sounds so different from either the smooth gospel of the Soul Stirrers or the harder gospel of the Blind Boys of Mississippi. "Crying in the Chapel" has little to do with ecstatic spirituality, and everything to do with finding a new way to represent black masculinity as smooth and sensitive, attractive and yet unthreatening. By using religiosity as an affect, rather than a source for stylistic appropriation or spiritual inspiration, the Orioles were carving out a position not unfamiliar to the black bourgeoisie. Franklin Frazier took a somewhat ambivalent position toward black religious life. On the one hand, he valued it as a mostly authentic expression of community that dated back to slavery, and whose mimicry of white values was only superficial. He also appreciated the moral influence of religious, its strictures against gambling and drinking, activities of which he heartily disproved. At the same time, however, he noted social stratification in the operation of churches.

Noting that most African Americans were essentially divided between Methodist and Baptist affiliations, Frazier argued that the former, with its hierarchal power structure, had "increasingly adopted a secular outlook toward the world and given support to the current values of black middle classes." Within the more diverse ranks of Baptist churches, he nevertheless noted that in many cities, middle-class Baptist congregations "sought to dissociate themselves from the emotional religious activities of the Negro masses."[61] Affirming or gaining class status through denominational choice was a strategy common in the United States after World War II. Vance Packard's pop-sociology tract of 1959 *The Status Seekers* would carefully map out the terrain of prestige. At the top of the list were Episcopalians; among other evidence, Packard noted that three-quarters of the weddings in the society pages of the *New York Times* occurred in Episcopal churches, and that a survey of top corporate executives found them ten times more likely to list Episcopal as their faith. Behind the Episcopalians came a second tier of Unitarians, Congregationalists, and Presbyterians, depending slightly on geographical region, then Methodists and Lutherans, and finally Baptists at the bottom.[62]

Belonging to some church became, at least in the popular imagination, an important piece of the postwar consensus, a marker of patriotic pride in the struggle against the atheistic Soviet Union and a convenient means of social organization in the many new communities springing up along the suburban fringe. As President Eisenhower famously remarked in 1954, "Our government makes no sense unless it is a founded in a deeply felt religious faith—and I don't care what it is."[63] For this reason, many scholars have argued, that the civil rights movement turned to hymnody and spirituals as its soundtrack, rather than more militant soul or even gospel music. Invoking Jesus in *a capella* harmony at the sit-in or on the freedom march neatly made the argument that if the United States claimed moral superiority in the Cold War, how could it ignore the oppressed fellow Christians back home?

But what seems crucial to me about "Crying in the Chapel" is its affect of sexual sublimation, even masquerade. This is not a particularly original reading, per se. Since its release, audiences have heard a simple trick at work in this song: if he sings devotionally to God, then those listeners who wish can imagine that Sonny is singing devotionally to them. That way nobody on either side of the color line need be threatened by the potent force of a sexually attractive black man. The Orioles prefigure here the famous trend in vocal groups toward increasingly juvenile subject matter and singers, culminating in the thirteen-year-old Frankie Lymon. As Brian Ward bluntly put it, "perfectly groomed blacks in their early teens could pass more easily as real-life incarnations of the submissive, emasculated black 'boy' of white rhetoric and imagination."[64] Sonny Til could not impersonate a teenager, but by choosing religiously themed material, he could provide himself a similar safety net.

This sleight of hand adds another layer of meaning to "Crying in the Chapel." The music of the Orioles is marked by their virtuosic handling of many expectations. They could express the upwardly mobile desires of the black bourgeoise. For Franklin Frazier, this might have been counterproductive politically, but it was nevertheless the sort of smooth, integrationist sentiment that led to the victory of *Brown v. Board of Education* in 1954. And even as their music provided the perfect soundtrack for the black bourgeoisie, the Orioles also tapped into an almost inaudible oppositional sentiment that resonated with the nascent African American youth culture, at least to those who wanted to hear it. As the protagonist of Ralph Ellison's 1952 novel *The Invisible Man* said of white passersby at the beginning of his journey, "when they approach me, they see only my surroundings, themselves or figments of their imagination—indeed everything and anything except me."[65]

The Blonde Who Knew Too Much

The Whiteness of Doris Day

The phrase "Doris Day" today evokes not so much an individuated person as a type, or more specifically, a phenotype. It is difficult to imagine any discussion of "Doris Day" proceeding without there occurring some reference to "blonde" and "blue-eyed." Together with that blondeness and blue-eyed-ness comes a certain character: perky, righteous, and virginal, together with a sense of what Wayne Koestenbaum once called her "hygienic frigidity."[1] Some know her best from the Rock Hudson comedies of the late 1965s and early 1960s, others know her better from her television show that ran from 1968 to 1973. Those born later, such as myself, know her not at all, except as blonde simulacrum. Those of my generation became familiar with the Doris Day parody first, the actual image later. I saw the 2003 homage *Down with Love* and heard the 1973 Sly and the Family Stone version of "Que Sera, Sera" before I had seen a single Doris Day film. And yet I knew enough of the Doris Day type to recognize these performances as the parodies they were.[2]

Such is not an unusual fate for Hollywood celebrities. As several generations of star studies scholarship have shown, the iconic performances
of film stars of her generation have been an extraordinarily productive
site for cultural formation and contestation. Doris Day's place within this
process is not unusual as a matter of technique; the creation of her persona
followed the typical progression of studio system pressures, individual
relationships, and the usual personal tragedies. Rather, the Doris Day type
looms especially large as the paradigmatic symbol of a particular kind of
white, middle-class femininity. For some, such as the neoconservative
critic Bruce Bawer she is a laudable symbol of wholesome innocence.[3] For
many second-wave feminists, that wholesome innocence was a burden—
Erica Jong famously bemoaned the whiplash of being "raised to be Doris
Day, yearning in our twenties to be Gloria Steinem, then doomed to raise
our midlife daughters in the age of Nancy Reagan and Princess Di."[4] As
early as 1980, the Doris Day persona became the subject of a recuperative
project by some feminist critics, but it's a project that has never quite taken
hold in the popular imagination. The staid, conservative image of Doris
Day might help to explain a relative paucity of scholarship on the star.
There simply is not a great deal of excitement there. It is perhaps understandable that in Richard Dyer's classic study of film celebrity *Heavenly
Bodies*, the role of the fifties blonde heroine goes to the other one, Marilyn
Monroe.[5]

And yet, we ignore Doris Day at our peril. If nothing else, as a historical
matter there is her absolutely phenomenal popularity in the 1950 and '60s.
Other stars might sometimes catch our eyes and ears more piquantly, but
at the height of her career Doris was arguably the most popular woman
performer of her time. Such things are difficult to quantize, but as every
Doris Day fan biography will tell you, even after thirty years of retire-
ment she is still today tied with Shirley Temple as the top money-making
woman film actor of all time, and during her heyday she was voted year
after year as the most popular actress by film critics. At a smaller but perhaps slightly more scientific level, a 1956 survey of 10,000 high school
students in New York City found that for boys Elvis Presley was the favor-
ite performer, but for girls it was Doris Day.[6] If for nothing else than her

mass-cultural importance, we ought to have a better understanding as to how the Doris Day type, as performed by Doris Day, was created.

That pivotal importance should be taken as a small matter. Historians of music have long been somewhat suspicious of artists who have achieved tremendous fame, especially those whose popularity occupies a middle-brow imagination. And certainly, the study of such tremendously popular figures can be very difficult; on the one hand there is an enormous amount of information, but on the other hand that information has been mediated to an extreme degree by the forces of celebrity. Day did not, for example, respond to my request for an interview, and any source claiming autobiographical authenticity must always be viewed somewhat suspiciously. At the same time, even if studying the mass popularity of Doris Day requires analysis from a certain distance, she has a great deal to tell us about the formation of identity in the 1950s. The particularities of this performance have quietly, almost subconsciously, formed a central part of cultural life in the United States. The Doris Day performance belongs to the subtle category of those that are so obvious as to escape attention, aspiring to an almost insidious quality of universality. Presumed unmarked, presumed normal, and yet cloaking a vast operation of labor to maintain those features. Even as Doris Day herself—or rather, perhaps we should say, Doris Mary Ann Kapellhoff, the woman who became Doris Day—receded from public view, the past three decades of absence have not diminished her influence.

Central to this performance of unmarked universality is the concept of whiteness. Whiteness is, of course, the ultimate universal, in the insidious sense of a category of identity that is forever unmarked, never noticed except in the presence of others. In fact, as critical race theory has long argued, whiteness does not actually exist in the same sense as our usual concepts of race and ethnicity. It is, rather, a system of power relationships, expansive enough to include newly emergent communities and devastating to those who still fall outside its boundaries. In the 1950s, the United States saw an acceleration of assimilation, spurred by the suburbanization of a growing middle class, that saw whiteness grow more expansive than ever before. I will be arguing that sentimental middlebrow performers such as Doris Day provided an important discursive role model for this new generation of whiteness.

To do so, I propose to take the artist at her own contention that her "type" was created not in the later Rock Hudson comedies or television show but in her first film musicals. I will, therefore, look in detail at three important singing roles early in her career: *Romance on the High Seas* (1948), *Calamity Jane* (1953), and *The Man Who Knew Too Much* (1956). The fact that many of these early roles were in some respect musicals strikes me as particularly important. As a biographical matter, her initial career as a singer is an often-overlooked aspect of her early popularity, but I think it also affords us a disciplinary opportunity to pay attention not just to the scopic regimes of her films but also to her own performance. Whiteness, after all, is not actually a skin color, but an embodied performance of fragile power. At least, that's how Doris did it.

■

In March of 1954, the well-respected journalist Edward R. Murrow and his producer Fred Friendly created an episode of the news program *See It Now* that has become one of the defining moments of early television history. Titled "A Report on Joseph McCarthy," the episode was not Murrow and Friendly's first public attack against the senator. The previous fall, an episode of *See It Now* had explored the case of Gordan Radulovitch, an Army Reservist who had been dismissed from service because of the political beliefs of his father and sister. This earlier broadcast had not attacked Joseph McCarthy himself; it had, rather, criticized the methods of the broader anti-communist movement that was already being called, to the senator's evident pride, "McCarthyism." The impersonal army appeals board bore no relation to McCarthy, and yet its use of secret evidence and hearsay in the prosecution of an innocent man was seen as part of a larger cultural moment of which Senator McCarthy was only a symbolic figurehead.

"A Report on Joseph McCarthy," on the other hand, narrowed the assault to one man. Carefully constructing their argument out of McCarthy's "own words and pictures," as Murrow dourly intoned at the beginning, the

producers assembled a range of filmstrips, audio recordings, and live television appearances to give the appearance of a man out of control. We see
McCarthy stuttering, sweating, yelling, contradicting himself, and even,
when finding himself the dedicatee of a laudatory speech, breaking into
tears. It was a skillful move on the part of Murrow and Friendly. Many
critics have pointed out that the effectiveness of the show relies upon the
very tactics McCarthy himself used. Andrea Friedman, for instance, has
pointed out that the broadcast traffics in gossip and innuendo to imply
that McCarthy's sexuality was somehow suspect. Anti-McCarthy tabloids
at the time made much of a supposed love triangle between McCarthy,
his assistant Roy Cohn, and Cohn's friend David Schine. The respectable Edward R. Murrow would never directly relate such gossip, but as
Friedman points out, he was also careful to include a shot of Roy Cohn
leaning in to whisper intimately in McCarthy's ear.[7]

There is another, less remarked upon aspect of the Murrow broadcast
that sheds light on the complex circulation of power in the United States
after World War II. As much as McCarthy's words are the centerpiece of
the broadcast, his actual body also plays a starring role. In contrast to
Murrow's elegant, lithe appearance, the depictions of McCarthy were of an
unruly body perpetually coming undone. We see his five o'clock shadow,
and the sweat glistening on his forehead. There is his rumpled, unpressed
suit and the tears welling up in his eyes. In a climactic scene, McCarthy is
shown listening to a witness in a hearing room. The scene begins with a
wide shot of the entire room. We then cut to a closer view of McCarthy;
it is now easier to see his physical discomfort in the crowded room. The
camera then zooms in closer still, focusing just on his sweaty face and
his dark, bushy eyebrows. Murrow's voiceover makes it clear that these
images are meant to signify racial difference. Quoting McCarthy's longtime enemy, Senator Ralph Flanders of Vermont, Murrow reads, "He dons
his war paint. He goes into his war dance. He goes forth to battle and
proudly returns with the scalp of a pink Army dentist."[8]

Here, Murrow voices one of the most popular lines of inquiry into
McCarthyism as a broad-based social movement. Senator McCarthy
was, of course, Irish American. During the 1950s, many critics analyzed

the rise of McCarthy in ethnic terms: the midwestern Irish Catholic, on the one hand, and on the other, was what Seymour Lipset later called "McCarthy's ideal-typical Communist enemy . . . an upper-class Eastern Episcopalian graduate of Harvard employed by the State Department."[9] This perspective on McCarthyism sees it as the politicization of a fundamentally ethnic conflict. McCarthy's base of support, according to an influential line of reasoning, were the huge numbers of Americans who, like McCarthy, came from immigrant communities that after World War II were being assimilated into the American mainstream. [10] His strength, the argument goes, was part of a relocation of political and economic power away from men of English and Scottish descent, who belonged to mainline Protestant denominations and were well-educated and well-off. Not only was McCarthy not assimilated into this traditional elite, he was able to transform their qualities into negative attributes. Personified by Alger Hiss, the eastern "elite" was seen as spineless and effete.

In racial terms, one might see competing definitions of whiteness. Murrow's attack is a famous example of how this discourse worked, but only one of many. Anti-McCarthy political cartoons were less subtle in their racialized portrayals of the senator (see figure 3.1). Cartoons always choose physical elements of featured politicians to exaggerate, and it is telling that nearly every anti-McCarthy cartoon chose to exaggerate his skin-darkening five o'clock shadow. Combined with frequent emphasis on his heavy brows, sweaty forehead, and simian hunch, the junior senator from Wisconsin was forcibly devolved into something between Neanderthal and ape.

The contestation of whiteness in politics was nothing new, but its particular inflection in the postwar era is our goal here. In July of 1950, the newly organized United Nations Economic and Social Organization (UNESCO) addressed one of the major legacies of World War II: the "race question," as it was called. After more than a century of scientific attempts to prove racial superiorities of various kinds, by one means or another, the liberal consensus was that the Nazi regime had proved the danger of the concept by extending such attempts to their logical and horrible conclusion. An international team of anthropologists and sociologists—including

Figure 3.1 Joseph McCarthy as Racialized Other.
A 1954 Herblock Cartoon, © The Herb Block Foundation.

Claude Lévi-Strauss, E. Franklin Frazier, and other luminaries—produced a report that concluded in terms of the utmost finality that there was no scientific evidence to prove one race was superior to another, or even that there were, scientifically speaking, different "races" beyond the generic *Homo sapiens*. Any differences, they argued, were the result of cultural upbringing. Quoting Confucius, the report argued that "Men's natures are alike; it is their habits that carry them far apart."[11] Rather than race, the report suggested, the term "ethnic groups" should more properly be used.

As discussed in the introduction to this book, the use of *ethnicity* rather than *race* was not a new invention, with the liberal notion of ethnicity as culture, rather than biology, largely dominating in mainstream discourse. Even as social science turned away from "race" and towards "ethnicity," however, ethnic groups themselves were coming under increasing internal and external pressure in the 1950s. Historians have identified this as the moment when many formerly distinct immigrant communities experienced hastened assimilation. The upward trajectory was not permanent, of course, and by the early 1960s critics like Daniel Moynihan began to speak of the "unmeltable ethnics"—those immigrant communities resisting the blandishments of the postwar consensus.[12] But these mid-sixties observations point toward the intense pressure to assimilate after World War II. Statistics tell the story: between 1942 and 1948, the number of radio stations broadcasting in a language other than English dropped by 40 percent. The number of Jewish Americans who changed or shortened their last names doubled over the same period.[13]

Richard Alba has argued that World War II itself played an important role in hastening the pace of assimilation. Although prejudice and antagonism toward German and Italian Americans did surface, such feelings were much more subdued than they had been a generation earlier, during the First World War. (Treatment of Japanese Americans, of course, was a vastly different story.) Alba points out that the waves of European immigration earlier in the century were thought to necessitate a more conciliatory approach on the home front. Government propaganda, for instance, such as the newsreels and photographs circulated by the Office of War Information, made a concerted effort to include images of Americans marked as visibly ethnic.[14]

Perhaps more important, however, was the enormous expansion of the American middle class. As Alba notes, from 1942 to 1948, the percentage of workers in white-collar employment nearly doubled, from 29.4 to 44.8 percent. This shift was assisted by a doubling of college enrollment, from 15 percent (of all men) in 1940 to 30 percent in 1954. Furthermore, the character of blue-collar employment changed as well, with skilled labor constituting greater and greater proportion of such work. By 1948, only 4.4 percent of the workforce was engaged in jobs defined as "unskilled labor."[15] We cannot completely ascribe ethnic assimilation to the expansion of the middle class, but the economic transformation did play an important role, especially in terms of geography. The millions of units of new housing being constructed on the edges of American cities were segregated, but only along the color line, in stark contrast to tightly knit ethnic neighborhoods before the war. To be sure, immigrant communities still tended to cluster in certain areas, but the geographic diffusion meant that institutions of coherence such as churches, neighborhood centers, social clubs, restaurants, and newspapers were increasingly difficult to maintain.

It should be noted, however, that this assimilation did not occur uniformly, nor without contestation. Assimilation was uneven, both geographically and within different ethnic groups. The relative "degree of assimilation"—a technical term in sociology of the period based largely on residency patterns—varied widely. In Cincinnati, for instance, the city where Doris Day entered the music business, one study found that while residential segregation of Italian Americans dropped precipitously from 1930 to 1950, residential segregation of Irish Americans actually rose in the first half of the century, and remained constant until well after World War II.[16]

Furthermore, American politics did not necessarily maintain pace with the liberal consensus of social science. Most crucial in this regard was the revision of immigration law in 1952 known as the McCarran-Walter Act. This legislation was the first successful "reform" to pass Congress since 1929, after a series of failed attempts in the 1940s to liberalize the avowedly anti-immigrant policies of the 1920s. McCarran-Walter, however, was in actuality a step back. Instead, it solidified the existing state of immigration policy that enforced a strict annual limit of visas. In this system, each European country was given an annual quota equal to one-sixth of 1 percent of citizens in the United States whose ancestry derived from that country, based on the 1920 census. Effectively dismissing all immigration of the previous three decades, this system had the effect of promoting immigration from Western and Northern Europe.

The only liberalization, if it can be called that, was that instead of banning Asian immigrants outright, a new quota of 2,000 annual visas was granted to immigrants of Asian ancestry. Unlike European visas, however, these visas were granted on the basis of race rather than nationality.

For example, a white English immigrant would apply for a visa as an Englishman, but a British citizen who was of Asian ancestry would count against the far more limited Asian quota. In addition, McCarran-Walter created new paranoid rules for immigrants: they could not be communists or drug addicts, and they had to annually report their address to the government for a central security file. Outgoing President Harry Truman vetoed this legislation, pointing out that there was a vested national interest in encouraging immigration from Eastern European countries endangered by an expansionist Soviet Union, but Congress easily overrode his veto.[17]

Economic forces do not tell the entire story of ethnic assimilation, nor do the hegemonic operations of large institutions such as federal legislation or property developers. Much has also been made of the cultural transformations wrought by assimilation—or perhaps it occurred conversely. Religion was a particular battleground. In an influential 1955 essay, the conservative essayist Will Herberg argued that "our cultural assimilation has taken place not in a 'melting pot,' but rather in a 'transmuting pot' in which all ingredients have been transformed and assimilated to an idealized 'Anglo-Saxon' model." This transformation, Herberg further wrote, was predicated upon a reconfiguration of religious values:

> To be a Protestant, a Catholic, or a Jew are today the alternative ways of being an American. This religious normality implies a certain religious unity in terms of a common "American religion" of which each of the three great religious communions is regarded as an equi-legitimate expression. Each on his part—the Protestant, the Catholic, the Jew—may regard his own "faith" as the best or even the truest, but unless he is a theologian or affected with a special theological interest, he will quite "naturally" look upon the other as sharing with his communion a common "spiritual" foundation of basic "ideals and values," the chief of these being religion itself. America thus has its underlying American Way of Life—of which the three conventional religions are somehow felt to be appropriate manifestations and expressions.[18]

Herberg's ideal "American Way of Life" is a good example of a discourse of universality. The cultural expression of whiteness here is both expansive and limiting. On the one hand, the rhetoric of assimilation allows for small cultural differences to be minimized; on the other, those whose religious practices are unable to assimilated are ever further outside of the mainstream, no longer part of the "way of life." Earlier American elites had in some respects been comfortable as a dominant minority, insulated from the masses in their men's clubs and Episcopal churches while easily retaining control over the means of production. By the 1950s, in Herberg's view, the dominant class is now theoretically the vast majority of the country.

The story of postwar ethnic assimilation explains some of the power relations behind whiteness, and also some of its peculiar cultural logic. Richard Dyer's 1997 *White*, the best and most influential film studies analysis of whiteness, shows how whiteness as a visual metaphor has its roots in religious iconography, colonialism, and what he terms a "culture of light."[19] With the advent of cinema, visuality became paramount to constructing a white race. In a fascinating chapter on representations of women in film, Dyer notes that the limitations of early photographic technology posed serious problems for white women: the first generation of black-and-white film stock processed shades of yellow very badly, often leading blonde hair to appear dark once developed. The solution was careful backlighting, giving a glowing Marian halo to an actresses head and hair. In addition, human skin did not reflect light properly, leading to the development of facial makeup specially designed to bounce light back at dazzling levels. Unless, of course, that skin was black, in which case the actor simply appeared as a dark, faceless shadow. Even after film stock improved greatly, and color was introduced, the highly controlled nature of a modern film set means that we are given a window into exactly how whiteness as a visual metaphor is created and contested.

Dyer makes a convincing case for the importance of visual representations of whiteness. It is also important, however, to remember that there is much more to whiteness than the visual. There are, after all, real bodies behind those hyper-white faces. Several recent critics have attempted to introduce other modalities of whiteness in film, as in Krin Gabbard's *Black*

Magic, which shows how African American music often stands in for the missing black bodies of all-white films.[20] Gwendolyn Audrey Foster's recent work has sought to reintroduce film as made up of *moving* images of whiteness—images with histories and trajectories.[21] Neither of these two works, however, deals sufficiently with corporeal realities—what bodies actually do in "real life."

Luckily, one of the other important locations of the critique of whiteness occurred in a discipline concerned above all with bodies and politics. Critical race theory was, in its inception, primarily a legal discourse. Its foundational figures, scholars such as Derrick Bell and Richard Delgado, were often also lawyers dealing with the dissolution of the civil rights movement in the 1970s, and the ensuing need to devise a new racial epistemology. Although the notion that race was a social construction had long circulated in academic settings, it now became a dominant axiom of legal reasoning. And with this newly critical discourse on race came the impulse to question whiteness itself—not in terms of representation, but in terms of power. This stream of whiteness studies is not solely limited to the law—George Lipsitz's *The Possessive Investment in Whiteness* is an excellent interdisciplinary example—but it is concerned with social and political realities, and less so with cultural representations.[22] Studying how whiteness can "sound" necessarily involves both matters of representation in cultural products and how those sounds are produced by actual people.

■

The performance career of Doris Day began in a minstrel show in Cincinnati in the 1920s. In her autobiography, written fifty years later, she still remembered the first lines she sang as a kindergartner:

I'se goin' down to the Cushville hop,
And there ain't no niggie goin' to make me stop.[23]

This was as far as she remembered, but the song is a well-known tune by Benjamin King, and would have continued:

> Missus gwine to deck me all up in white,
> So watch de step dat I's getting' in to-night.
> Um-hm, mah honey, tain' no use;
> Um-hm, mah honey, turn me loose,
> Um-hm, mah honey, watch me shine
> When mah foot am a-shakin' in de ole coonjine[24]

There is also no record or memory of whether she performed the awkward shuffling of the coonjine dance, or indeed of whether she blacked up for this performance. In her recounting, the story is told not to emphasize the minstrelsy but, rather, to narrate an intense childhood shame of having visibly wet herself just before going on stage. The story is followed, however, by tales of the casual racism of growing up in the German American neighborhood of Evanston, in Cincinnati. Twisting around shame, regret, and ignorance, the foundational performance places Doris squarely in the context of the tangled legacy of racial borrowing and betrayal in popular music, a legacy that her mature persona would do much to transform.

The performance also places Doris squarely within the mainstream of singers of her generation. The great majority of popular singers, especially women, who were successful in the 1950s came from similar midwestern and southern backgrounds, and like Doris they got their starts in local variety shows and the amateur hours of regional radio stations, before joining the traveling dance bands of the late swing era and then eventually striking off on their own. One might compare her story to that of Peggy Lee, who grew up in North Dakota, sang on the local station KOVC, and toured with Benny Goodman before going solo in 1943. Or Patti Page, who grew in Oklahoma, sang on Tulsa's KTUL, toured with the Jimmy Joy Band, and struck it big on her own in 1947 with the single "Confess." Or even more directly, Rosemary Clooney, a fellow native of the Cincinnati region who won a spot on that city's WLW station, toured with the Tony Pastor Orchestra, and signed a solo contract with Columbia Records in 1949.

One basic fact of the period is the demise of the large swing orchestras that had dominated the airwaves and jukeboxes before the war. Many

explanations have been essayed for this development, beginning with the
fact that so many young musicians were drafted during the war; simple
lack of manpower forced many ensembles out of business. There was also
a series of violent disputes between artists, managers, and record companies that led to the American Federation of Musicians calling a strike
against record companies that lasted from 1942 to 1944. Coupled with
wartime shortages of shellac, and a general industry-wide fear of intro-
ducing new acts during wartime, the market for dance music produced by
large bands declined precipitously.

As the story goes, the musicians dropped from these big bands went
in three different directions. Some became members of stripped-down
ensembles that used only one instrument where previously there might
have been a section, such as Louis Jordan and his Tympany Five. A small
coterie of jazz musicians went the even more minimalist route of "modern jazz," the virtuosic chamber music called bebop.[25] Most crucially for
our narrative, however, the vocalists of large dance bands began to strike
out on their own. Previously, big band vocalists had been relegated to a
supporting role, usually stepping in for a verse or two, in the context of a
longer number mostly dominated by instrumentals. Led by Frank Sinatra,
who left the Tommy Dorsey Orchestra in 1942, these vocalists began to
strike out on their own during the recording ban, and as the war ended,
pop vocalists began to dominate the charts.

But in the next decade, the ecology of the pop charts underwent a subtle
shift. Frank Sinatra's initial burst of popularity faded away, and there arose
a new phenomenon of "girl singers." Table 3.1 compares the ten bestselling
artists of 1947 with those of 1954.

In 1947, the only women in this top ten are Dinah Shore and Jo Stafford.
By 1954, there are four women, three of whom share near identical biographies. Patti Page, Rosemary Clooney, and Doris Day were young blonde
women from the interior of the country who began singing on local radio
shows, graduated to supporting vocals in a dance band, and finally headed
out on their own in the early 1950s, beginning phenomenally successful
solo careers. Together, these women were referred to as the "girl singers,"
and it is their success, rather than the male vocalists such as Sinatra and

TABLE 3.1   THE RISE OF THE "GIRL SINGERS"

1947	1954
1. Eddy Howard	1. Eddie Fisher
2. Ted Weems	2. Four Aces
3. Perry Como	3. Patti Page
4. Frank Sinatra	4. Perry Como
5. Dinah Shore	5. Rosemary Clooney
6. Jo Stafford	6. The Gaylords
7. Vaughn Monroe	7. The Crew-Cuts
8. Bing Crosby	8. Kitty Kallen
9. Johnny Mercer	9. Nat "King" Cole
10. Guy Lombardo	10. Doris Day

SOURCE: Joel Whitburne, ed., *Billboard Pop Hits Singles and Albums, 1940–1954* (Menomonee Falls, WI: Record Research, 2002), 198, 258.

Nat "King" Cole, that came to be seen as emblematic of the parlous state of popular music before rock and roll. The racial uniformity of their histories is notable: male vocalists could be marked as Italian, or even, in the unique case of Nat "King" Cole, African American. A female pop vocalist, however, *had* to be white.[26] Conspicuous whiteness marked not only their appearance but also their singing styles and on-screen personae, and this became integral to the story of "pop" music.

After an early attempt at a career in dancing was ruined by an injury, Day won a contest to appear on WLW, which she parlayed into a series of touring gigs that culminated with becoming the vocalist for the Les Brown Orchestra. On early recordings with Les Brown, such as the hit "Sentimental Journey" (1944), her voice is almost unrecognizable, throaty and dark, with a tight vibrato that at certain moments makes her a dead ringer for her idol Ella Fitzgerald. How did this singing body eventually become the singer of "Que Sera, Sera"? Doris herself once pondered the question, in her putative autobiography, the precise origins of her own type. For her, the answer was not in the Rock Hudson comedies, or in the television shows, and certainly not in her early career as a big band singer. Rather, she hypothesized that it had something to do with her early film career at Warner Brothers, in a series of music-centered roles that began with her breakthrough *Romance on the High Seas* (1948) and continued through seventeen films in just six years. Doris Day argues that it is in these low-budget and often hastily produced movies that she became Doris Day.

The legend of Doris's entry into Hollywood began with a party in Los Angeles, at the home of composer Jule Styne. Having been turned down by both Judy Garland and Betty Hutton, Styne and his writing partner Sammy Cohn were looking for a singer to take the lead role in a forthcoming musical at Warner Brothers, *Romance on the High Seas*. At Styne's party, Doris sang "Embraceable You" for the crowd, and was immediately invited to audition for the role in front of director Michael Curtiz, of *Casablanca* fame. In the audition, both the makeup team and Curtiz himself attempted to position Day as a Betty Hutton type, bouncy and energetic with makeup "that made me look as if I were wearing a mask." Doris, however, rejected that approach, in favor of a kind of personal authenticity that rejected both Hollywood star craft and the more psychologized "Method" techniques then percolating in the New York avant-garde.

> When we did the scene, I did it my own way. I guess I instinctively understood something then that was to sustain me through all the years of acting that followed—to thine own self be true. Don't imitate. Don't try to imagine how someone else might feel. Project your honest response to your movie situation, quite the same as you would respond honestly to a life situation. I have never been one for artifice.[27]

Once filming began, Curtiz apparently embraced her low-key style, putting a stop to acting lessons she had been taking with longtime studio coach Sophie Rosenstein. "You have there a natural thing there in you," he apparently told her.[28] Such sentiments aside, the end result of Doris Day's performance in *Romance on the High Seas* came down heavily on the side of artifice. Speaking of her look in this first film, Doris says it best: "There I was on the screen, a pancaked, lacquered Hollywood purse made out of a Cincinnati sow's ear."[29] Indeed, the plot of the film requires the character of Georgia Garrett to be down on her luck and from humble origins. And yet, the filming and marketing of the film required that same character to be beautiful and glamorous. Thus, in a classic Hollywood juxtaposition, Doris was made to speak in labored contemporary slang, chewing gum vigorously, even as the Warner Brothers team scraped a particularly thick application of pancake makeup on to her face and dressed her in a series of elaborate blonde wigs and even more elaborate shoulder pads.

In the wake of *Romance on the High Seas*, Doris Day was immediately cast by Warner Brothers in an interestingly diverse set of musicals. For example, 1950 saw three films released: *Young Man with a Horn, Tea for Two*, and *West Point Story*. The latter two were light musical comedies, but the first was a lightly fictionalized account of the life of Bix Beiderbecke, with explicit treatment of his alcoholism. Until ending her contract with Warner Brothers in 1954, Doris's performances would lurch back and forth between the dark and the light, providing her ample room to expand upon her dramatic skills while still expanding her fan base. Ironically, it is one of her lightest and silliest roles, the title role of *Calamity Jane* in 1953, that has provoked some of the most interesting critical discussion of her evolving persona.

Calamity Jane was produced by Warner Brothers as a direct result of the successful 1950 film version of the western musical *Annie Get Your Gun*, which had starred Betty Hutton as a last-minute replacement for a drug-addled Judy Garland. Not only does *Calamity Jane* share with *Annie Get Your Gun* a historical setting and a love interest—musical theater star Howard Keel in both—the central plot device is the same: a rough tomboy is transformed, not without difficulty, into a married woman. This narrative, of course, mirrors the broader trend in American culture of the period, as women were "redomesticated" and withdrew from the workforce in the aftermath of World War II. In *Annie Get Your Gun*, Annie Oakley is a bumptious trick shooter who earns the jealousy of rival Frank Butler. Ultimately, Annie must resort to throwing a shooting contest so Frank feels sufficiently masculine enough to be able to woo her. As Raymond Knapp has pointed out, this story arc maneuvers its way through a filmic world filled with a variety of identificatory possibilities for Annie—Indians, city-dwellers, African Americans, Europeans, and so on.[30] In the end, Annie chooses as her new identity a universalized model of domesticated white femininity, a choice that clashes distractingly in the film with Betty Hutton's brashness and self-presence.

Day's Calamity Jane faces similar choices. Her character is again a tomboy, although less naïve than Annie. Whereas Annie only shoots animals and clay pigeons, Calamity protects stagecoaches from Indian attacks, a job that she pursues with enthusiasm: for much of the beginning of the film we assume that she is exaggerating when she brags of killing Indians, but during one of the stagecoach rides, we watch as she shoots several of them. Furthermore, the untroubled heterosexuality of Betty Hutton's Annie Oakley is—at least initially—problematized for Day's Calamity Jane. In *Annie Get Your Gun*, Annie's transformation into desiring woman begins the instant she sees the handsome figure of Howard Keel. In *Calamity Jane*, the transformation is set in motion not by a man but by a woman. Calamity is sent on a mission to Chicago to bring back a pretty actress for the amusement of Deadwood's men. In a scene that almost exactly duplicates the meeting of Annie Oakley and Frank Butler, Calamity Jane finds Katie Brown backstage at a theater. "Gosh, you're pretty," says the awestruck frontierswoman. Back in Deadwood, the two women take up together in a cabin in the woods, and it is Katie, not Wild Bill Hickok, who inspires Calamity to finally try on a dress over the course of the aptly-named song, "It Takes a Woman's Touch." In the end, the two women pair off with their respective men, and all four ride off into the sunset together.

Calamity Jane is, on the whole, a much more woman-positive story than *Annie Get Your Gun*. Calamity is not some backwoods naïf waiting for feminization; she is a genuine butch who can take care of herself (and others). Even after she assumes normative femininity, she can still chase down a stagecoach. In fact, she performs the song of the film coded as most feminine, "Secret Love," not in a dress but in a very sensible beige pantsuit, and singing to a horse who is at best uninterested. And yet, some of the patriarchal elements of *Annie Get Your Gun* surface, albeit in a subtler manner. Although it is the pretty actress, Katie Brown, who teaches Calamity what is involved in being a (white) woman, the transformation doesn't actually take root in Calamity until heterosexuality asserts itself. Her initial attempt at wearing a dress to a formal dance is unsuccessful, and it is only when she falls in love with Wild Bill that the transformation takes hold. As in *Annie Get Your Gun*, the normative turning point is caused by symbolic disarming—Wild Bill shoots a glass out of Calamity's hand, forcing her to realize that her sharpshooting skills won't ever match his, and more important, won't ever gain her love.

Calamity Jane is one of the most-analyzed works in the Doris canon, beginning with a pioneering British Film Institute (BFI) retrospective in 1980 and an accompanying set of essays, and important critical response by sociologist Teresa Perkins published the following year.[31] As with much of the Doris Day literature, the focus is almost exclusively on her femininity, especially in the context of the playful cross-dressing and explicit gender performativity in *Calamity Jane*. The central question was the same as under discussion here: situating Doris's performance in relationship to post-*Feminine Mystique* feminism. All are agreed that Doris had come to symbolize a certain retrograde view of femininity, but the BFI authors—Diana Simmonds, Jane Clarke, and Mandy Merck—sought a somewhat recuperative perspective, emphasizing the nonnormative aspects of her performances. Perkins, on the other hand, remained more circumspect. In a nuanced reading of *Calamity Jane*, she argues that some of the resistant elements in the star's performance reassured gender norms as much as they challenged them, especially given the attempt of the films to seemingly implicate the viewer in mocking and judging the butch Calamity.

A later generation of film critics have continued to emphasize the slippery play of performativity in the role. Eric Savoy, for example, writes that "the stubborn insistence of Doris Day's queerness remains far in excess of the narrative's heterosexist attempts at containment and 'feminization.'"[32] Savoy argues, rightfully, that while generic conventions might require certain heteronormative plot twists, this by no means is the only stage on which to read *Calamity Jane*, and that the film's resolutely incoherent play costume, awkward dance numbers, and polysemic lines in the script resist the solely conventional, even by the standards of its time.

Writing a decade later, Robert Corber places *Calamity Jane* within the larger framework of her other career, arguing that Doris's tomboyism in roles such as this were an important part of her persona in the 1950s, although one that needed to be repressed by the end of the decade as she entered the *Pillow Talk* phase of her career. Interestingly, Corber suggests that Calamity's most important identificatory role may not be as a lesbian but as a man. The film, he argues does not present her masculinity as some kind of simulacrum but, rather, as the real thing that indeed threatens the masculinity of other supporting characters.[33] Indeed, perhaps "Secret Love" might be understood not in lesbian terms but as another sort of queer: "If the song's lyrics announce an epistemology of anything, it is that of the gay male closet. Because of her cross-dressing and because she is singing about Hickok, Calamity resembles a gay man more than a butch lesbian."[34]

Missing from these discussions is the fact that it is not a universal femininity that is under debate in analyzing the Doris Day persona. Rather, crucial to the performance of Doris Day is her performance of whiteness. How much of *Calamity Jane* is about her accepting or rejecting the feminine mystique, and how much is about her becoming white? The answer, of course, is that the two can't actually be separated. Becoming a proper woman in this context means becoming properly white. There is no better example of that process than the famous scene in which Calamity presents herself to the men wearing a dress for the first time. The gesture of femininity is ignored because she has fallen down in some mud—her white face is literally blackened, as if with minstrel cork. Her mode of dressing remains, but her skin color has changed, and the illusion of heterosexual normativity fails.

There are innumerable film stars from the 1950s for whom their gendered performance is notable; I argue that it is the whiteness of Doris Day that has marked her as remarkable. It is not actually the color of her hair, her eyes, and her skin that signals her as remarkably white—blonde, blue-eyed actresses have never been in short supply in Hollywood—but, rather, her specific performance of those characteristics that open up a particular hermeneutic window into the Doris Day persona. Dyer's work on cinematic constructions of whiteness discussed earlier is particularly useful here.[35] The first half of the film is dominated by scenes shot in the large stage and bar of the Deadwood Hotel. Cinematic character lighting typically features a general light source from above, a soft "fill" light to suppress shadows, and backlighting to help separate the actor's body from the background.[36] In the filmic world of the hotel, fill lighting is almost nonexistent. Harsh shadows play across the faces of all the actors, including Doris (see figure 3.2). In fact, if anything she is more harshly lit than others, thanks to the shadows created by her ever-present hat. This highly directional lighting continues to haunt Doris the tomboy, whether inside or out; when Calamity escorts Katie to the cabin in the woods, direct downward lighting follows them.

The transformative moment comes as Calamity realizes she loves Wild Bill, and sings the movie's showstopper, "Secret Love." Although the filming is taking place in the exact same location where she had earlier

Figure 3.2 Calamity Jane protects Katie Brown, shot under harsh lighting.
Courtesy of Warner Home Video.

escorted Katie to her cabin in the woods, her lighting has been drastically changed; only now is it soft and evenly balanced, and a light from behind Day pinpoints her blonde hair, causing it to glow (see figure 3.3). As the camera zooms in for a close-up, Day tilts her head, leans on a tree branch, and gazes upward into the light dreamily. It is only at this moment that we *see* she is truly white.

This much one can learn from Dyer's scopic analysis. But a careful listener to popular music signification can also *hear* Doris Day/Calamity Jane's passage to whiteness. As one might expect, there is a clear difference in vocal style between Calamity the tomboy and Jane the domesticated white woman. The tomboy songs, most noticeably the opening number "Whip Crack Away," feature Day singing at the bottom of her range with an exaggerated "western" accent. This vocal quality, which she used for spoken dialogue as well as the singing, was Day's own invention. She later wrote that she spoke in her normal register on the first day of shooting, but after screening dailies decided her voice was incongruous with the tomboy clothing, and changed it accordingly for the remainder of the shoot.[37]

Figure 3.3 The white Calamity Jane, with more flattering lighting.
Courtesy of Warner Home Video.

Her singing in these opening numbers is accompanied by an intense, even aggressive physicality. Doris throws her body around the set with reckless abandon, jumping up on the bar, sliding across the floor, pushing men out of the way, and shooting away with her pistol. Her jaw is thrust out, her arms swing wildly, and she fairly buzzes with energy. The physical exertion is obvious to the audience. As the film critic James Harvey once observed of Day in *Calamity Jane*, "even at rest she was a strenuous presence."[38] The manic energy of the pre-transformation Calamity, in her singing and in her movement, helps to illuminate an effusive corporeality that characterizes both the freshly whitened Jane and Doris herself in many of her later roles. For as we watch Calamity become Jane, we notice that her level of physical energy does not actually drop, even though she has become a woman. Her movements become more measured, to be sure, and the singing is no longer performed with the guttural voice and a western twang. Audibly and visibly, however, she is still working hard.

Consider the film's climactic musical number, "Secret Love." On the surface, all is calm. Day walks slowly down a hill leading a horse, and pauses by the creek to assume the carefully lit glamour pose as shown in figure 3.3. But as she sings the beginning verse, her quiet, tight vibrato, reminiscent of "Sentimental Journey," seems ready to explode. And explode it does, as she swoops up an octave to sing, "Now I shout it from the highest hills." The chorus is belted out almost harshly before she cups the sound inward, shading back into a *sotto voce* that is probably supposed to sound "pretty," but instead transmits an affect of barely controlled energy. This dynamic, of tightly constrained quietness interrupted by startling outbursts, seems crucial to understanding the Doris Day model of white interiority.

Those outbursts, her vocal leaps into the chorus, became Doris's trademark. "Secret Love" was an enormous hit, but the same startling outbursts prevail in an even more famous musical number. And as in *Calamity Jane*, the Doris Day type is performed alongside a narrative of racial confusion, now in an international context. The setting is 1956, in the Alfred Hitchcock film *The Man Who Knew Too Much*. This was actually a remake of a film from earlier in Hitchcock's career; in updating the movie from the 1930s to 1956, he sought to explicitly dramatize a number of elements

we find crucial. First, he most obviously changed the geopolitics, moving the opening location from a ski resort in Switzerland to Marrakesh,
Morocco, against the backdrop of that country's colonial resistance movement, the crooks of the original film replaced by a shadowy political group
whose allegiances seem vaguely revolutionary.[39] In other words, the setting is now the Cold War.

Also crucially, however, Hitchcock alters the plot to explicitly thema-
tize an element seen in *Calamity Jane*, and much critiqued by Perkins—
an interpretation of the Cold War as a generalized threat toward white
middle-class family structure, and therefore a reactionary reassertion of
domesticity. And indeed, the plot of *The Man Who Knew Too Much* reads
as if it could be a case study in Elaine Tyler May's *Homeward Bound*: Doris
Day playing a musical star who has given up her career on Broadway to
live in the dreary Midwest and perform motherhood. That motherhood,
however, comes under attack when abroad: she loses her son to kidnappers. As Michael Rogan has argued, this representation of motherhood
under attack is extremely common in Cold War cinema, mirroring this
idea of domesticity as a bulwark against various foreign menaces. But what
is in some ways more interesting is another aspect of Rogin's argument—
equally typical for this period, if the maternal instinct goes too far, if it
becomes too hysterical, it needs to be contained. One of the most famous
scenes from this film, and a real triumph for Doris as an actor, is that
in which her doctor husband secretly drugs her before breaking the bad
news of her son's kidnapping to her.[40,41]

Rogin makes the point that motherhood is not a symptom of
containment—it's not the *result* of this larger ideology—but, rather, a strategy for implementing it. And although reading this ideology onto actual
human lives is a trickier business than reading into texts, other strategies
of containment were a very real fact of life for performers like Doris Day,
especially in the 1950s as the studio system was, in many respects, having to work harder at maintaining control over its subjects. The tools at
its disposal were mainly money and the promise of fame, but one must
also include the pills, the alcohol, the medical procedures, and for many
women the controlling influence of abusive spouses. Doris had married

a low-level agent named Marty Melcher in 1951, who quickly took control over her financial and creative decisions. Most important, he pressured her not to renew her contract with Warner Brothers in 1954, leading directly to her ability to sign for *The Man Who Knew Too Much.*

This thematization of Cold War politics and the domestic revival is undercut throughout with tropes of anxiety. While feelings of foreboding dread are obviously present in most Hitchcock films, *The Man Who Knew Too Much* doesn't just "use" anxiety as a cinematic device; it is actually "about" anxiety, from the drugging scene to the musically choreographed buildup of dread in the foiled assassination attempt at the Royal Albert Hall, to the famous clattering footsteps that invisibly track Jimmy Stewart through the streets of London. Note that most of these examples involve sound: if anxiety is in essence fear of the unknown, Hitchcock constantly manipulates our sense of dread through an acousmatic soundscape that hints at danger without ever revealing its exact nature.

Finally, the film thematizes what Brian Edwards has called its "strong racialized unconscious."[42] In a penetrating analysis of Hitchcock's Marrakesh, Edwards points us toward scenes of masking. [43] In the opening scene, the white American couple and their son travel on a bus. Fascinated by a woman's face covering, the boy accidentally pulls it off, provoking an angry reaction that is resolved only by the presence of a mysterious stand-in for French colonial authorities, Louis Bernard. Later, in the incident which triggers the film's plot machinations, that same Frenchman blacks up in a manner we might fruitfully compare to the mud on Doris's face in *Calamity Jane.* In the earlier film, the mud applies itself accidentally to Doris's face to thwart her attempted femininity. Here, we only see the end of the racial performance. Bernard, cloaked not only in dark makeup but also in a face-covering robe, is stabbed to death. He falls into the arms of Jimmy Stewart, in the process uncloaking himself. Stewart finishes by rubbing the makeup off his face, revealing the Frenchman underneath. Calamity Jane's blackface trafficked in a easily understood black–white/man–woman set of binaries; the blackface in *The Man Who Knew Too Much* opens up a globalized scene of racial confusion that won't ever be resolved.

Into this perfect encapsulation of the racialized Cold War age of anxiety, enter Tin Pan Alley. "Que Sera Sera" was written by Hollywood songwriters Ray Evans and Jay Livingston, who had the good fortune of being
represented by the same agent as Jimmy Stewart and Doris Day. Hitchcock
asked them for a popular song that could be "sung to a little boy" and,
furthermore, that "it would be nice if it had a foreign title."[44] Early in the
film, the song marks a moment of bonding between mother, father and
son. The most famous moment, however, comes at the end. Hank, the little
boy, is being held by kidnappers upstairs at the embassy, while Doris and
Jimmy are downstairs at a cocktail party. Doris is asked to sing her trademark number to entertain the guests, and suspecting that Hank is being
held somewhere nearby, Jimmy suggests that she sing as loudly as possible
so as to root him out.

There has been a tremendous amount of ink spilled about this scene,
especially as regards postwar domesticity and womanhood. Murray
Pomerance, rather amusingly calling it a "desperate yodel for her lost
son," reads in this performance a tension between the purposeful artifice
of the performance—loud, "stagey," the "stuff of theater"—and her more
authentic desire as a parent to find her son: she must be artificial to be
authentic.[45] Elsie Michie, like Pomerance, reads this moment as embodying the dialectic of containment, of her former career as a singer saving
the day.[46]

One other reading we might make on this scene is the way in which anxiety is once again foregrounded, but now in a more positive light. Earlier,
Stewart drugged Doris for fear that her anxiety would make the situation worse. Now, however, at the climactic moment, Doris Day's anxiety
is unleashed. In her panicky, strident, anxiety-ridden singing, she saves
the day. This is significant because we should not view "anxiety" as a uni-
laterally negative phenomenon, especially in historical context. Although
it was not a majority view, there was a significant critical element that
viewed anxiety as a productive, useful tool.

The name most famously associated with this stand was Rollo May, a
young psychologist who would later in life become something of an icon,
thanks to works such as *Love and Will* (1969). His first book, however, was

a bestselling adaptation of his doctoral dissertation, titled *The Meaning of Anxiety*, published in 1950 and an interesting contemporary counterpart to Erikson's *Childhood and Society*. The heart of his theory was the relatively straightforward idea that anxiety results from a "from a cleave or contradiction between expectations and reality," or in other words, when we are afraid of things that aren't there.[47] However, May was a profoundly literate thinker and not prone to medicalization; the introduction to *The Meaning of Anxiety* begins with a long exegesis of W. H. Auden's *The Age of Anxiety*, and in American psychology he is best known as a conduit for the existential ideas of Kierkegaard and Sartre into this country. Drawing on those sorts of Continental ideas, May views anxiety as a crucial part of human development: "the positive aspects of selfhood develop as the individual confronts, moves through, and overcomes anxiety-creating experiences."[48] We become ourselves through experiencing anxiety, learning the strategies we need to mature and grow as adults. So "anxiety" in the age of anxiety is not monolithic; even at the height of a rather controlling medicalized discourse, the anxious Doris Day can triumph over Jimmy Stewart and his bottle of pills.

Race seems absent in these accounts of "Que Sera, Sera," but then, of course it would be. But if Day's voice bears the marks of Cold War anxiety, it is also indisputably racialized. In this moment we begin to hear the wear and tear of assimilation. The octave leap heard in "Secret Love" has now become even more explosive, the disjunction between the vocal timbre of the chorus and verse even more disjunctive. Hughson Mooney, writing in 1954, described the "earthy" voices of Day and her contemporaries in political terms:

> It may not be coincidence that in these days of Senator McCarthy's sort of Americanism, the newest type of hit . . . on the *Hit Parade* concurrently in the winter of 1953–54, is blatantly orthodox in structure and sentiment. Even such ditties, however, partake of that warm, folksy, often reverent quality captured in the childlike primitives of Grandma Moses as well as in the robust, earthy, thoroughly American voices of Guy Mitchell, Rosemary Clooney,

Champ Butler, Rusty Draper, Doris Day—a simple wide-eyed extroverted delight in the familiar. With Babbitt no longer reviled but respected, many of these tunes are the kind he can sing at Rotary luncheons.[49]

Mooney's words here, and Day's hit songs, are reminders that frequently the sound of the girl singers in the 1950s is surprisingly "earthy," as he puts it. While most of them were very capable of—and even preferred to, personally—producing sentimental ballads in a very smooth style, they often found their biggest success outside that stylistic terrain. Unlike the overwhelmingly smooth sound world of R&B vocal groups such as the Orioles, the white girl singers were pushed into extreme vocal effects, encouraged to sing at the very broadest extremes of their registers, and often placed visually, in marketing, television shows, or movie appearances, to emphasize their comedic abilities. I argue that the specific articulation of whiteness here is indicative of a larger tension: attempting for a performance of naturalized authenticity, but doing so in a conflicted relationship with its femininity, especially when it came to sexuality.

Before returning to Doris Day, consider the similar case of Rosemary Clooney. Raised in a small Kentucky town near Cincinnatti by her Irish grandparents after her parents divorced, Clooney followed the same path into musical stardom as Day: early success singing jingles for a local radio station, in her case the same station—WLW in Cincinnati—that had launched Day a few years earlier. In 1945, this led to a touring engagement with the Tony Pastor Band, as one of the Clooney Sisters. By the time the Pastor Orchestra arrived in New York City in 1948, Rosemary had matured enough to continue on her own, and she signed with Columbia Records under the management of legendary impresario Mitch Miller.

Rosemary had her first hit in January in 1951, with "Beautiful Brown Eyes," which sold a respectable 400,000 copies. Her greatest success, however, came in July of that same year, when she recorded "Come on-a My House," under the direction of Miller. Famously, Rosemary had wanted none of it, envisioning a career of more genteel love songs instead of this "weird novelty fluff," as she called it. The song was based on an Armenian folk song, and had been penned a decade earlier by two recent Armenian immigrants: William Saroyan, the playwright and author of *The Human Comedy* who famously refused a Pulitzer Prize because it was too tainted with commerce, and his cousin Ross Bagdasarian, even more famous for creating, under the name David Seville, Alvin and the Chipmunks.

Mitch Miller was a great fan of the novelty song, and he rightly predicted that Rosemary's exuberant personality could handle the most outlandish songs and arrangements, in this case for jazz harpsichord. A harpsichord was borrowed from Juilliard, and the pianist Stan Freeman was drafted to play it, despite no prior experience with the instrument. The resulting song was an overwhelming success, staying at #1 on the pop charts for eight weeks. The lyrics are a surrealistic mixture of fairy tale and sexual innuendo:

> Come on-a my house my house, I'm gonna give you candy
> Come on-a my house, my house, I'm gonna give a-you
> Apple-a plum and a apricot-a too eh
> Come on-a my house, my house-a come on
> Come on-a my house, my house-a come on
> Come on-a my house, my house I'm gonna give a you
> Figs and dates and grapes and cakes eh!

Bagdasarian and Saroyan's song, written for their unsuccessful off-Broadway musical *The Son*, is actually written from the point of view of a "lonely immigrant boy." In a slow introduction left out by Clooney and Miller, the boy is going home from work when he spies a "fine U.S. number one girlie" and falls in love with her. Unsure of how to approach her, he speaks to her "in old country way," which leads into the chorus of "Come on-a my house." In the original version, the song ends with the boy singing "Come on-a My house-a, all-a your life, come on, come on and-a be my wife."

Armenian folk tale or not, the image evoked in Miller's version of the song is a sirenic Hansel and Gretel, with Clooney cast as a particularly seductive witch luring the listener into her food-laden house. Whereas the original Armenian boy asked the listener to be his wife, Clooney ends the song by promising us in a throaty voice that if we come into her house, she'll give us "everything." She chants this word three times, before ending on a coquettish exclamation of "Come on-a my house!" Although other versions of this song recorded by artists from Della Reese (1952) to Madonna (2002) have emphasized the seductive, as crooned by Clooney over the clattering plectra, "Come on-a My House" is equal parts sexuality and menace, even implying that the two might be one and the same.

Seductiveness was quite easy to achieve thanks to Clooney's personal charms, but analyzing this atmosphere of menace is more involved. Consider, for instance, the complete lack of contrasting material. Most pop songs of this period followed traditional Tin Pan Alley structures, especially the classic thirty-two bar AABA or ABAB verse-chorus arrangements. The only other hit song of 1951 to lack a strongly contrasting B section was a traditional number from a completely different time, the Weaver's strophic folk song "On Top of Old Smoky." With the slow introduction stripped out of "Come on-a My House," the only break from to Clooney's voice is provided by the harpsichord solo, which riffs on the same material. The reverberations of the echo chamber used in the recording further destabilize the listener, adding ambience but also emphasizing the already slippery cross rhythms of the vocal line. When the harpsichord solo comes, it feels as if the machine is beginning to break down. Closely miked and clumsily played, Freeman's harpsichord break sounds on the edge of breakdown. As he attempts faster and faster figuration, melodic content fades into the sound of overworked plectra clacking away.

The putatively Armenian dialect of "Come on-a My House" was heard by most contemporary listeners as Italian, an impression assisted by Clooney's later hits such as "Botch-A-Me (Ba-ba-baciami Piccina)," a cover of an Italian pop song that spent seventeen weeks on the charts in 1952, and "Mambo Italiano," which charted for twelve weeks in 1954. Given her ambiguous last name, many listeners assumed that Clooney was herself Italian. In addition, her (two) marriages to Puerto Rican actor José Ferrer added a *frisson* of ethnicity to Clooney's popular image. Her first major movie role was in *The Stars are Singing* (1953), a musical farce that lightly thematized the confusions of ethnic assimilation in the wake of the McCarran-Walter Immigration Act of 1952: the protagonist is teenaged Polish immigrant Katri Walenski (played, in true Hollywood melting-pot fashion, by Italian actress Anna Maria Alberghetti) living illegally in the United States while trying to break into show business. She lives in a Greenwich Village tenement full of other Broadway hopefuls, including Clooney, who plays herself as Irish American pop singer "Terry Brennan," even singing a version of "Come on-a My House." Walenski eventually wins a televised amateur contest singing under the assumed name "Mamie Jones." In the process, however, she is revealed as an illegal alien and is arrested along with most of her friends—with the exception of Clooney, whose blonde good looks keep her out of trouble. None other than President Eisenhower saves the day, moved by public outcry to grant Walenski a last-minute residency permit.

A generation earlier, Clooney's persona would have found a comfortable niche in a venerable ethnic novelty-song tradition. An Irish performer singing an Armenian song in an Italian accent bears an obvious debt to earlier performers like Blanche Ring and Sophie Tucker, who in 1928 could famously sing a line like "My mother is Jewish / my father is Irish / Which proves that I'm Spanish." The ethnic novelty song, however, went into steep decline after World War II, when the surge in assimilation mentioned earlier made it difficult to find a market for unmeltably ethnic music. Josh Kun has written movingly about this process in his book *Audiotopia*. Although Jewish comedians like Milton Berle and George Burns were tremendously popular in the early days of television, Kun points out that overt performance of Jewishness died out almost overnight. Kun memorializes singer Micky Katz, who made his living with Yiddish parody versions of pop songs—he did one of "Come on-a My House"—and live performances that often featured klezmer hoedowns midway through a song. Katz's insistence on remaining unassimilated resulted in widespread rejection by the Jewish community in the 1950s.

How, then, did Clooney succeed with these "outdated" ethnic novelty songs? Simply by virtue of her distance from them. Unlike the "too Jewish" Katz, blonde, blue-eyed Clooney performed ethnicity from an ironic distance. Raised poor in a southern midwestern town, her career goal was to become an urbane performer of jazz standards, a goal reached when her sentimental version of "Hey There" hit #1 in 1954. Even as audiences appreciated the zany antics of "Come on-a My House" and the other novelty songs, they understood that her music was simply playing with signifiers of ethnicity, not actually inhabiting them—that she was really just white. This is made clear in the very first episode of *The Rosemary Clooney Show*, which premiered in 1955. The musical number of this show was a montage of "Come on-a My House" with "Mambo Italiano" and a version of the old Rat Pack standard "Love and Marriage." Exoticisms abound, with Clooney wearing a garish striped dress and pointing seductively at baskets of fruit. However, the baskets of fruit and other elements of the Italianesque set are not naturalistically presented; they are large cartoon mock-ups, obviously empty underneath. Clooney's 1950s pop career shows that not only was ethnicity made invisible but it had also become so thoroughly detached from corporeal reality that it could become nothing more than a harmless play of signifiers.

There was one lingering after-effect of this playfully performative ethnicity, however, and it allowed Clooney to distinguish herself from the even whiter Doris Day. Unlike her peers, Clooney utilized a slightly more sexually explicit persona. For Day, her sexuality had to be spoken silently by her body; her music hardly broached the subject. Clooney, as in the songs just discussed, was able to at least wield an occasional double-entendre in a winking fashion. It might useful to think of her particular kind of sexualization in the context of Anne Helen Petersen's essay on the Hollywood "Cool Girl."[50] Taking Jennifer Lawrence as her starting point, Petersen theorizes a star type that is at once "one of the guys" while remaining both sexually appealing and, crucially, figured as sexually available. Lawrence's genealogy stretches back from Jane Fonda, to Carole Lombard, to Clara Bow. It's important to note that Petersen's timeline actually skips the 1950s. While surely not intended to be comprehensive, it's not a coincidence. The "Cool Girl" is distinctly not possible in the immediate postwar aesthetic, at least not for white performers. Clooney, however, comes close, and it was precisely her ethnic play that allowed her to do so. Her career in the 1950s, despite its winking parody of the old ethnic novelty song, still retained just enough of that racialized difference to allow for a small window of performed sexuality.

Day, however, in her early film musical career and beyond, aspires for a wider audience than that of a Cool Girl, and to do so she radically flattens her performance. To draw again upon more recent culture, it is useful to compare her cultural work with that described by philosopher Robin James in her essay on Donald Trump and Adele's hit song "Hello" (2105), a pair not so dissimilar from Senator McCarthy and Doris Day. James points out that these two performances—the politician and the hit single—gain their power from "immediate, friction-less emotional and intuitive identification" with their audiences.[51] Rather than appealing to more intellectualized forms of knowledge—empirical facts in the case of Trump, and specific musical trends in the case of Adele—we simply let their performances wash over us and validate our existing feelings. Both aspire, very successfully, to the largest possible audiences using a rhetoric of naturalness and authenticity, juxtaposed against the unnatural and inauthentic (Hillary Clinton, Auto-tune). James's "experiential homogeneity" is precisely what Doris Day worked so hard to maintain in her performances. By accessing a seemingly "natural" form of acting and singing that was devoid of any particular marked characteristic, the whiteness of this naturalness could wash over an enormous fan base equally as interested in the same day-to-day performance of whiteness. The difference between Doris Day and Adele, however, is not unlike the differences between Joseph McCarthy and Donald Trump. Audiences, and their whiteness, were actually quite different in the 1950s, and the anxiety, cracks, and strains shown by McCarthy and Day construct a whiteness still in formation, still bearing the marks of violence in its recent past.

This Promise of Paradise

Identity and Performance in the Pacific Theater

oward the end of *South Pacific*, the phenomenally successful 1949 musical created by Richard Rodgers and Oscar Hammerstein, the French plantation owner Emile de Becque has a long, searching scene with the American Lieutenant Joseph Cable. In the midst of war, both men have found themselves in love with women outside the accepted boundaries of conventional romance. Cable, a white American of privileged upbringing, is in love with Liat, the beautiful daughter of a crafty local vendor of grass skirts. De Becque, on the other hand, is in love with a white American, and although as a wealthy French immigrant de Becque himself might have been acceptable to social conventions, his previous marriage to and children with a Polynesian woman mark him as racially tainted. Cable's song reacting to this frustrating dilemma is one of the musical's signature numbers, "You've Got to Be Carefully Taught." As Jim Lovensheimer's excellent study of the show tells it, the song was one of the reasons Rodgers and Hammerstein had conceived of the show in the first place.[1] Both committed activists for racial equality in the United States, the two men saw *South Pacific* as a chance to stage, in a sometimes oblique and displaced manner, questions of race and integration. Those politics, as mild as they eventually emerged in the show, were controversial in 1949, and even today conservative critics such as Terry Teachout still find the show to be "preachy" when it comes to racial tolerance.[2]

Immediately after Cable's famous number, however, de Becque offers his reaction: "This Nearly Was Mine." Ornamented with occasional reminiscence motives from "Some Enchanted Evening," he sings a short number that elides failed romance and imaginary geography.

> One dream in my heart,
> One love to be living for
> One love to be living for,
> This nearly was mine

> One girl for my dream,
> One partner in paradise,
> This promise of paradise
> This nearly was mine.

If "You've Got to Carefully Taught" is an allusion to the question of civil rights in the United States, its companion number transports us back to the geographical specificity of *South Pacific*. As the character of Nellie Forbush becomes linked with the place of paradise, we're reminded that the particular setting of the musical does actually matter. Emile de Becque is not a white American; his failed romance takes place in a zone of hostile interculturalism, and the collision of couples ill-fated in love is the result not of Shakespearean machinations or arbitrary coincidence but, rather, because of the cold, technical calculations of war.

While Rodgers and Hammerstein were looking for a location that was far removed from contemporary American debates, the better to quasi-orientalize the question of racial tolerance, life in the actual South Pacific was a concrete reality for many U.S. citizens in 1949. Millions of American

soldiers served in the Pacific theater during World War II, bringing home
with them an experience of racialized difference unlike those in which
they had previously participated. Even as World War II came to a close,
geopolitics conspired to cause confrontations between the United States
and a range of political actors in Asia. The immediate postwar era of the
1940s and 1950s saw what Christina Klein has called an "expansive material and symbolic investment in Asia and the Pacific."[3] *South Pacific* lived
its life amid a series of early Cold War flare-ups, from the final communist
victory in China in 1949 to the outbreak of the Korean War in 1950. War
is an unpleasant hermeneutic window, but as the name implies, it is also
an unavoidable fact of performance in the postwar era.

At the same time, if the musical staged the experience of white
Americans newly encountering the Pacific rim, and if the early Cold War
brought a new focus to the country's relationships with Asia, for many
Americans these Pacific rim relationships were more longstanding, as well
as personal. While they were not a large numerical presence in the United
States, the perspective of Asian Americans is not often explored within
these dynamics, which often conflate Americanness with whiteness. This
chapter thus looks at intercultural performances in the wake of World War
II's Pacific theater.

I use the term "intercultural" advisedly; as a theoretical concept it
dates from the 1970s, and much academic discourse around the topic
deals with more conscious attempts on the part of artists to cross traditional boundaries of nation and culture.[4] However, as much of this
study is concerned with a somewhat teleological perspective of examining the roots of cultural trends that came into much wider view later in
the twentieth century, I find it useful to place the series of performances
analyzed in this chapter in this rubric of interculturalism. Rather than
the more reified and inherently orientalized notion of "cultural contact
between East and West," interculturalism allows us to speak of more
fragmented and hybridizing operations. The art historian Jonathan
Hay has found interculturalism not only to encompass the relationship
between cultures but also as pointing to the "constitutively hybrid nature
of any culture."[5]

Thanks to the work of scholars such as Christina Klein, Jim Lovensheimer, and many others, the orientalist musicals of Rodgers and Hammerstein—*South Pacific* (1949), *The King and I* (1951), and *Flower Drum Song* (1958)—have been thoroughly explored, both in their musical details and in their historical contexts. A more intercultural analysis, however, might ask a further question: What is the relationship of these musicals not just to white Americans' perspective on Asian issues but also to the perspective of Asian Americans? I hope to press against a notion of middlebrow American culture as being presumptively white, with subcultural African American performance offered as a binary other. Asian Americans also saw themselves being performed on these stages, and their relationship to these performances was not always what one might expect. Tracing the complex matrix of these performances across the multiplicity of color lines, comparing and contrasting white cultural engagement with Asian themes, and the reality of Asian American performances, allows us to see the mutually constitutive nature of racialized identity through performance.

■

The term "postwar" accomplishes a curious sort of cultural work. On the one hand, it implies a historiography of which many of us are rightfully suspicious: the periodization of human history based on conflict. To mobilize "postwar" seems to imply that war is the defining feature of the culture in question, and as decades of social history have shown, this is not necessarily the case for the average person At the same time, "postwar" has become a particularly influential term referring to a very specific conflict, World War II, and thus to one particular historical moment, a long moment that in fact includes myriad other wars, from the Cold War to the Korean War to the Vietnam War. Here arises the curiosity, however: the original "war" that defines this "postwar" moment is remarkably oblique. Famously, the federal government did even begin the process of planning a national memorial to the war until 1987, well after the introduction of the Vietnam Memorial on the mall, and construction of the memorial was finished only in 2004. Contrast this with the proliferation of memorials, holidays, and artistic creations that sprung up in the wake of the First World War. As a number of studies have shown, the process of mourning and commemorating the Great War became an enormous undertaking, much contested by elites and populists alike.[6]

Such work was also attempted after World War II, but in much more limited ways. I briefly outline a few examples of such performances, tracing within each our theme of identity. I am especially interested here in how the dominant white culture of mainstream and middlebrow performances reflected a heightened sense of globalization in the wake of the war. For a great deal of the late 1940s and 1950s, this globalization was inseparable from the growth of the Cold War and specific conflicts such as the Korean War. Senator Joseph McCarthy famously drew upon his service in the Pacific theater as a key part of the mythology that brought him to power. At the time of Pearl Harbor, McCarthy was serving as a circuit judge in Wisconsin. Realizing early on that a man with political ambitions would need military experience, he quickly volunteered for the Marines. As David Oshinsky recounts, McCarthy spent three years as an intelligence officer debriefing pilots.[7] In his spare time he participated in the underground black market embodied in *South Pacific* by the character of Bloody Mary, procuring liquor and exotic food. Still thinking of his political career back home, he began sending back news reports of his activities, in particular claiming to have become a tail gunner on dangerous bombing missions. He received an Air Medal, four stars, and the Distinguished Flying Cross, and a citation from Admiral Nimitz for carrying on with his duties despite having been severely wounded in action. During the rest of his career, McCarthy would often roll up his pants leg to show his shrapnel scar to friends and enemies.

The stories were all fake. Shortly into his national career, reporters discovered the truth—that during lulls in wartime action, McCarthy would occasionally tag along on less dangerous missions for fun. Wanting to break the record for most ammunition used in a single mission, he was "strapped into a tail-gunner's sea, sent aloft, and allowed to blast away at the coconut trees."[8] His wound, it soon emerged, came not from a combat mission but from a hazing ritual onboard a ship that was crossing the

Equator. He slipped and fell down a flight of stairs, and broke his leg in three places. War stories such as these, both real and fabricated, were a common part of the American political imagination. In a country where 12 percent of the population had served in the armed forces during World War II, such performances were inevitable. After all, when McCarthy was up for reelection in 1952, the country as a whole voted for former Supreme Commander of Allied Forces in Europe Dwight Eisenhower for president, a man's whose military performance was much more authentic, but nevertheless just as much consumed by his audience as theater.

McCarthy was an extreme example of a politician exaggerating wartime exploits in service to strident anti-communist war mongering, but political elites of many stripes realized early on the importance of framing the historical reception of the world war in service to contemporary realities. Probably the most influential such attempt was the twenty-six episodes of the miniseries *Victory at Sea*, which aired on NBC beginning in the fall of 1952. Ostensibly a documentary, Peter Rollins has called it a "dangerously seductive epic of the Cold War era."[9] Put together from American filmography of the war—captured German and Japanese films, training films, and the occasional dramatic recreation—*Victory at Sea* was the result of the Roosevelt-Truman administration's attempt to control the historiography of World War II. As Rollins recounts, the series creator, Henry Salomon, part of a team of mostly Harvard graduates working in the public relations division of the U.S. Navy, was commissioned by the Roosevelt administration to create a living history of naval operations. Salomon himself participated in six major battles in the Pacific, and he was given access by Naval Intelligence to interview Japanese leaders after the war. The ultimate product was a fifteen-volume history of the naval aspect of World War II.

In 1948, Salomon began collaborating with NBC on a television series based on the historical work. The series would eventually air on Sunday afternoons, and according to news accounts of the time, family viewings of the show became sacrosanct times in many households, with children around the country admonished to keep quiet and pay careful attention to the war stories. Rollins argues that the overall message of the series was narrowly patriotic, often uncritical, and sometimes needlessly venomous in its portrayal of German and Japanese enemies. Sophisticated editing and the use of a glorious musical soundtrack by Robert Russell Bennet (based loosely on themes by Richard Rodgers[10]) allowed for a dramatic narrative of liberation to iron out the particularities of historical detail; as Rollins pointed out, some of the scenes of liberation being portrayed were actually in service of maintaining the "liberty" of the British colonial empire. In one particularly awkward moment, a clip unself-consciously lifted from a *March of Time* documentary about the plight of African American tenant farmers in the U.S. South is used as an example of Americans contributing to the war effort.

Rollins argues that some of the most egregious historiographic efforts came in episode thirteen, "Malanesian Nightmare."[11] The episode dramatizes the New Guinea campaign, an ongoing attempt by Imperial Japan to assert control over the entirety of New Guinea and which involved American, Japanese, and Australian forces. The Japanese and the joint American-Australian effort took turns pushing each other back and forth across the island. Partway through, the Japanese attempted to sneak 3,000 reinforcements into their base from a nearby island. In the dramatic high point of the episode, reconnaissance planes spot the largely undefended Japanese ships, and in a rather orgiastic display of air superiority, American bombers completely destroy the troop shipment, killing thousands. With Bennet's soaring, martial score, we are wrapped up in the action. As Rollins rightfully points out, the decision to forgo almost all diegetic sounds—no antiaircraft firing, no bombs dropping, no dialogue—allowed the series creators to tightly control the emotional narrative of moments such as this. There is simply no space left in the soundtrack for viewers to form an emotion on their own. Bennet's score is widely acclaimed in this regard, and it must be said that to its credit the music does not traffic in as many orientalisms as one might expect. To be sure, there are plenty of moments; a repetitive pentatonic melody voiced by the oboe serves as accompaniment both for the natural dangers of the jungle and for the local people. Describing American attempts to win them over, the narrator solemnly intones, "The New Guinea natives primitive and warlike, headhunting and sorcery are part of their lives. But an enlightened colonial administration has won their loyalty." That said, we can be thankful there are no real attempts at some sort of Puccini-esque imitation of Japanese musical styles.

The episode ends with an interesting quasi-anthropological portrayal of American versus Japanese attitudes toward death. American soldiers are shown kneeling at white crosses in an island cemetery, while the narrator speaks in religious terms: "God grant they know thy victory." This is juxtaposed against a series of clips that portray the Japanese in terms both radically other and somewhat dehumanized. We are first shown scenes of Japanese officers cheering in control rooms; they have been deceived, we are told, by their superiors into thinking their side was victorious. The camera then moves to a horrendous image of hundreds of dead bodies, presumably Japanese, lying in mud and water, as proof that the Americans were indeed victorious. Then to show the other side of the previous image of American gravestones, we are given brief glimpses of a ceremony in which the cremated ashes of Japanese soldiers are given to young women in kimonos, presumably family members receiving the remains of loved ones. Rollins flags for us a small amount of contempt in the narration at this point, not just for the Japanese defeat but also for their different relationship with their dead. Referencing their Buddhist beliefs, the narrator announces, "Welcome home, young man. . . . You are no more. Suns may set and rise, but you must sleep on, during one never-ending night." The episode fades into the large "V" for victory that begins and ends each show.

This American dismay and fascination with the cultural differences of the Japanese formed another important thread of this story. One of the most famous texts of the period was Ruth Benedict's 1946 study *The Chrysanthemum and the Sword*. As its marketing copy read, the book was "an investigation of the pattern of Japanese culture which suggests a program for new understanding among nations."[12] The very first chapter, "The Japanese in the War," addresses some of the same issues as that episode of *Victory at Sea*. Japanese soldiers, we are told, "were taught that death itself was a victory of the spirit."[13] Benedict is able to spin out this attitude to explain why the Japanese paid very little attention to medical care for their own soldiers, let alone for prisoners of war. As she puts it, "According to our standards the Japanese were guilty of atrocities to their own men as well as their prisoners."[14]

As with *Victory at Sea*, *The Chrysanthemum and the Sword* was the direct result of wartime work. Benedict was invited to begin the research project in 1944, and she in fact became influential in military planning as it grew clear that Allied victory was at hand, and that occupation and negotiations were in the near future. She is credited, for example, with supporting the notion that preserving the role of the emperor in Japanese society was a worthy concession. A student of Franz Boas and close friend and colleague of Margaret Meade, Benedict represented the new anthropology that was coalescing around the idea of the "culture concept." The basic idea was one of cultural relativism. As Timothy Taylor puts it in his gloss of Benedict's earlier work *Patterns of Culture* (1934), rather than being different in some sort of evolutionary or racial sense, "cultures were merely different from one another, neither superior nor inferior, existing in a pluralist world."[15]

Christopher Shannon has a more critical perspective on Benedict's contribution to cultural tolerance. Pointing out that a great deal of Benedict's wartime work took place in the context of developing intelligence strategies for psychological warfare, he wonders what power relations are built into the discipline of anthropology as envisioned by Boas and Benedict. Anthropology, he points out, ends up replacing the earlier concept of "civilization" as a "universal standard by which to judge all the peoples of the world."[16] While scrupulously maintaining a sense of detachment in making her observations about Japanese culture—and it should be noted, as she does, that these observations were necessarily made from afar, rather than through fieldwork—Benedict cannot help but instill her American values of individuality in her hopes for Japan's future. Shannon flags a number of such moments, but most tellingly the very metaphor of the chrysanthemum, which provides the book's title and closing anecdote. Telling the story of a Japanese woman given the rare opportunity to plant a "wild" garden rather than the traditional Japanese garden of rigorous order, she writes:

This simulated wildness stood to her for the simulated freedom of will in which she had been trained. . . . [C]hrysanthemums are grown in pots and arranged for the annual flower shows all over Japan with each perfect petal separately disposed by the grower's hand and often held in place by a tiny invisible wire rack inserted in the living flower. Mrs. Sugimoto's intoxication when she was offered a chance to put aside the wire rack was happy and innocent. The chrysanthemum . . . discovered pure joy in being natural.[17]

As Shannon puts it, rather eloquently, "the peace of the world depends not on a liberal intellectual elite controlling world events but on the peoples of the world controlling themselves in accord with the values of that elite."[18]

As the examples of *Victory at Sea* and *The Chrysanthemum and the Sword* show, political and intellectual elites tried to walk a fine line in the years after World War II when it came to representing racial difference. The time of overt propaganda was in the past; there was no need to rally Americans against an Asian enemy, or at least not in quite the same manner as had been thought necessary during the war. Gradually, however, the same Cold War tensions that had fueled the rise of McCarthy began to work their way into new representations. On the whole, representations of Asian people were quite rare. One notable exception was a short-lived series starring the Chinese American actor Anna May Wong, who would later be featured in the film version of *Flower Drum Song*. Called *The Gallery of Mme. Liu Tsong*, the show told the story of an amateur detective with a day job as an art dealer.[19] Eleven episodes were aired in the fall of 1951 on the short-lived Dumont Television network. Unfortunately, almost no records of the show were kept, let alone any actual footage, and therefore it is difficult to know what actually transpired in the program. By description, however, it seems not to have been particularly related to either the Pacific theater or the Cold War.

A more direct example, however was *The Manchurian Candidate*, a 1959 novel by Richard Condon in which several white American soldiers are captured during the Korean War.[20] The group is taken to Communist China and brainwashed into becoming sleeper agents for a joint Chinese-Soviet espionage mission in the United States. Their leader, Sergeant Raymond Shaw, is the son of a domineering woman who is both a KGB spy and married to a U.S. senator and vice presidential candidate, him-self a thinly veiled portrayal of Joseph McCarthy. The plan is for Shaw to assassinate the leading candidate for president, thus allowing the Soviet-controlled senator to assume power and declare martial law.

The Manchurian Candidate, particularly in its 1962 film adaption star-ring Frank Sinatra and Angela Lansbury, is a classic text of Cold War stud-ies, and we need not repeat these analyses too much. As Michael Rogin has pointed out, for example, the book and film helped reanimate Cold War tensions in the wake of McCarthy's fall, the end of the Korean War, and what might have been a cooling down of tensions with the Soviet Union. As he puts it, "Like Kennedy, The Manchurian Candidate warns against both right-wing hysteria and bureaucratic complacency. Both the film and the administration aimed to breathe new life into the cold war."[21]

Certainly the most explicit themes here are of Cold War paranoia and anxiety, not so different from many of the issues in Hitchcock's The Man Who Knew Too Much discussed in chapter 3. At the same time, as with South Pacific, the geographic specificity of the opening gambit matters. Coming a year after the publication of The Ugly American, a fictional-ized account of our early descent into the Vietnam War, The Manchurian Candidate reverts to somewhat pre-Benedict representation of Asian peo-ple as inscrutable and mysterious. Condon's novel begins with an intro-ductory scene in which an elderly Chinese scientist, Yen Lo, is presented as the mastermind behind the entire operation. Even the Soviet allies fear him, not knowing if he has brainwashed others, or even themselves, into his submission. Yen Lo gives a long, erudite speech on his methods, and displays both cruelty and an affected sense of dignity, commanding Shaw to kill two men, but curling his lip dismissively when the Soviet officer asks for one of the murders to be committed with his bare hands. Throughout, the Soviets are brutish and the Chinese are cunning masterminds, paral-leling the political sense of many conservatives that if the Soviets were the normative enemy, the Chinese were the truly dangerous foes in the world.

Subtler forms of harnessing racialized encounter for Cold War pur-poses circulated throughout popular culture, as Christina Klein's master-ful study Cold War Orientalism has shown.[22] For example, middlebrow publications such as *Reader's Digest* and *Saturday Review* explicitly tailored their content for the particular brand of Republican internationalism espoused by the Eisenhower administration. This internationalism, to be clear, was of a very different sort from the foreign policy of right-wing activists like McCarthy. As part of the larger liberal consensus of which Benedict's scholarship was an example, the Eisenhower administration wished to promote an atmosphere of respectful engagement with different cultures around the world. As Klein puts it, culture work in this sentimental mode allowed the country to articulate itself as "a familiar, legitimate, nonthreatening, and beneficial presence in the decolonizing world."[23]

At this point, I make a rather abrupt shift. We have been discussing a range of cultural work that engaged with the intercultural moment brought on by the Pacific theater. It is clear that there was no monolithic response here; although certain larger tropes appear commonly throughout, we should resist the temptation to generalize too widely. However, there is one particular thread that all of these performances share: all came from the perspective of white Americans. This is to be expected, for many reasons. For one, white Americans were objectively the largest group in the United States. According to the 1950 Census, "native whites" made up 83 percent of the population; in this census, the category "white" included those of Hispanic ancestry. "Negroes" were just barely 10 percent of the population, and "other races" barely registered at half of a percent.[24] And more to the point, as has been well established, mass culture in the 1950s almost exclusively adopted the viewpoints and aspirations of a white middle-class hegemony both imaginary and also very real.

At the same time, what of those 729,717 Americans counted as "other races" in the 1950 Census? In this particular census, "other races" referred largely to those of Asian descent, including South Asian, East Asian, and Pacific Islander residents. While numerically small, examining the perspective of Asian Americans on postwar interculturalism is not only morally important but also crucial for understanding the "constitutive hybrid" nature of these performances, to recall Jonathan Hay's description. Their perspective also helps complicate the often binary historiography of racial identity in the postwar era. Chapter 3 described one of the most well-known tropes of the Cold War: the process of suburbanization. Beginning with the famous Levittown developments in New York and Pennsylvania, planned suburban communities offered a pastoral, automobile-oriented model of residential living, especially targeting the enormous expansion of the middle class that occurred in the wake of World War II. Whereas before we were mostly concerned with the effects this suburbanization had on the assimilation of white ethnic immigrant groups, we can also now observe that a very similar process happened to Asian communities, especially the long-established Chinese American community in the San Francisco Bay area. As Charlotte Brooks has shown in her study of the transformation of Asian American housing in California, San Francisco's Chinatown was one of the most dense and most segregated neighborhoods in the entire country, comparable to the worst conditions endured by immigrants to New York in the nineteenth century, but persisting well into the twentieth century. According to Brooks, in 1890 more than 80 percent of San Francisco's citizens of Chinese ancestry lived in a single assembly district. By 1939, the situation was actually even more segregated, with 4,787 of the 4,858 Chinese American households in the city located in the Chinatown district.[25]

During the war, this long-established segregation was thrown into an uproar. To be sure, the essential divide between white and nonwhite housing areas remained unchanged; Brooks quotes one homeowner's committee member as saying, "We don't feel like it is our patriotic duty to take a loss on our property values."[26] Within minority areas, however, much was in flux, triggered by two large upheavals: the internment of Japanese Americans and the migration of African Americans from the South. Traditional boundary lines began to be crossed, and with an exploding Chinese American population thanks to the war and the repeal of the Chinese Exclusion Act in 1943, there was stiff competition among all groups to find adequate housing. Unlike in the rest of the country, where work on fighting housing discrimination was largely the province of black activists, in California a multi-racial coalition of Chinese, Filipino,

Korean, and Mexican residents combined forces with the NAACP to work for housing integration.[27]

However, at the close of World War II, as with much of the left, such alliances began to crumble. The political values of the Chinese American community were as inflected by the Cold War as were anyone else's. As Charlotte Brooks argues in a more recent study, *Between Mao and McCarthy*, the community was placed in a particularly difficult position.[28] On the one hand, as minorities in a country where racial discrimination was actively practiced, Chinese Americans were of necessity active in the civil rights movement, fighting especially against housing and employment discrimination. As such, similar to the experience of African American civil rights activists described in chapter 2, mainstream political battles often hinged on whether such political activity was un-American, possibly a front for communist activity, or an example of liberal tolerance to be shown to the world as proof of the country's values of freedom and liberty. However, unlike African American activists, Chinese American activists also bore the politicized brunt of immigration, moving from a communist country. McCarthyite Republicans tried, sometimes successfully, to link black activists such as Paul Robeson to radical left groups, but it was rarely argued that they were somehow "foreign." Chinese activists had no such safety net, and the natural immigrant experience of sharing a sense of simultaneous identification with one's new home and one's homeland was fraught with political tension. While there were small groups of left-wing activists who did indeed support the People's Republic of China, and similar small groups supporting the most reactionary aspects of the Nationalist movement in Taiwan, Brooks argues that the vast majority of Chinese Americans embraced a resolutely centrist politics.[29]

This centrism is related to other aspects of Chinese American cultural work that reflected larger postwar narratives. Jennifer Fang has argued that the Chinese American experience of suburbanization, especially in the San Francisco Bay area, helps complicate commonly held notions of the suburbs.[30] Thanks to the kind of liberal multiculturalism encouraged by ideas such as those of Ruth Benedict, and also thanks to the emerging rhetoric of the "model minority," Chinese Americans were able to carve out for themselves a uniquely selective sort of assimilation, separate from the old Chinatown model and yet retaining more elements of their Chinese heritage than other ethnic groups were able to do in similar circumstances. Today, Fang points out, Chinese Americans are more likely than any other nonwhite ethnic group to live in the suburbs, with more than half residing outside central cities.

An important consequence of suburbanization was the development of an identity that was truly Chinese American, in a hybridized and bicultural sense. To a certain extent the relative isolation and lack of access to cultural resources for Chinese immigrants who moved to the suburbs helped account for this formation, as did the fact that many of them had come from a wealthier and more elite position than the poor residents of Chinatowns. Fang, however, also ties this hybrid identity more specifically to "the conflation of Cold War liberal ideals of cultural pluralism and consumerism."[31] As she demonstrates, the liberal ideology of pluralism explored in the first half of this chapter allowed for ethnic minorities such as the Chinese American to aspire, at least theoretically, to white assimilation. This pluralism, however, was largely articulated through practices of consumption that transformed traditional Chinese cultural products in important ways. The development of Chinese American cuisine is a famous example of this transformation—one celebrated in the musical number "Chop Suey" in *Flower Drum Song*—but Fang also traces this Chinese American middle-class identity in such practices as New Year celebrations, the development of Chinese Christian churches, and the spread of Chinese language schools.[32] Unlike in the dense and often unassimilated culture of urban Chinatowns, these forms of cultural work blended Chinese traditions with the middle-class values of Cold War pluralism.

One other consequence of this suburbanization was a disruption of the traditional forms of performance in San Francisco. Mina Yang's study of the music of Asian immigrant communities in California shows a long-standing traditional Cantonese opera, aimed both at the community itself and at the tourist trade. The first opera troupe visited as early as 1852, and by the 1920s there were two professional theaters featuring opera, with famous performers from China frequently visiting for sold-out engagements. By World War II, however, suburban migration and other disruptions meant waning interest in traditional Chinese opera. Traditional music-making remained, but rather than a professional affair it became the province of amateurs in more informal formats.[33]

This brings us to the question of what performance options were available to Asian Americans after World War II. Here I will sketch out some of the possibilities, making particular note of how the postwar moment transformed the process of identification. The greatest amount of scholarly attention on Asian American performance after World War II has focused on work largely authored and produced by white artists, chief among them the orientalist trilogy of Rodgers and Hammerstein mentioned earlier. Although our attention will eventually want to turn elsewhere, the politics of representation in these musicals is indeed important. The third of these musicals, *Flower Drum Song* (1958), is of particular interest because unlike the previous two, the show is actually based on a novel by the Chinese American writer Chin Yang Lee, and with some important exceptions, was cast with Asian American actors. It therefore gives us better access to the scene of representation available to actual Asian American people in the period.

Chin Yang Lee's novel, published in 1957, was a runaway bestseller, inaugurating a tradition of Asian American literature that would include such postwar classics as John Okada's *No No Boy* (1957) and Louis Chu's *Eat a Bowl of Tea* (1961). Playwright David Henry Hwang, in a preface to a recent edition of the book, remembers as a child being awed when seeing the 1961 film with its Asian cast. As an adult reading the book for the first time, however, he was thrilled to find that even more than the musical, *Flower Drum Song* contained "characters, cultures, and situations that I knew well but had never expected to encounter so intimately on a published page."[34] The novel, Hwang argues, is nothing less than the birth of a new literary genre, the Chinese American novel. Furthermore, it was an "amazingly daring and evocative portrait of Asian American sexuality during a critical period of fundamental transition in the Chinatown community."[35]

The plot of the novel and musical centers on Wang Chi-yang, a wealthy anti-communist immigrant who refuses to assimilate into American culture, but has two sons who are rapidly Americanizing. The oldest son, Wang Ta, is trying to find a bride; in the novel, he is in a relationship with three women: a nightclub dancer who overwhelms his more traditional values, an unattractive seamstress who commits suicide, and a young woman newly arrived from China. The three women are presented sympathetically and in a complex manner. None of them fits into any easy archetype, with the nightclub dancer surprisingly naïve, the eventual wife surprisingly aggressive, and the seamstress embodying, as Hwang says, an extremely rare character type of "an unattractive Asian woman, rejected even by men of her own society."[36] The men are also complicated people, their actions often constrained by racist American policies and prejudices, and highly conscious of the drama of ongoing assimilation. As a whole, the novel is an excellent example of what Lisa Lowe calls a "horizontal" portrait of the Asian American community.[37] Rather than a "vertical" story in which cultural traditions are passed down through generations, and are thus presented as static entities being thrust into white assimilation, we are instead shown the unevenness and contingency of Asian American cultural practices at one moment in time.

Unsurprisingly, Oscar Hammerstein, together his collaborator Joseph Fields, simplified these characters, and to a certain extent reinserted a more white perspective in the creation of archetypes. Mei Li, Ta's eventual wife, adheres much more closely to the "lotus blossom" stereotype of a dutiful, submissive Asian woman; and the nightclub dancer, Linda Low, is much more sexually sophisticated and assertive. Even reviewers in the mainstream white press noticed the flattening of characters. The *New Yorker* review commented that "the authors' attitude toward exotic peoples in general seems to have changed hardly at all since they wrote 'South Pacific' and 'The King and I.' . . . It seems to have worried neither Mr. Rodgers nor Mr. Hammerstein very much that the behavior of war-torn Pacific islanders and nineteenth-century Siamese might be slightly different from that of Chinese residents of present-day California."[38] In his critique of the film version of the musical, Robert Lee is unhesitating: "*Flower Drum Song's*

China town is a yellowface version of *State Fair*'s small-town America. . . . Ironically, in a film in which ethnicity displaces race and cultural transformation is a measure of assimilation, it is race—and the tradition of not being able to tell one Asian from another—that lends the film its supposed authenticity."[39]

As Lee indicates here, although *Flower Drum Song* was famous for its all-Asian casting (with the exception of Juanita Hill, to be discussed presently), only one of the actors was actually Chinese American. The cast included Japanese, Hawaiian, Filipino, Korean, and biracial actors. Lee argues that the women of the musical bear special brunt of becoming a vehicle for Rodgers and Hammerstein's commitment to liberal pragmatism. The characters of Linda Low, Mei Li, and Aunt Liang, the sister-in-law of the elder Wang, are the most successful assimilationists, he points out. While the musical allows them to retain a façade of individuality in their happy endings, they can do so only by succumbing to white middle-class values, especially consumption and compulsory heteronormativity. Indeed, in a twist at the end of the film, it is revealed that the dutiful, traditional Mei Li has been watching American television and has internalized enough knowledge to be able to strategize a way into marriage with Wang Ta. We might be reminded of Christopher Shannon's critique of Ruth Benedict: according to liberal values, assimilation into white culture should not be forced on anyone, but somehow it nevertheless must be magically internalized into one's own value system.

I certainly share Lee's criticisms, and those of many others who have found the transformation from novel to musical of *Flower Drum Song* to be deeply problematic. At the same time, these questions of representations and narratives are only one kind of analysis, and as always, I am concerned here to think more closely about the actual people implicated in these performances. As has been explored time and time again, from Gershwin's casting of African American actors in *Porgy and Bess* (1934) to Aziz Ansari's lightly fictionalized study of Hollywood casting of Indian actors in his television series *Master of None* (2015), roles in a show such as *Flower Drum Song* involved many negotiations. On the one hand, performers were required to erase aspects of their individuality to a degree never expected of white performers, to don stereotypical accents, and often to play into white audiences's worst fears of an ethnic group. The case of the actress Anna May Wong, noted earlier for having starred in a short-lived television series, is a notorious example of the pitfalls that could befall an Asian celebrity. Having achieved international stardom during the silent film era, she spent the rest of her career having to constantly fight for dignified roles. Anti-miscegenation rules in the Hayes film code meant that she could almost never be cast as a romantic lead, and in one famous moment, a film studio dubbed her "too Chinese to play a Chinese."[40]

On the other hand, it meant work in a world with precious few roles for Asian American actors. And for some, as in David Henry Hwang's recounting of his childhood awe at the film's relative lack of the worst of Hollywood stereotyping, there was much to be said for simply seeing one's self represented on the screen at all. For many Asian American actors, the Rodgers and Hammerstein trilogy provided a lifeblood of support during the 1950s. For example, the original Ngana, the daughter of Emile de Becque who opens the show singing "Dites-moi," was played by Barbara Luna, who would go on to be one of the Siamese children in *The King and I*.[41] The young Filipino American actor Patrick Adiarte in turn played one of the Siamese princes in *The King and I*, and six years later was given the role of Wang San in *Flower Drum Song*.[42] The other famous instance of casting continuity was the presence of Juanita Hall. A native of New Jersey and the child of Irish and African American parents, Hall was a popular singer associated with blues songs and the Harlem Renaissance, and whose career skyrocketed in the white mainstream after her casting as Bloody Mary.[43] In a perceptive study of her career, Sam Baltimore has noted her orientalist homoexoticism. In the role of Bloody Mary where she is paired dramatically with the campy figure of Luther Billis, Baltimore argues, "Mary's queer signification is fully triangulated—she is the female opposite of a character coded as a gay man, she is exoticized as part of the dangerously homosexual Orient, and she is embodied by a woman whose primary musical identity connects her to a history of queer Black women."[44]

At this point, however, I set aside Rodgers and Hammerstein, whose famous musicals have a tendency, as they do in this chapter, to overwhelm discussions of Asian American performance in the 1950s. As important a venue as they might have been for many Asian American actors and musicians, and as influential as their narrative representations were, ultimately there is a great deal to be gained from looking at performances not only casting Asian Americans but produced by them as well. I make this shift not in an attempt to essentialize these performances as any less intercultural and hybridized than *South Pacific*, but for the simple reason that their perspective adds a great deal of richness to the question of identity formation on the Pacific rim. Unfortunately, the analytical options in this regard are quite limited. Involving an extremely diverse and often fragmented minority community, limited largely to a few geographical areas on the West Coast and New York, the historical archive of preserved performances is quite small. As Yang reminds us, even the strongest and most-heavily organized postwar Asian American community, Chinese Americans in the San Francisco Bay area, saw a great deal of fragmentation after World War II, as many performances of traditional opera moved into amateur and private spaces largely lost to a contemporary scholar.

We are lucky, however, that at least one performance community has been fairly well documented, thanks to the activist work of the brother-and-sister team of filmmaker Arthur Dong and scholar Lorraine Dong. Ironically, it is a musical world that was represented in fictional form in *Flower Drum Song*: Chinese American nightclubs in San Francisco. While few contemporaneous recordings survive, thanks to a series of interviews with performers recorded by Dong and published both in a 1989 documentary and in a 2014 book, we have remarkable access to the social world of Asian American working musicians and dancers operating in the postwar era.[45] I spend the rest of the chapter outlining some of this history, and considering many of the same matters as were discussed for texts such as *Flower Drum Song*: "vertical" versus "horizontal" modes of context, the gendering of racial stereotypes, and the question of identification.

The story of Chinese nightclubs in San Francisco is not so dissimilar to that of the overall rise of nightclubs in the swing era. There was a precedent of "dine and dance" clubs in Chinatown dating back to the turn of the century; during Prohibition, these clubs emphasized food and dancing rather than alcohol. The Mandarin Café, for example, offered "Chinese and American menus" on a supper special, followed by dancing with music provided by the Mandarin Orchestra and the Famous Yee Woo Yuen Trio.[46] Many of the performing musicians came from the vaudeville circuit; publicity photos show young men dressed in traditional Chinese clothing posing with instruments typical of jazz bands of the 1920s. Krystyn Moon, however, points out that many of these vaudeville performers did aspire to break out of the "yellowface" stereotype ascribed to them. Their costumes, although emphasizing their Chinese heritage, were chosen to add a sense of dignity to their performances, and were more colorful and attractive than those worn by Chinese impersonators.[47]

With the end of Prohibition in 1933, legal nightlife around the country boomed. In San Francisco, the first Chinese cocktail bar opened in 1936. Its owner, Charlie Low, arranged for some musical entertainment, especially featuring the singer Li Tei Ming, whom he eventually married. The entertainment side was so successful that Low looked to expand, and in 1938 opened the Forbidden City nightclub, just outside of Chinatown proper, near Union Square. As the Dongs write, business was initially slow until 1940, when he discovered Noel Toy, a student at the University of California. Toy had no experience in dance, but developed a routine in which she walked around the club mostly nude carrying a large latex balloon. It was christened the "bubble dance" after a similar routine by the white burlesque dancer Sally Rand, and soon business was thriving.[48]

Later that year, *Life* magazine ran a feature story on Forbidden City, in an issue that also featured a photo essay on the army's new venture "training its first conscript army in its peacetime history."[49] A year before Pearl Harbor, it was clear that for the white audience of the magazine, war was only a matter of time. The magazine talks of little else; in addition to a photo essay on the new draft, there are small news updates on the situation in Europe, reproductions of a number of posters urging the country to join in support of Britain, a discussion of German air force aces, a look at the vulnerability of the British colony on Gibraltar, and the transcript of a "secret Nazi speech," provided as a "fair sample of the kinds of doctrine that is currently being voiced by highly placed members of the Nazi government."[50] While most of the focus is on Europe, the longest article in the issue is an in-depth profile of Fumimaro Konoe, the current Japanese prime minister. Written by Ernest O. Hauser, the essay takes a quasi-anthropological approach to placing Fumimaro's power in the context of Japanese history, while also using psychoanalytic language to discuss the politician's many foibles.[51]

Soon after, Forbidden City is given three pages of photographs, with a short accompanying text:

> Here each evening Californians flock to watch a talented floor show that ranges from slumberous oriental modes to hot Western swing. San Francisco is numerically ill-equipped with Broadway-style cabarets. Its citizenry eats at home, dances at hotels. When "Forbidden City" opened two years ago, it filled a local cultural need. It has prospered ever since. In décor, "Forbidden City" blandly jumbles rice-paper screens, lighted fishbowls, college colors and football trophies. Somehow the net result is satisfactory. Its tri-nightly floor show as blandly scrambles congas, tangos, tap numbers and snaky tuff from the Far East. Chinese girls have an extraordinary aptitude for Western dance forms. As singers, not many achieve success according to occidental standards. But slim of body, trim of leg, they dance to any tempo with a fragile charm distinctive to their race.[52]

The accompanying images take a similar tone. Some show a white clientele enjoying their orientalizing experience: two Stanford students awkwardly attempting to eat chow mein with chopsticks, and then dancing with Asian women. Li Tei Ming is shown mid-song, Jadine Wong poses in a skimpy outfit next to a gong. There is even a carefully cropped photo of Noel Toy with her balloon, captioned "Noel Toy ('The Chinese Sally Rand') majored in French at U. of C. until money ran out. She doesn't drink, go out with men. One night last week her bubble broke."[53]

With the U.S. entry into World War II, the popularity of the Chinese nightclubs only skyrocketed. As was shown in the discussion of housing, the sudden forced removal of Japanese Americans to internment camps created a fluid environment—ironically, one with many new opportunities for other members of the Asian American community. As one racist headline in the *American Weekly* newspaper supplement put it, "The Japanese Dolls are Vanishing, Leaving the Playful Gentlemen Who Like to Be Seen Around With Exotic Slant-eyed Lovelies, to Seek the Company of the Chinese, Filipino and Hawaiian Charmers."[54] The constant influx of service members headed for the Pacific theater only contributed to the success of the clubs.

Women performers were in a special place in this nightclub economy. The awkwardness of the dancer Linda Low's character in the novel version of *Flower Drum Song* was actually a fairly realistic depiction of the challenges faced by Asian American women performers. As Lorraine Dong points out, women's options were constrained by a variety of historical forces unusual to their situation.[55] For one, the legacy of the Chinese Exclusion Act with its ban on immigration by women meant that the very presence of women in San Francisco's Chinatown was comparatively rare. Many of those who did make it were, like Mei Li, illegal immigrants from rural and impoverished areas of China, and who therefore were less affected by the women's rights movements brewing in China, let alone those in the United States. And performers faced steep opposition from moralizing traditional Chinese society, which considered performance to be only just above prostitution, as well as the stereotyping in Hollywood of Asian women as either subservient or as evil dragon ladies. As Dong puts it, "mere entry into the profession was automatically condemned by both Euro-American and Chinese American patriarchal cultures. Working outside the vocations prescribed for them at the time . . . let alone singing, dancing, and displaying one's body, was simply unacceptable."[56]

Robert Lee's critique of the character of Linda Low in *Flower Drum Song* is relevant here. Reading the nightclub scene in the movie, which was of course set in a thinly fictionalized version of Forbidden City, he points out that Low's sexuality is "contained and domesticated by its transformation into consumption." Comparing her to the creation of the Barbie fashion doll, which was released that same year, Lee figures Low's own desires as "transparent, understandable, and (for the middle-class wage earner) readily satisfied."[57] I agree whole-heartedly with this critique of the fictional character, but it is interesting to apply it to the real-life version of Linda Low. In Noel Toy's interview with Arthur Dong, we meet a woman of great poise and political savvy.[58] She grew up in Marin County, the only Chinese family represented in her high school. Contact with San Francisco's Chinatown came only annually for Chinese New Year, and it wasn't until attending junior college and meeting other Asian Americans that she began to self-identify as "oriental." She won a scholarship to the University of California at Berkeley, but as her family was very poor she continued to work as a waitress. She was approached to work as a nude model at the Candid Camera attraction at the Golden Gate International Exposition on Treasure Island; the pay was thirty-five dollars a week. She and fellow models would assume a pose on stage, and visitors could pay to photograph them naked. Charlie Low offered her fifty dollars a week to appear in a burlesque act at Forbidden City, and despite no dance experience she was happy for the raise.

The more experienced dancer Jadin Wong put together an act for Toy, which mostly involved walking around stage assuming elegant poses with her five-foot latex balloon. While the soft focus of nostalgia surely plays a part in her memories, Toy describes herself as self-assured, happy to exploit the ignorance of her white customers. A common racist belief of the era was that the genitalia of Asian American women was in some mysterious way structured horizontally. Toy performed nude except for a tiny piece of moleskin required by San Francisco law, which often disappointed customers who had came to see for themselves if the rumors were true. Toy promoted the mystery:

There was this weird concept that Oriental women were built differently. And so consequently I had a song written which said, "Is it true what they say about Chinese women?" And one of the lines was, "Do the streetcars run North and South or East and

West?". . . I mean, I didn't get annoyed at it, and I'd play along with
it. They'd say, "Is it true what they say about Chinese girls?" And I'd
say, "oh sure, didn't you know? It's just like eating corn on the cob!"
[*Laughs*][59]

While acknowledging the deeply racist and sexist structures that lay
behind their performance careers, it is also remarkable to see how individual women were able to find their moments of agency. Toy was able to
parlay her bubble dance skills into a very successful dance career. She had
no trouble leaving Forbidden City after only a year when offered a sizable
raise to appear at the rival Chinese Sky Room. Six months after this move,
she began receiving sizable bookings to appear at clubs in New York City
and elsewhere on the East Coast, becoming a fixture in gossip columns
and eventually making five hundred dollars a week. After marriage to a
white husband who wanted her to focus on clothed performance, she had
a series of small parts in Hollywood films and television productions. Her
only complaint about her treatment was to argue that Asian American
women needed to be more aggressive in seeking out roles: "The only
thing that I see is that the Orientals aren't out there beating their breasts
and screaming. 'Look, we want to be in the mainstream of everything.
You've got to put us in every picture, that every chorus line should have an
Oriental in it.' We haven't screamed enough."[60]

Singers had a more subsidiary role in this nightclub economy. The
lucrative but racist white fascination with the sexualized Asian body
tended to land more on dancers such as Toy; singers were a necessary
part of the entertainment but less well received in the press. Singers also
tended to more firmly reject exoticizing costumes in favor of resolutely
white performance styles. The most famous singer to emerge from the
Chinese nightclubs was Larry Ching, a young Hawaiian man of Chinese
ancestry who was marketed as the "Chinese Frank Sinatra." If truth be
told, his voice sounded very little like Sinatra, with a sweet tenor voice that
tended toward a more crooning style.[61] Toy Yat Mar, on the other hand,
was known as the "Chinese Sophie Tucker." Born and raised in Seattle,
Mar probably earned this moniker less for any musical characteristic than

because of her own road-hardened toughness. As a young girl she began a singing career in small-town bars in rural areas. Frequently the white bands with which she toured would cross the border into Canada; unable to cross the border because of her ethnicity, the teenaged Mar would be left to fend for herself for weeks at a time working odd jobs until the band came back through. By the time she made it to San Francisco and Forbidden City, she was a force to be reckoned with, unafraid to stand up to Charlie Low when necessary.

In a sensitive reading of performances at Forbidden City, Anthony Lee makes the most important point about all this cultural work: rather than simply staging orientalism for a white audience, performers were accomplishing complex work of their own. The acts, he argues, did double duty, "displaying not only the racial difference imposed on the performers by a culture that wanted desperately to resolve their appearance but also a more complex racial identity constructed by the players themselves—that is, the working out of 'Chinese American' from within."[62] As an example, Lee looks at the dancing and choreography of Jack Mei Ling. Arthur Dong's interview with Ling does not make this fact explicit—not that it is too difficult to read between the lines—but Ling was gay, and Lee reads in his performance a somewhat campy orientalism that took full advantage of the queer space orientalism often provided. Exoticizing orientalist conventions were often thwarted with gestures from ballet and ballroom dance, and in one popular number, "The Girl in the Gilded Cage," Ling played a harem master who acts almost exclusively in tropes drawn from Hollywood films.[63] As Lee writes, "San Francisco's Chinatown at midcentury was a battleground of representation. . . . Indeed, as the Forbidden City players tell us, hybridity—that strange commingling of difference and desire—may be Chinatown's most powerful legacy."

Making Sense of Silence

John Cage's Queer Avant-Garde

T he Maverick Concert Hall sits in a forest on the outskirts of
Woodstock, the famous arts colony a few hours north of New York
City, in the Catskills. The approach to the hall today involves a
number of heavily wooded county highways, and the turnoff is easy to
miss even in broad daylight. For much of the building's history, a tall
wooden sculpture crowned by a twisting horse marked the entrance from
the highway, but fear of damage from the weather eventually led to the
removal of the statue to inside the hall. These days, a prospective visitor
needs good directions and some extra time.

Designed to resemble a barn, the ninety-year-old building rests easily in
a symbiotic relationship with the surrounding woods. It was constructed,
roughly and amateurishly, of local wood, with large diamond-paned win-
dows at the top to let in light. In good weather, the audience sits both
inside and out of the wooden building, whose back wall is a series of large
doors that open out onto the woods. Paying customers sit on wooden

benches, the nonpaying gather around a tree just beyond. On one side of the building, the moss-covered roof of an overhang has been carefully cut away to allow a tree to grow through. It is difficult to tell where the concert hall ends and the forest begins (see figure 5.1).

The symbolism of the concert hall—iconic architecture laden with several centuries' worth of power and prestige, opening up to, even allowing itself to be taken over by, the surrounding natural environment—resonates with the most famous piece of music premiered at the Maverick: John Cage's *4′33″*. On August 29, 1952, David Tudor sat down at the piano for the penultimate piece of a lengthy piano recital. Starting a stopwatch, he carefully closed the lid of the piano and sat quietly, his eyes scanning a score. Every so often, he carefully turned a page. After thirty seconds, he stopped the clock and opened the lid of piano. After a brief pause, Tudor closed the lid again, and sat quietly for two minutes and twenty-three seconds. Another pause with the lid open, and then the final movement: one minute and forty seconds. During the first pause, the wind outside the

Figure 5.1 Maverick Concert Hall, in Woodstock, New York.
Photograph by author.

concert hall could be heard picking up; during the second, rain began to fall.

As Lydia Goehr later wrote, "Cage's 'work' reflects an attempt to shed music of institutionalized constraints imposed by composer, performer, and concert hall. He aims to bring music back into the real or natural world of everyday sounds."[1] This is the traditional interpretation of the piece, found in every music textbook, most critical discourse, and indeed Cage's writings as well. It's a powerful and evocative concept that has captured the imaginations of many, a seemingly universal statement on the relationship between sound and silence that could theoretically be performed by any person, in any space, and at any time.

Consider, however, another performance of *4'33"*. In 1973, the artist Nam Jun Paik compiled a series of video works as *A Tribute to John Cage*. In one, Cage and Paik devise a performance of *4'33"* using chance procedures and a map of New York City to choose locations for a four-movement version of the piece. The last three movements were performed without problem, filmed at, respectively, a vacant lot overlooking the Harlem River, Times Square, and Bleecker Street. For each movement, Cage stood quietly on a city sidewalk while Paik taped the surrounding visual and aural environment. For the first movement, though, chance procedures took them to a location considerably farther uptown from Cage's neighborhood—the 2100 block of Third Avenue. Here, the sight of Paik's video camera and Cage's stoic stance attracted the attention of several African American teenage boys. They mug for the camera briefly, and then one turns to Cage and asks what is being taped. Cage looks briefly stricken at having to break his silence, but quickly—and nervously—smiles and explains what he is doing. It is difficult to imagine Cage similarly breaking his silence at the Maverick, or Lincoln Center, but this is East Harlem in 1973, and he is out of his comfort zone. Race matters, even for John Cage.

Taking its cue from Cage's own rhetoric, critical discussion of *4'33"* has long privileged its universality, hailing it as a piece of music that can theoretically be performed by any performers and in any context. But staging *4'33"* in Harlem required a new performance practice: rather than being aware of rain pattering on the roof, Cage was now required to be conscious of the urban streetscape, and of social difference. And although these two performances are extreme examples, we need to remember that every performance of 4′33″ will be different, and will require different interpretive strategies. After all, if there were ever a piece of music whose "meaning" depended upon its context, it would be 4′33″. Without historicization, 4′33″ too easily becomes a quite literally empty philosophical statement, abstract and ahistorical, robbed of any possible political momentum within the period of its creation.

What politics could possibly be performed by four and a half minutes of silence? This chapter argues that while there might not be a simple answer to this question, listening closely to the premiere of 4′33″ opens a window into the tense negotiations between one's private sense of self and one's relationship with the world. In other words, the question of identity. The silent piece might seem an odd choice for this. Comparatively speaking, it is much easier to think through strategies of identity when performance involves expression, even when, as has been the case in many of the preceding chapters, that expression can't always be taken at face value. Not so for Cage; his aesthetic has consistently been described as anti-expressionist. Cage's famous rejection of "ego" in music would seem to negate any possibility that the composer's identity might surface somewhere in the music. However, as has been shown throughout this book, the question of politics in music is not always about finding meaning in work. Instead, we are better served by asking ourselves: What does the act of composing, performing, or listening to this music *do*? And in the case of 4′33″, I argue that a great deal of political work was accomplished.

Still, what politics? 4′33″ is the work in question here not simply because of its special, quasi-mythic role within twentieth-century American music. As he prepared the piece, John Cage was himself struggling precisely with the question of identity. Cage was not heterosexual, either in identity or practice. Neither was he homosexual, especially at this moment in his life and in a historical moment of considerable flux in sexual categories. Just a few years prior, across the country his old friend Harry Hay was founding what would become the first successful gay rights organization, the

Mattachine Society. By the end of his life, Cage would indeed come to view himself as part of this more formalized gay identity, but in the late 1940s it was just one of many options during a time of heightened suppression of sexual deviance. As we reconstruct the specific circumstances around the making of *4'33"*, we'll see how Cage responded and what that silence had to say.

On August 29, 1952, the front page of the *New York Times* displayed its usual jumble of local and national articles. In the borough of Queens, $1.65 million in taxes intended to upgrade the sewer system were in jeopardy owing to faulty inspections. Dwight Eisenhower assured local political leaders that after Labor Day, he would "come out swinging" in his campaign for the presidency, despite his slow pace thus far. A *New York Times* reporter managed to sneak into the new headquarters of the United Nations to observe progress on a series of murals being painted in the assembly hall by the French artist Ferdinand Léger. In mock solemnity, he warns us that "visitors will waste a lot of time trying to figure out what the murals look like," before informing us that "actually, the murals are in the abstract school and are meant to be designs in color rather than a portrayal of any subject."[2] In international news, there were reports from Korea on the treatment of prisoners of war, a story about Truman's refusal to heed the call of the American Legion to fire Secretary of State Dean Acheson, and the notice that the growing trade imbalance with Europe was possibly a more severe threat to postwar stability than Soviet aggression.

That evening, one hundred miles upstate, the Woodstock Artists Association sponsored a concert by David Tudor and John Cage. The association, which had been formed decades earlier to support local painters and sculptors, conducted a series of Friday evening events to benefit their Artists Welfare Fund. Previous Fridays had included a speech by Buckminster Fuller, a lecture on "Art and Psychiatry" by a Dr. Robert Beim, and a roundtable discussion with several young artists. Most events were held in the association's gallery space in downtown Woodstock, but for musical events, they would often rent the Maverick Concert Hall for the night. Admission, in this case, was one dollar, and the postcards were sent to association members advertising a "concert and lecture-demonstration."[3] The program consisted largely of works by the so-called New York School—John Cage, Christian Wolff, Morton Feldman, Earle Brown—with the addition of Pierre Boulez's Piano Sonata No. 1, and Henry Cowell's classic *The Banshee*. The penultimate selection, a new work by Cage, was confusingly titled "4 pieces," and had as its subtitle four timings: 4'33", 30", 2'33", and 1'40." This now seems to have been a misprint; the first timing was of course the title, and the latter three were the lengths of each of the three movements. In any case, audience reaction was decidedly negative. Over the following decades, Cage described the premiere in many interviews:

> They missed the point. There's no such thing as silence. What they thought was silence [in *4'33"*], because they didn't know how to listen, was full of accidental sounds. You could hear the wind stirring outside during the first movement [in the premiere]. During the second, raindrops began pattering the roof, and during the third the people themselves made all kinds of interesting sounds as they talked or walked out. (1968)

> People began whispering to one another, and some people began to walk out. They didn't laugh—they were irritated when they realized nothing was going to happen, and they haven't forgotten it 30 years later: they're still angry. (1982)

> I had friends whose friendship I valued and whose friendship I lost because of that. They thought that calling something you hadn't done, so to speak, music was a form of pulling the wool over their eyes, I guess. (1985)[4]

Cage was not exaggerating the loss of friendship. Typical was the response of his friend Helene Wolff, who wrote the composer an impassioned letter in 1953:

> Musically I am an ignoramus, and heaven forbid that I pretend to more than I know. But one doesn't have to be a musician in order to

understand this kind of thing, which actually is a schoolboy's prank, and can give pleasure only to an immature position of yourself which apparently delights in baiting artists and audience. . . .

I very earnestly beg of you, John, to reconsider your decision and not to cheapen your worth by what is merely a trick. If you are quite honest with yourself, you must admit that you are only trying to knock and bedevil people.

I feel very strongly about this—so strongly that had I known what was up your sleeve, I would have refrained from sending out, to a number of personal friends, with personal notes, invitations to the recital. I don't relish the thought of having all these people's noses thumbed—for that is what it amounts to, if we are at all honest about it.[5]

What exactly were people so angry about? We unfortunately do not have many eyewitness accounts of the Maverick Hall concert beyond that of Cage and his circle. The only voice to have emerged from the audience members is an oft-repeated anecdote of an anonymous voice from the back of the hall: "Good people of Woodstock, let's run these people out of town!"[6] No newspaper reviewed the concert; the closest to a contemporary review came two years later, when the *Times* and the *Herald-Tribune* reviewed the work's New York premiere at Carl Fischer Hall. In an article titled "Look, No Hands! And It's 'Music.'" the *Times* reviewer has much the same reaction as the Woodstock audience: "Works of this sort have nothing in common with the disciplined art of Palestrina, Handel, Mozart and the obvious B's; they are hollow, sham, pretentious Greenwich Village exhibitionism."[7]

These traces of voices from the audience of $4'33''$, scattered and incomplete though they are, begin to reveal a sense of anger that seems rather disproportionate to a concert-going experience that, after all, only lasted four and a half minutes and did not involve the usual audience-provoking devices of the musical avant-garde, such as loud volumes and harsh sounds. And it was not that this particular audience was unaware of Cage's music, or even predisposed to dislike him. In fact, just the year before, the Woodstock Artists Association had hosted a film festival that awarded Cage a certificate for "Best Musical Score" based on his composition accompanying the film *Works of Calder*.[8] Although the patrons and artists associated with the artist colonies in Woodstock were decidedly bohemians of an earlier generation, they no doubt considered themselves open-minded supporters of new music. And yet, on this particular night, the same group of people was clearly not happy.

There are two possibilities for this unease. On the one hand, perhaps Helene was right: maybe they felt tricked and cheated. Cage was certainly not above providing shock value; as his mother once wrote in a letter, apropos of a recent recital, "The reviews were disparaging, but then John likes that."[9] Correspondence between Cage and his intimates was consistently infused with caustic commentary on bourgeois taste and bland values of middle-class America, their knowledge of which came largely from their own families. While perhaps not a camp wit at the level of his mentor Virgil Thomson, Cage was nevertheless the type of artistic personality who liberally sprinkled French phrases and obtuse allusions into his daily speech. Perhaps the aged bohemians of Woodstock, largely well-to-do and living comfortably, were an inviting target for a radical young neo-Dadaist. Perhaps noses were, indeed, being thumbed.

On the other hand, there is the possibility that the threat being silently voiced at Woodstock was a bit more serious. Or, if *serious* seems like the wrong word, perhaps the threat being voiced was not Cage's alone, but that of a new aesthetic bearing witness to the passivity of its time in an attempt to resist it. Next to Robert Rauschenberg's white paintings, Jasper John's darkly coded collages, and Merce Cunningham's stridently anti-expressive choreography, *4′33″* begins to seem less a moment of *épater les bourgeois* and more a carefully chosen statement of principle. This has been the conclusion of an influential mode of art criticism in the last three decades. Although this discourse takes place after the period in question, it nevertheless provides an extraordinarily useful framework for understanding certain cultural politics in the composition and reception of *4′33″*, and I should like to trace this framework's history and contours in some detail.

This position was perhaps first articulated by the noted essayist Susan Sontag. Writing in 1967 for the avant-garde multimedia journal *Aspen*, Sontag observed that contemporary art was trapped in a conflict between its possibility for mythic transcendence and the very concreteness of its materials. "Art," she wrote, "becomes the enemy of the artist, for it denies him the realization—the transcendence—he desires."[10] Philosophical silence, for Sontag, therefore becomes an important gesture for an artist, whereby he may "free himself from servile bondage to the world." Despite such lofty goals, however, acts of silence retain a highly social character, and ultimately contain considerable political content. Writing specifically about Cage and Jasper Johns, Sontag manages to link what she terms a "cautious" mode of silence with the specific historical moment:

> [Cage and Johns] are saying something equally drastic. They are reacting to the same idea of art's absolute aspirations (by programmatic disavowals of art); they share the same disdain for the "meanings" established by bourgeois-rationalist culture, indeed for culture itself in the familiar sense. What is voiced by the Futurists, some of the Dada artists, and Burroughs as a harsh despair and perverse vision of apocalypse is no less serious for being proclaimed in a polite voice and as a sequence of playful affirmations. Indeed, it could be argued that silence is likely to remain a viable notion for modern art and consciousness only if deployed with a considerable, near systematic irony.[11]

The last sentence is key, for it is here that Sontag harkens to a more famous essay of hers, the "Notes on 'Camp'" of 1964, which famously proclaimed the victory of irony over sincerity, and begins to perhaps trace a connection between Cage's sexual identity and his music. Although Sontag sought to downplay the queer heritage of camp in this earlier essay, it is clear that she is linking their complicated modernist programs to an implicitly queer discourse—as well as claiming for it a serious political critique of bourgeois modernity.

Sontag's analysis inspired a fuller treatment in the 1970s by the feminist art critic Moira Roth, who coined the memorable phrase "aesthetic of indifference" to describe the art of Cage, Cunningham, Rauschenberg, and Johns. Like Sontag, Roth described this aesthetic as characterized by "neutrality, passivity, irony and, often, negation."[12] Unlike Sontag, Roth was concerned with placing this artistic movement in a very specific cultural context: McCarthyism, and its "psychological ambience" of alienation. That is to say, as the political sphere was becoming an increasingly untenable home for meaningful activity, cultural producers turned inward and upon themselves. Whereas the previous generation of American writers and intellectual, working in the midst of the Depression and then World War II, had searched exhaustively for politicized art, the postwar generation gave up the cause.[13] For Roth, this was the period of *Catcher in the Rye*'s Holden Caulfield (1951), and of James Dean's iconically confused and passive character in *Rebel Without a Cause* (1955). It was also, however, a period when the blood-drenched detective novels of Mickey Spillane relished in vigilante justice against communists. Roth quotes a famous monologue from Spillane's *One Lonely Night* (1951): "I killed more people tonight than I have fingers on my hands. I shot them in cold blood and enjoyed every minute of it. I pumped slugs into the nastiest bunch of bastards you ever saw and here I am calmer than I've ever been and happy too. They were Commies, Lee."[14]

In Roth's analysis, there were two basic options available to an artist during McCarthyism: "bigoted conviction" or "embittered passivity," the diametrically opposed paths of Mickey Spillane and Holden Caulfield. In the world of modern art, Roth's dichotomy encompasses two crucial figures of the postwar art world, Jackson Pollack and Marcel Duchamp. Pollack, with his swaggering and often violent personality, was the Mickey Spillane of the avant-garde. (Cage: "I more tried to avoid him. He was generally so drunk, and he was actually an unpleasant person for me to encounter."[15]) His paint-drenched canvases seemed to perfectly combine that sense of violence—not for nothing was he nicknamed "Jack the Dripper"—with a rhetoric of individualism, and it was no coincidence that the Abstract Expressionist school became the favored benefactor of overseas shows sponsored by the U.S. government in its propaganda war against the Soviet Union. Duchamp, on the other hand, refused all that which Pollack stood for. He was French, dandyish, bisexual, and often dressed in drag as his alter-ego "Rose Sélavy." His readymades embraced mass production and commercialism, and explicitly rejected any sense of individualism or personal taste. Cage and his cohort looked up to Duchamp as a father figure; the title of Cage's 1968 composition featuring himself and Duchamp playing chess was *Reunion*. That is, their performance reunited two artistic sensibilities long sympathetic to one another.

Roth's essay only briefly notes another characteristic of Cage's New York crowd that also opposed them to the Abstract Expressionists: Cage, Johns, Cunningham, and Rauschenberg were all gay men. Their gayness was not a question of their sexual behavior; if their sexuality was determined only by performance in the bedroom, all four would, like Duchamp, be more accurately termed bisexual. Rather, the performance that gave these men their gay identity was that of everyday life. Their mannerisms, their speech, their dress—and yes, their art—visibly and audibly displayed their gayness to those who knew to look for such cues. Cage's gayness was most obviously represented by his voice, which he maintained at a high pitch and with an effusive verbosity characteristic of urban gay men in the 1950s. Morton Feldman referred to him in print, affectionately, as a "squealing monkey."[16] David Tudor once complained privately in a letter to a friend that "John does very well in Paris . . . sometimes I think I will retch if I hear another word about chance or control or 'very interesting' or 'very *importante parce que*.' "[17] Listening to one of the many recordings of Cage's voice, such as on his 1959 recording of *Indeterminacy*, one is struck by the similarity of his voice to that of Truman Capote, with its lisping, arched pronunciations. Or simply, as Richard Koestelanetz put it, "Everyone who knew John Cage thought him gay; the suspicion of homosexuality probably crossed the mind of nearly everyone hearing his peculiar voice."[18]

Cage's public display of his homosexuality lends another layer to the threats faced under McCarthyism. It was not only alienation and a lack of political purpose that drove Cage and his cohorts into embittered passivity. Cage's performance of a gay subject position posed a real danger in 1952. As is now well documented, McCarthyism was not merely concerned with the threat of communism. Sexual deviance—in particular, male homosexuality—was an obsession of governmental and institutional powers. Two years before the premiere of *4'33"*, a U.S. Senate committee report, *Employment of Homosexuals and Other Sex Perverts in Government*, concluded that "even one sex pervert in a Government agency tends to have a corrosive influence upon his fellow employees. These perverts will frequently attempt to entice normal individuals to engage in perverted practices."[19] Thanks to this report and a few widely publicized incidences of spies who were both homosexual and communist, President Dwight D. Eisenhower signed the infamous Executive Order 1050, which added "sexual perversion" to the list of activities prohibited for federal employees. The private sector and academia followed his lead, and thousands of gay men were dismissed from their jobs—many more than were ever directly fired for Communist Party affiliation.[20]

Cage was fortunate that during this period his sources of income came not from large institutional structures such as universities and foundations but from a wide range of freelance activities: lectures, commissions, dance accompaniment, and perhaps most significantly, assistance from his parents. This is not to say that his livelihood would have been unaffected had his sexuality been more publicly known, of course. For one, Cage's mother, with whom he was very close, was known to be quite homophobic.[21] And one did not receive grants from the Guggenheim Foundation, as Cage did in 1949, without some measure of discretion. Cage's display of homosexuality was always a tightrope walk. On the one hand, his everyday queer performance sustained him intellectually and personally, gave him entry into important social networks, and was probably the mode of expression that seemed to him most authentic. But go too far, and the weight of public and private repressions stood ready to push him back.

The art historian and activist Jonathan D. Katz has provided us the most extensive theorizing to date on what Cage's homosexuality, and his performance thereof, might mean in terms of his music.[22] Katz points out that there is an unavoidable "coincidence" in Cage's biography: in the late 1940s and early 1950s, Cage divorced his wife of ten years, Xenia Kashevaroff, and began a permanent relationship with Merce Cunningham. At the same time, he began to turn toward Zen Buddhism and the use of chance techniques. In addition to pulling together the numerous hints of Cage's homosexuality in one place for the first time, Katz goes on to give us a nuanced and provocative reading of the queer politics of silence under McCarthyism. [23] For Katz, Cage's silence was not simply passivity and neutrality in dangerous times; it was also a calculated act that complicated the very means by which we hear music. "Silent music," he writes, "inaugurated a process of reading that moved the listener, potentially, from unselfconscious complicity with dominant forms of expression (in which the expressive was passively registered as inherent in the music) toward a degree of self-consciousness about one's role as a listener or a maker of meaning."[24]

Katz's narrative of the postwar Cage is highly compelling.[25] One possible objection is that the neat grouping of postwar American artists into binarisms of straight/gay or expressionist/indifferent is quickly complicated by the predominance of heterosexual composers in the so-called New York School to which Cage belonged. Morton Feldman, Earle Brown, Christian Wolff, and David Tudor were all heterosexual men. This is a reasonable objection, even if the heterosexuality of some of these men was often far from simple: although in a heterosexual relationship with Mary Caroline Richards during the early 1950s, David Tudor later gave up on sex altogether, leaving Richards for celibacy.[26] Feldman might have been heterosexual, but also famously flew into a somewhat disproportionate jealous rage when Cage befriended Brown. And Wolff was a teenager for much of the period in question. Nevertheless, the straight/gay binarism at work in this circle must necessarily be viewed somewhat heuristically.

There is another strand, however, that complicates things somewhat, and that is the status of male homosexuality, as well as how Cage conceived of his own identity within that status. In short, did Cage consider his sexuality to be part of his oppositionality? His music, to be sure, was oppositional; that much seems clear. But when Cage constructed this oppositional music, was his sexuality a part of it? Or was it simply, for him, an unrelated factor? To answer this, I step back and take a more detailed look at the relationship between white male homosexuality and identity in 1952.

It is doubtlessly true that institutional power was overwhelmingly repressive during this time of McCarthyism, and that this repression was no doubt felt by nearly all persons engaged in "sexually deviant" behavior such as homosexuality. However, recent historical work has given us a much fuller picture of the possibilities and options available to gay men in the 1950s. There is, after all, no one narrative of gay male life in the United States. There are simply too many intersecting issues of race, class, family background, geography, psychology, and any other number of factors for this to be true. After the pioneering recuperative efforts of early gay historians who necessarily constructed overarching frameworks, historical scholarship has now reached a point where these many smaller narratives, communities, and possibilities are beginning to be explored. Let us consider some of the narratives and movements with which Cage might be identified.

One of the most obvious possibilities for Cage's self-identification is that represented by a childhood friend of Cage's, the fellow Angeleno Harry Hay. Cage and Hay had gone to high school together; and in 1931, after Cage returned home to California from travels in Europe, he and Hay immediately reconnected. Cage and his then-boyfriend, Don Sample, often hosted Hay and his various boyfriends at their home for parties and salons, sharing an interest in modern art and music, the homoerotic photographs of Baron von Gloeden, and as Hay put it, "merry drag performances."[27] Although their close friendship soon foundered—as did many of Cage's friendships in this period—for years their lives followed parallel paths. Both married women in the late 1930s, and then divorced them in the late 1940s.

Hay had long been involved in left-wing political causes, and for many years was an active member of the Communist Party. By 1948 he, like many other leftist artists, had departed the party, but took with him an intimate knowledge of the mechanics of political organizing, especially of campaigns that required a measure of secrecy. Thus, in 1950, he was well positioned to found the first successful gay rights organization in the

United States, the Mattachine Society. Among the many achievements of this group was the first analysis of homosexuality as a minority identitarian community. As John D'Emilio put it, the Society theorized that "homosexuals . . . were trapped by false consciousness, by a hegemonic ideology that labeled their eroticism an individual aberration. The first task of a homosexual emancipation movement, then, was to challenge the internalization of this view by homosexuals and to develop among the gay population an awareness of its status as an oppressed minority."[28]

The importance of this new theory of homosexual identity cannot be overstated. For the past several decades in America, the main cultural debate over homosexuality had been about whether it was a condition that deserved criminalization or pathologization, whether jail or a mental hospital. The most liberal theorists of homosexuality after World War II— academic researchers such as Alfred Kinsey and Evelyn Hooker—were considered radical for simply suggesting that gay men might perhaps not be pathological. To claim, as the Mattachine Society did, a nascent sense of *pride* in homosexuality as a marker of one's identity, was truly revolutionary. In the tumultuous climate of the 1950s, this idea spread rapidly around the country. Mattachine chapters sprung up in most major cities, a lesbian organization with similar ideology called the "Daughters of Bilitis" was formed, and the venerable magazine *ONE* was founded in Los Angeles to connect those in more isolated areas. The initial communist influence of the founding members was soon downplayed, and indeed Hay was eventually purged from the organization; but the homophile movement—socalled in an attempt to distance itself from the pathologizing tendencies of the word *homosexual*—remained an enduring presence until the late sixties. Echoes of its radical philosophy of group identity and the need for civil rights can still clearly be heard in today's mainstream gay and lesbian political movement.

The homophile movement, however, with its radical theorizing of homosexual pride in the face of oppression, was always a minority position within the growing number of people in the United States who identified themselves as homosexual. For one, the membership of the Mattachine Society was almost entirely white, middle class, and urban.

More important, for our purposes, is the fact that this new construction of a homophile identity simply did not strike a chord with many gay men, even if they, like Cage, were themselves white, middle class, and urban. As the historian George Chauncey has shown, in the wake of post-Stonewall identity politics, we have tended to privilege a model of sexual identity that assumes every person has a stable, coherent sexuality, at least internally, and that any variation in one's identity is simply a matter of secrecy versus openness. This is, of course, the idea of the closet: the act of "coming out" is the moment when one's hidden, internal sense of sexual identity is finally expressed openly. Chauncey's recent work on gay male life in New York City after World War II, however, points out that for many men in the post-WWII era, the notion of being married with children and then visiting underground gay bathhouses and clubs on the weekend was not simply a question of being "in the closet." Although secrecy was involved, there was not necessarily a concomitant split-subjectivity and sense of inner conflict. Rather, these men were more or less content to inhabit "dual spheres," as Chauncey puts it. Different social settings required different modes of performance and different forms of identity. As long as the two did not mix, everything was fine.[29]

We might also call this the "open secret" model, to use the more common phrase often applied to many of Cage's musical contemporaries in New York City: Aaron Copland, Virgil Thomson, Samuel Barber, and so on. This musical world, carefully delineated in Nadine Hubbs's recent book *The Queer Composition of America's Sound*, operated not "in the closet" but in a realm of deniability. That is to say, their performances of homosexuality took different forms in different spaces. In more public spaces, meanings were often left abstract and unspecified. However, as Hubbs points out, abstraction can be read as "deferring rather than obviating meaning—and deferring it until such time as its audiences might be capable of receiving it."[30] The world of the dual spheres was therefore not without political motivations, and perhaps even a desire for political change. However, I would not consider this world to be oppositional, per se. Oppositionality is, for sure, a tricky categorical concept, but to use Raymond Williams's framework of anti-hegemonic movements, I read the dual spheres to be an alternative culture: creating and maintaining an alternate political reality, but not necessarily actively working toward making that reality mainstream.[31] It is the sense of being "active" that I assign specifically to oppositionality. The cultural work being done by those in the dual spheres should not be underestimated, but as a matter of form, it seems a different sort of work than that of an oppositional stance.

The third narrative to be considered here is one recently proposed by the critic Henry Abelove, who has pointed out that an enormous number of American writers and artists, mostly men and mostly white, but not exclusively so, chose neither the model of the dual spheres nor the model of homophile activism.[32] Rather, they chose to exile themselves outside the country, to locales where if homosexuality was not exactly celebrated, it was at least left alone, more or less. The most popular such places were Paris, North Africa, and Mexico City. The queer artists in exile included a wide range of mostly New York–based artists who were all contemporaries of John Cage: William Burroughs, Ned Rorem, Paul Goodman, Paul and Jane Bowles, Allen Ginsberg, Frank O'Hara, and James Baldwin are the specific artists Abelove cites. As Abelove points out, these artists contributed to a queer discourse that is often missing from histories and theories of gay and lesbian politics: the integration of what was to be called gay liberation within a broader anticolonial framework. That is, there was a rejection of the idea of identity politics, as promulgated by the homophile movement, in favor of wider political action. As Abelove writes, the movement "was not predicated on a commitment to a supposititiously stable or definite identity. It was rather predicated on a commitment to a worldwide struggle for decolonization and its potential human benefits."[33] This group of artists, often considered in the same breath as those living in dual spheres, seem to me to be operating in a very different political mode. It is these artists who most often give us explicit representations of homosexuality in their work—consider, for example, the novels of James Baldwin, the published diaries of Ned Rorem, or Paul Goodman's famous essay from 1967, "The Politics of Being Queer."[34] Rather than deferring meaning, they force their own meanings into the present. In other words, it is a much more oppositional movement.

Cage's biography interweaves aspects of all three narrative options. In his early Los Angeles days, as documented in Thomas Hines's important biographical essay, Cage was a typical member of the social milieu that gave rise to the Mattachine Society.[35] Instrumental to the success of the Mattachine Society was a culture of artists, actors, and socialites, a bohemian set that arose in Los Angeles in the thirties thanks to the confluence of Hollywood money and the emigration of European intellectuals and artists fleeing Hitler. As already noted, Cage and Mattachine founder Harry Hay were good friends in the thirties, with Hay later claiming to have premiered some of Cage's earliest works.

Cage's life in New York City in the fifties, however, hews closer to the dual-spheres narrative. He certainly was never involved in any sort of political activism related to sexuality, unlike his old friend Lou Harrison, who joined a homophile organization in San Francisco.[36] And as I noted earlier, although his personality and mannerisms communicated certain messages to those in the know, he largely maintained a discreet lifestyle his entire life. As Katz relates, even in the 1980s, when asked to characterize his relationship with Cunningham, his stock response was "I cook, and Merce does the dishes."[37] Certainly in the early 1950s, such coy discretion was maintained at all times, even in comfortable surroundings. Very little correspondence between Cage and Cunningham remains from this period. What little we do have barely hints at anything other than friendship, with only occasional indications of something more. In one such example from 1953, we see how even those moments bear traces of dueling worlds. Cunningham, writing from Black Mountain College where he was once more on the summer session faculty, apologizes for being formal when the two spoke on the phone: "When I phoned you, I couldn't say endearments because of groups around, but I say them now, and miss you very much, and send you all my best love, and great kisses."[38]

And what of the other narrative of gay male history, the "queer commuter" model offered by Henry Abelove? Here, there seem to be less obvious connections. Cage was not particularly close, socially or artistically, to the artists Abelove lists. He was rather curiously uninvolved with the student rebellions of the late sixties and early seventies. Unlike Paul

Goodman, Allen Ginsberg, or William Burroughs—all heroes to varying
degrees of the counterculture movement—Cage was not so closely linked
with that later historical moment. He was surely seen as sympathetic, but
not to the point where he achieved the sort of stature as had his friend
Norman O. Brown. Rooted in the modernism wars of an earlier period,
and with his often elitist attitude toward issues of cultural production,
Cage was simply missing in action during many of the political struggles
of the period. An anecdote Cage recounts from the period is telling: in
the late sixties, Cage was asked to participate in a teach-in at Cornell
University organized by the school's Revolutionary Student Congress.
Cage was game enough to participate, but when he tried to telephone the
group, he was unable to reach anyone because the group lacked enough
phone lines. No doubt true, but Cage took this lack of technological prow-
ess to be a fundamental flaw in the entire student youth movement, and he
withdrew from participating.[39]

Nor did Cage ever actually exile himself during the fifties, although one
could possibly read his move from New York City to the wilds of Stony
Point, in upstate New York, as an escape of sorts. His youthful travels
to Europe in the thirties were part of a much different cultural moment
than that described by Abelove—more of an exercise in modernist peda-
gogy than an education in anticolonial experience. One important connection can be found in Cage's later attraction to the writings of Henry
David Thoreau, a writer many of these queer commuters saw as a sympathetic literary ancestor.[40] However, what I find most compelling about
this queer-commuter narrative is the way it complicates our understanding of the dual-spheres model. Anti-identitarian politics work both within
and against the notion of dual spheres: on the one hand, the two narratives share a reaction against the homophile movement's positing of
sexual behavior as the most important component of a political identity.
On the other hand, the queer commuters did not reject sexual identity in
favor of an apolitical one, even if the political identity they substituted—
anticolonialism—was often politically naïve.

The politics of Cage's own anti-identitarian identification similarly
negotiate between the political and the apolitical, and between the naïve

and the sophisticated. Cage certainly refused identity politics on a regular basis. According to one account, when asked point-blank about his sexuality in the late 1980s, he admitted that he was gay, but said that he "didn't like to be political about it."[41] And when asked in the 1960s about the potential of the black power movement, he replied in the negative: all the black power movement was doing, he said, was replacing one source of power with another. It was not, however, that Cage refused the political; he was in fact quite committed to his anarchist politics, as utopian as they might be. Like the queer commuters, he simply refused to make self-identification a part of those politics, either his own identity or that of any other.

There is indeed a naiveté here, both in Cage and in the queer commuters. Marginalized in some respect by their sexual behavior and performance, Cage and the queer commuters were also privileged in many other respects—it was, I would suggest, easier for them to refute a notion of identity than it might have been for those involved in the black power movement. However, by playing these three narratives off against one another, we see that Cage's subject position was often more subtly articulated than a simple "closeted" model of sexuality would give us.

■

If Cage's political relationship with identification was complex, where does that leave silence? As with homosexuality, later approaches to 4′33″ have seeped into our historical understanding of the piece. The aesthetic of indifference, for example, begins with the assumption that the work is indeed silent, or at least noncommunicative. Is that the case? As Kyle Gann has pointed out, there is a curious gap in the historical record with regard to 4′33″.[42] After the work's premiere in 1952, and a follow-up performance in New York City in 1954, no more was heard about the work. It was not until the publication of his essay collection *Silence* in 1961 that the piece became widely known, and positioned at the heart of his compositional philosophy. And in the meantime, the work itself had been transformed.

Generations of music textbooks have promulgated the idea that the score of 4′33″ is the familiar "Tacet" edition. Published in 1967 as part

of C. F. Peters's complete John Cage edition, the "Tacet" edition consists
of three movements marked on a single piece of paper, each movement
labeled with the traditional signal for orchestral players that their services are not required: *tacet*. An explanatory note at the bottom gives the
timings used by David Tudor at the premiere, but gives the performer
(or performers) free rein to choose new timings, and to use any combi-
nation of instruments. This is not the score Tudor used in 1952; nor did
he use the version Cage made as a gift to Irwin Kremen in 1953, and later
published by *Source* magazine in 1967. This edition was a simple graphi-
cal notation—a vertical line runs down an otherwise blank page, with the
note that "1 page = 7 inches = 56 seconds."

Like so many other artifacts of the original performance of *4′33″*, the
original score used by Tudor was lost, possibly within days of the performance. Tudor, however, made a copy from memory, and so we have a
fairly accurate idea of what it must have looked like. As Cage said, it used
the same notational system as his *Music of Changes*. Conventional manuscript paper was used, and the notation was quite traditional: each system
is made up of two lines, with treble and bass clefs carefully added throughout. The only nontraditional element—besides, of course, the absence of
notes!—is the written indication that every 2.5 centimeters of staff line
equals sixty seconds, thereby creating a primitive graphic notation.[43]

Compare this score with the one most familiar to us, the "Tacet" edition. Elegant in its simplicity, it is the "Tacet" edition that has produced the
traditional interpretation of *4′33″*: as a concept, not as music. For music
requires people, and there are no people present in the "Tacet" edition.
Or, put another way, there is literally no relationship between performer
and score. The piece of paper upon which the score is printed is not actually needed to perform the piece—even those traditionalists who perform
4′33″ on a piano in the manner of Tudor's premiere rarely keep the score
on the piano. It is enough to remember the three timings, and to keep a
clock handy. If anything, the idea behind the piece is better transmitted
to the performer by a simple verbal explanation. The "Tacet" edition of
4′33″ is an idea about music, not music itself. This is the prime difference between the "Tacet" edition and the original autograph. The original

was actually meant to be played. It carries with it the corporeal traces of its original performance: it is six pages long, and so not only were eyes required to scan its graphic score, but fingers were required to turn its pages. The slight shuffling of paper were added to the sonic mix, and the white fluttering of that paper and skin became part of the visual scene, marking the passage of time. In short, the performing body was present. If the "Tacet" edition symbolizes the abstract, the original score symbolizes the social.

The real stumbling block, I imagine, to musicological study of *4′33″* is its troubling status as a musical object and what this means for our conception of Cage's place in musical hierarchies—and our ability to use musical analysis to validate those hierarchies. As Patricia Carpenter pointed out many years ago in an influential phenomenology of "the musical object," musicological study has only seemed possible when a musical object is created, when "sheer musical process or activity" is constructed as having a space of its own.[44] And indeed, to take one example, James Pritchett's important study of Cage's music makes quite strenuous claims that the composer output needs to be treated as a set of musical objects—coherent works with beginnings and ends, composed with "a unique and very beautiful sense of musical style."[45] This leads Pritchett to avoid *4′33″* and favor "work-like" creations like the *Concerto for Prepared Piano and Orchestra*. The existential instability of *4′33″* strongly resists objectification. If creating a musical object requires us to "transform sound from vital sensation into tone that has an objective character," as Carpenter wrote, then *4′33″* does exactly the opposite: a musical object is reversed until it becomes "vital sensation."[46] A bundle of radically contingent events and sensations utterly fails to provide objectified grist for the music-analytical mill.

So what is there to analyze? Those musicologists who have attempted to deal with *4′33″* in detail have done so by bracketing the piece as an example of theater, not music. Michael Broyles, for instance, has created a binary framework for understanding Cage's compositions: a piece is either "musical" or "theatrical." The musical pieces are those intended for the traditional concert hall, and they are primarily aural experiences. Theatrical pieces are more visual in nature, and they are often presented in nontraditional venues and using several different mediums. For Broyles, *4′33″* and the Black Mountain College Happening of the same year, mark the start of Cage's theatrical output.

William Fetterman's 1996 study includes one of the most detailed published accounts of *4′33″* to date. Like Broyles, he distinguishes between Cage's theatrical and musical pieces, and places *4′33″* within the context of multimedia works such as *Water Music*, the *Song Books*, the Black Mountain College Happening, *Theater Piece*, the *Musicircuses*, and the *Europeras*. Fetterman defines "theater pieces" by quoting Cage: "Something which engages both the eye and the ear," and designates *Water Music* (1952) as the first true theatrical piece.[47] Fetterman's categorization of *4′33″* as theater allows him to focus on analyzing the physical gestures performers have used in performing it. David Tudor's later performances, for instance, were notably graceful and solemn, with a rounded quality to his hand movements as he turned pages. Margaret Lang Tan, on the other hand, often keeps keys on the piano depressed while the seconds tick by, giving a more laborious affect to the experience. Others have gone for farce, dressing performers in costumes. A performance televised by the BBC and often-circulated on social media features an entire symphony orchestra poised ready to play for the duration.

Theater, or music? An oversimplified binarism it may be, but the question nevertheless unlocks an important hermeneutic window into *4′33″*. Fetterman's decision to treat *4′33″* primarily as "theater" leads him to what a musicologist might call "performance practice," focusing especially on the diversity of approaches performers have taken to the piece over the years. This is a promising line of investigation, but one that draws us away from the historical moment of the Black Mountain College premiere. Did Cage himself view *4′33″* as a work of theater?

It is important to note that most of Cage's own statements on the relationship between music and theater were made well after the composition of *4′33″*. In 1957, when addressing the National Association of Music Teachers, he decisively called for composers to turn toward theater, arguing that theater, "more than music, resembles nature."[48] And 1960 saw the premiere of his *Theater Piece*, perhaps his first explicit attempt to create a performance event that was primarily visual in nature. By the end of the 1960s and into the 1970s, Cage was spending the majority of his time working on large-scale multimedia works such as *HPSCHD* (1969), the various *Musicircuses*, and the *Lecture on the Weather* (1976). However, as James Pritchett and others have noted, there was a decisive shift in Cage's life and works in the years 1956 and 1958, the point at which Cage moved to a residential commune in Stony Point, New York, and when a notorious retrospective concert of his works finally brought him widespread attention. So, *4′33″* was written in 1952, at a very different time in his life. In many respects, it points backward into the 1940s, not forward into the 1960s.

This is not to say that in 1952 Cage was a stranger to the mixing of artistic media. Cage participated in numerous modernist collaborations; indeed, his early career was marked by a number of theatrical experiments and collaborations with dancers and poets. As Tamara Levitz has shown, Cage's first work with the prepared piano was inspired not only by the logistics of re-creating the sound of a percussion ensemble with a piano but also formally and aesthetically by the dancer Sylvia Fort.[49] In fact, most of his composing throughout the 1940s was intended to accompany dance performances, especially those by Merce Cunningham. And in the same month as the premiere of *4′33″*, Cage created an unabashedly theatrical work, the famous *Black Mountain Piece* that inspired the Happenings movement of the later 1950s.[50]

Nevertheless, I argue that when Cage composed *4′33″*, he intended it as a piece of *music*, written specifically for the piano. I realize that this goes against the grain of Cage's own statements on the piece, which value the very qualities of theatricality I have been criticizing. However, Cage's position on the matter changed over the years, and we will obtain a more accurate knowledge of the piece's framing if we look more closely at the historical record. In 1952, although Cage was relatively well known within new music circles as a composer for percussion, almost all his music was still being performed in concerts organized by Cage himself. These concerts were either solo recitals by David Tudor or they took place in conjunction with dance recitals by Merce Cunningham.[51] Although Tudor usually played in the dance recitals, and Cunningham was often involved in helping to organize Tudor's solo recitals, there was an interesting division of repertoire between the two types of performance. Cunningham at this point was still creating dances for many of Cage's earlier prepared piano works, like *Daughters of the Lonesome Isle* (1945) or more recent electronic works like *Imaginary Landscape No. 5*. Tudor, however, focused his recitals almost exclusively on recent works by contemporary composers for unprepared piano. By August 1952, in fact, Tudor had developed a fairly stable repertoire of piano works that changed little from concert to concert: he would play a Boulez piano sonata, a movement or two of Cage's *Music of Changes*, and a number of shorter piano works by Morton Feldman and Christian Wolff. A two-night series of recitals at Black Mountain College on August 9 and 12 almost exactly mirrors the program at the Maverick two weeks later. (See table 5.1.) There are a few works for prepared piano, and the multimedia *Water Music* (titled, according to Cage's custom, by the date of the performance), but the centerpieces of the Black Mountain program are clearly the Boulez Piano Sonata No. 1, and Cage's *Music of Changes* performed in its entirety. Both are works of considerable length and complexity, and were virtuosic showpieces for Tudor.

Thinking carefully about the musical status of *4′33″*, we might ask why Tudor included it on the August 29 program at Woodstock but not on the August 9 or 12 performances at Black Mountain College. Although it is not certain just when Cage composed *4′33″*, it had been gestating for months, if not years, prior to that August; it is reasonable to assume Cage could have included it on the earlier program if he had wanted to. It would seem that the audience at Black Mountain College was "wrong" for Cage's purposes. Cage, Cunningham, M. C. Richards, and Tudor were all teaching at Black Mountain College's summer sessions, and they had helped to nurture an atmosphere that was remarkably open-minded and tolerant of artistic experiments. Just days prior to Tudor's recital, Cage and his colleagues had organized the famous *Black Mountain Piece* mentioned earlier, a proto-happening that involved the artistic—and theatrical—talents of many of the artists in residence. In short, I suggest that the audience at Black Mountain was too well-prepared to receive *4′33″* as "theater." Having just

TABLE 5.1   DAVID TUDOR'S BLACK MOUNTAIN COLLEGE
RECITAL PROGRAMS

August 9, 1952	August 12, 1952
Morton Feldman, *Extensions* no. 3	Stefan Wolpe, Presto furioso
Christian Wolff, *For Piano*	John Cage, Two Pastorales
John Cage, *Music of Changes* (four parts)	Pierre Boulez, Premiere Sonate
	Morton Feldman, *Intermissions* Nos. 4 and 5
	Stefan Wolpe, Passacaglia
	John Cage, August 12, 1952
	Henry Cowell, *The Banshee*

attended an event in which Cunningham danced through the audience, the poet Charles Olsen recited poetry from a stepladder, and movies and slides were projected on the walls, the Black Mountain audience would have seen *4′33′* for just that which Cage did not want it to be: a theatrical spectacle. To premiere *4′33″* in such close proximity to the *Black Mountain Piece* would have stripped the work of its specifically musical presence. Instead, Cage chose to premiere *4′33″* far from the experimentation of Black Mountain College, in the confines of the Maverick Concert Hall at Woodstock.

From the way Cage programmed the piece, surrounding it with other pieces of piano music at a relatively traditional concert venue, one can infer that he initially intended *4′33″* as a piece of music. His intentions might not be the most important part of our analysis, and the "music" side of this artificial binarism is not the ultimate point I wish to make. But if we think—at least provisionally—about *4′33″* as Cage did—as music—a number of new avenues for analysis open up. For instance, *4″33″* might not have the "vital sensation of tone" that Patricia Carpenter argued for, but it nevertheless has a number of musical characteristics that might well submit to the traditional analytical tools of musicology. After all, *4′33″* does have two of the most important preconditions for a traditional musicological work: it exists in (several) written scores, and it has a pivotal position within a specific stylistic lineage of similar musical works.

Let us consider the second musicological question first. If *4'33"* is a piece for the piano, where does it fit in relation to other piano works by Cage, and where do these works fit within Cage's oeuvre? By 1951, Cage had largely stopped performing percussion music, and even his work for the prepared piano was being performed less often than his electronic music and his work for unprepared piano. De-emphasizing the physicality of his instruments, he began to concentrate almost exclusively on the abstract organization of sounds. He first began to turn toward chance procedures in 1950 for the last movement of his *Concerto for Prepared Piano and Orchestra*. Building upon this experiment, Cage then attempted to create an entire work using chance: the *Music of Changes*. As James Pritchett describes the process, Cage constructed a series of charts, each eight rows across and eight rows down, giving sixty-four cells to correspond to the sixty-four possible hexagrams of the *I Ching*. Of the two primary charts, the first determined sonority—in other words, pitch content, although a cell on the chart could give either one pitch or multiple pitches—either in the form of chords or as short phrases he called "constellations." In addition, half of the sixty-four cells contained silence. The second primary chart contained duration. For each bar, Cage would toss coins to achieve a number between 1 and 64, and use it to choose a duration. Then he would toss coins again to choose a rhythm, and attempt to fuse the two; despite the severity of the method, this was actually accomplished somewhat freely, with Cage allowing himself to use only part of the duration if the fit was too unwieldy.[52]

With these two elements, Cage created the main musical material of the piece. Other charts were consulted to put things together. Dynamics and tempo were a simple matter of again throwing coins for each bar. To complicate the density of the piece, Cage constructed another chart that would specify how many layers each unit of the piece would have. If a unit needed six layers, for instance, he would repeat his compositional process six times and then attempt to combine the result into two playable lines. Furthermore, to vary the choice of musical materials—with only sixty-four possible sonorities, repetition over forty-five minutes could have grown quite noticeable—Cage utilized one of the less understood aspects of the *I Ching*: the quality of hexagrams to be either "mobile" or "immobile." When immobile hexagrams are achieved, the chart remains the same. But when a mobile hexagram is achieved, the cell to which it points is refreshed with new material.

Amid all this organization, which elements of composition remained in the hands of John Cage himself? As David Bernstein has noted, the *Music of Changes* was "as much a product of the composer's intentions and pre-compositional decisions as of his chance operations."[53] Certain decisions were left to be freely notated, such as the fitting together of sonorities and durations, and also the use of pedals, which Cage simply added according to his own taste. Most important, however, the initial sonorities and durations were solely a matter of Cage's own judgment. The element of chance here is actually quite restricted: it inheres not in the performance of the piece, which is quite fixed, nor in the original musical materials, which were determined aesthetically. The indeterminate aspect of the piece is solely the organization, the structuring of material.

Another notable aspect of the *Music of Changes* is its sense of narrative. This need not be so surprising, given that it was written in the wake of the *Concerto for Prepared Piano*, which explicitly set itself up as a dialogue between piano and orchestra. Here, the main narratographic element is the distinction between pitched, traditional keyboard sounds and the sounds produced by extended techniques such as slamming the keyboard lid or strumming the strings (see table 5.2). Listening to the piece as a whole, one hears these as two contrasting musical areas in dialogue. This is metaphor, to be sure, but it could be argued that Cage intended to produce this

TABLE 5.2   UNPITCHED SONORITIES IN *MUSIC OF CHANGES*

Movement	Length	Unpitched Sonorities
I	3:37	0
II	16:30	27
III	10:30	24
IV	10:30	30

effect: the first movement of the work contains no unpitched elements, and the piece traces a clear trajectory toward more such sonorities.

This trajectory is something Cage easily could have controlled, despite the indeterminate organization. The original charts from which Cage constructed the piece are unfortunately incomplete, showing only the first iteration of each chart; they do not show the process by which Cage replaced sonorities when instructed to do so by the *I Ching*. The first chart we have consists entirely of pitched sonorities—the sounds we hear in the first movement. The evidence of the finished work makes one suspect that whenever Cage drew a mobile hexagram, and thus had the freedom to replace a pitched sonority, he chose to substitute an unpitched sound. This is conjecture, but it would have been easy for Cage both to respect the workings of "chance" and to gradually and intentionally increase the ratio of unpitched to pitched sounds as the piece progressed.

How might we interpret this teleological drive toward noise? It seems that even among the abstract modernism of the compositional practice, Cage is still concerned with emphasizing the physicality of the piano. Even without the presence of the unpitched elements, there is evidence of such concern in this piece. Often, in *Music of Changes*, Cage will give special emphasis to solitary notes followed by silence. The juxtaposition of isolated notes and silence is the work of the *I Ching*. The pedaling instructions, however were Cage's own choice. As I noted earlier, there was no chart for such performance practices; Cage simply went through the score and used his own judgment. Therefore, the decision to *hold* a solitary note, and to manipulate its resonance by gradually decreasing the pedal, was an aesthetic choice by Cage, who always loved the sound of gradual decay. Indeed, might we trace his choice to use this chart method, which produces sudden juxtapositions of silence after loud clamor, to an aesthetic enjoyment of sound resonating through space?

It might seem strange to place *4′33″* within this lineage. *Music of Changes*, after all, is an extended score of considerable formal complexity, which requires a pianist of exceptional technical abilities. But there is clear evidence that Cage did intend *4′33″* to be heard in the same context. In fact, in a 1991 interview with William Fetterman, Cage claimed that the two works were something of a matched pair:

I wrote it note by note, just like the *Music of Changes*. That's how I knew how long it was, when I added all the notes up. It was done just like a piece of music, except there were no sounds—but there were durations. It was dealing these cards—shuffling them, on which there were durations, and then dealing them—and using the Tarot to know how to use them. The card-spread was a complicated one, something big.[54]

Whatever we might glean from the composer's vague memories, it is undeniable that the simple choice of instrument in *4′33″* connects it to earlier piano works. One of Cage's crucial concerns from the 1930s onward was the physicality of his instruments. As Christopher Shultis has pointed out, his 1940s percussion music showed an extraordinary sensitivity toward the physical materials being used.[55] In the 1950s, it might be easy to decide that Cage lost this physical connection with instruments, especially as he turned increasingly toward electronic sources. However, I argue that rather than leaving this concern for materiality behind, Cage simply redirected it into abstraction: the physicality in question is no longer the instrument, but the sounds themselves. In this I read a certain longing to connect with a larger audience. Cage's percussion music could be performed only by his own instruments and performers, necessitating the transport and operation of large numbers of percussion instruments back and forth across the country. Even the prepared piano, invented to circumvent just these sorts of logistical challenges, required a large inventory of devices that were not only increasingly inaccessible over the years but difficult to learn how to use appropriately if one did not personally know Cage. Abstraction meant widening the scope of physicality to include both commonly available instruments and sound itself, thereby making Cage's ideas accessible to a greater number of people.[56]

Thus, *4′33″* is the ultimate abstraction of materiality, not requiring competence at the piano or even a properly working instrument. And yet, the sonic substance of the work is nevertheless the physical shape of sound, framed by the concert hall. Here, the "music" versus "theater" binarism begins to break down. Focusing on *4′33″* as music, we neglect the actual performance of the work's premiere. Paradoxically, it is the score of *4′33″*

that leads us further away from music—or, at least, music as conceived thus far—and toward a model of *4'33"* that relies upon those ephemeral sounds, gestures, and meanings that have so far eluded us.

We need to return to that audience at Woodstock. Consider the specific line the *New York Times* reviewer used to dismiss the later performance of the piece: "Greenwich Village exhibitionism." Or the shout by the anonymous concertgoer: "Good people of Woodstock, let's run these people out of town!" The tone of these responses tells me that many in the audience did indeed sense something threatening in Cage's music, and felt the need to protect their communities from whatever that mysterious threat was. In short, what sets Cage apart from many of his contemporaries in New York City was a willingness to be oppositional, and not only that but also a desire on Cage's part to attract others to his cause. Let's consider one more response, this time to a Cage-Tudor concert in 1954, at Wesleyan University, a small all-male college in Connecticut. The program is unfortunately unknown, but *4'33"* does not seem to have been on it. Regardless, it gives us a sense of the politics Cage seems to have attempted to create in his music. What follows is an eyewitness recall of the concert, several decades later: "The mood of the audience that jammed Memorial Chapel was festive and hair-trigger. Just below the surface lay maniacal eagerness to laugh, yell, jeer, applaud."

Then, Cage invited the audience to the stage to witness him preparing the piano:

> The hall exploded. People lunged toward the stage, some of them racing across the backs of pews, their feet occasionally dropping down to break hymnbook racks. Students in the balcony climbed over the rail, hung by their hands, then dropped, to be caught by friends below. The stage filled up instantly.[57]

Such were the scenes of mass seduction that greeted Cage, Tudor, and his colleagues as they toured the United States in the early 1950s. Swayed by more recent memories of Cage as a genial elderly man, I think we often forget the evangelical young Cage, the grandson of a Methodist preacher who poured all his energy into convincing the world that he held the key to the future of music. The "aesthetic of indifference" hardly captures the purposefully seductive power of Cage's performances. There are no codes to be deciphered here, no meanings deferred until a later date, as Nadine Hubbs put it. But also unlike the similar seductive power of a then-contemporary musician like Sonny Til or Elvis Presley, this particular enactment of seduction was intended to be pedagogical. The audience was not to be swept away, it was to be educated. Cage's own idea of oppositionality, I think, did not involve the overt politics of the queer commuters, or even the dream of a different political reality perhaps shared by those living in two worlds. Rather, his oppositionality was a utopian desire to educate his audiences, to change the way they thought. And yet, it is a sort of education not everyone appreciates. As David Tudor remained motionless at the keyboard in 1952, the Woodstock audience felt itself exposed in an uncomfortable position. If Cage had succeeded in creating a musical space that was at once pedagogical and perhaps faintly erotic, what exactly was being taught? And with what conditions?

I first experienced *4'33"* when I was fifteen years old. It was at a summer arts program sponsored by the State of California, in which artistically minded high schoolers spent four weeks on the campus of the California Institute of the Arts. On the first night, alone and not having made any friends yet, I saw an announcement for a concert of new music and decided to attend. The pianist Gaylord Mowrey was performing, and he announced to the audience that the concert would be a tribute to John Cage, who, he told us, had passed away just three years prior. I had no idea who this was, but I was intrigued by his promise that the piece he was about to perform was one of the most important works ever written.

Sure enough, Mowrey sat quietly at the piano for four and a half minutes, occasionally pausing to close and open the piano lid. The audience of young teenagers remained stock-still for the duration, no doubt confused by the work, and not sure enough of themselves to be outraged or to know how to act. For me, it was an intensely vivid moment. For most of us it was the first time we had been in the company of others like ourselves—which is to say, artistically minded and, for many of us, exploring our sexualities for the first time in an era before Gay-Straight Alliances. Away from parents and our normal communities, for four and a half minutes we contemplated the physical presence of strangers breathing next to us, strangers willing to also sit quietly and listen to the silence.

I want to end the chapter by directing our attention back to the sounds of that original performance on August 29, 1952. What were the sounds of that premiere? Recall Cage's description: "You could hear the wind stirring outside during the first movement. During the second, raindrops began patterning the roof, and during the third the people themselves made all kinds of interesting sounds as they talked or walked out."

What are these sounds? Some are ecological, some are the sound of the concert space responding to the environment. But most "interesting," Cage tells us, was the sounds "the people themselves" made. There actually is a universality to $4'33''$ that ties a great number of its performances together: the sounds of human bodies. Not the sound of the concert hall or the environment, but the sounds of people. That shuffling, coughing, murmuring, and breathing makes up the sonic substance of $4'33''$, and ultimately it is people who make up Cage's real world of sounds. The performance theorist Jill Dolan theorized the search for utopia as "the desire to be part of the intense present."[58] There, $4'33''$ offered, however briefly and perhaps inarticulately, the chance of intense presence with others.

Epilogue

The Practice of Identity

The four case studies presented in the preceding chapters have offered strikingly different visions for the cultural work of music and identity. Keeping in mind the original Eriksonian definition, we remember that identity is the practice of an individual but also the practice of an individual in relationship to a larger specific group in society. The context of the larger group matters, so that a John Cage might have a different relationship with the concept of identity than would a Sonny Til, or a Doris Day, or a Larry Ching. Scholars sometimes hesitate to push individual agency to the forefront of historical narratives—rightfully so, if it means losing track of larger social forces. But one of the goals of a performance-based history is to allow more and different voices to creep into the historical narrative. Giving people their chance to breathe and express themselves, as individuals, in a historical narrative helps ensure that the complexity of macro-level analysis is maintained. It also, I hope, provides us as individuals with a sense of political hope.

In this book I have tried to avoid too much engagement with contemporary debates on identity politics, but it seems only fair at this point to admit that I admire their transformational power. I don't believe that identity politics have been responsible for the demise of class-based and labor organizing, nor do I agree that they produce political citizens too narrowly focused on single issues. At their best, identity politics have been a chance for individuals to find a political voice for themselves in a context that leads to the mass mobilization necessary for larger change. To be sure, as such these politics are not the endgame, but they have been a crucial tool, and I hope will continue to be so.

Thus, I close this book by leaping ahead to the present, presenting one more articulation of music and identity, as well as the possibilities of identity politics. One of the greatest musical sensations of 2015 was the opening of the hit Broadway musical *Hamilton*. The show was conceived by Lin-Manuel Miranda, a young Nuyorican composer, actor, and rapper who had won a Tony award in 2008 for his previous musical *In the Heights*, set in the Latino immigrant communities of New York City's Washington Heights. *Hamilton*, however is set in the eighteenth century, and is famous for two acts of audacity across the color line. The actors cast to play the founding fathers—Washington, Jefferson, and, of course, Alexander Hamilton—are not the traditional, mostly white performers of Broadway nor the traditional, mostly white men of historical fantasies but, rather, people of color. Similarly, the music they perform is not the traditional Broadway musical tradition but, rather, that of hip-hop. These two choices break not only with the performance practice of your average Broadway musical but also with this nation's standard performance practice of itself.

At the same time, the immediate political context for *Hamilton* was a sense of division on the left. The rise of *Hamilton*'s popularity was roughly coterminous with the 2016 Democratic Party primary, which for many on the left became a referendum on the old binary of identity versus class politics. Hillary Clinton's successful mobilization of feminist and African American political networks seemed perfectly juxtaposed to Bernie Sanders strongly voiced critique of a corrupt financial system. As the primary campaign wore on, writers and activists on the left became increasingly divided and antagonistic, with many otherwise-natural allies reduced to online screaming matches. *Hamilton* became something of a touchstone in this debate, with the musical's creators throwing their support to Clinton—most visibly in a special performance for a Clinton fundraising event complete with the candidate speaking from the stage of the Richard Rodgers Theater.[1] Sanders supporters, for their part, zeroed in on the show's high-priced tickets and liberal aspirational politics. As socialist writer Amber A'Lee Frost put it, *Hamilton* was "reactionary nostalgia wrapped in affirmative action."[2]

Frost and other leftist critics of *Hamilton* have a point, and I would argue that Clinton's mobilization of identity politics, or "trickle down feminism," to use the evocative phrase of Sarah Jaffe, was indeed fairly cynical.[3] As is often the case, however, many on the left misunderstand the relationship between the cultural work of a musical like *Hamilton* and the broader political sphere. Cultural work, especially of the mass-cultural variety, remains frivolous for too many activists on the newly revived socialist left. As Raymond Williams wrote almost four decades ago in his famous essay, "Base and Superstructure in Marxist Cultural Theory,"

> We have to revalue "superstructure" towards a related range of cultural practices, and away from a reflected, reproduced or specifically dependent content. And, crucially, we have to revalue "the base" away from the notion of a fixed economic or technological abstraction, and towards the specific activities of men in real social and economic relationships, containing fundamental contradictions and variations and therefore always in a state of dynamic process.[4]

Kendra James has connected *Hamilton* to the Black Lives Matter and immigration debates, and its particular sensibility toward "the urgency to force change."[5] She also, however, points to a phenomenon tracked by many observers, which is the sense of ownership engendered by the casting choices: "Lin-Manuel Miranda has done what many history curricula fail to do: allow young people of color to see themselves in history." The poet Saeed Jones made a similar observation, tweeting "Watching HAMILTON was the first time in my life I felt like the history of our Founding Fathers was being told with me in mind."[6] It's a special kind of historiography that accomplishes this feat of belonging.

What precisely does it mean to feel an emotional connection to history? I suspect many musicologists are familiar with the sensation. Elisabeth Le Guin has written of the sense of reciprocity we might feel as we perform and study old music, the intimate and emotional connections we find with long-dead composers.[7] What if the magic of *Hamilton* is to inject more identity politics into these intimate moments of connection-through-performance? Of course, maybe all history is a performance, inflected with politics. As Diana Taylor once wrote, "history, like performance, is never for the first time, but it too is actualized in the present."[8] By way of example, I offer myself: on my mother's side I'm descended from a branch of the Schuyler family. My mother's first name is Elizabeth, and mine is Philip. When Eliza introduces young Philip Schuyler for the first time in *Hamilton*, my breath catches a little.

It's a very tangible, intimate connection with the past. But of course it is an entirely fictional one; there's no sort of empirical meaningfulness to a family connection like that, and I'm equally descended from thousands of other ostensibly less interesting people. And yet it is a connection with very real, material advantages. That's how whiteness works, after all. As chapter 3 argued, there's really no such empirical thing as being white; the founding fathers were not "white" in any kind of real sense. Whiteness is a system, and one of the rewards of that system is a sense of ownership. "Look," whiteness seems to say, "all of this is yours. Christianity is yours. The cultural heritage of Western Europe is yours. The Founding Fathers are yours." This is why the identity politics that emerged in the 1960s were so transformational, and why these symbols of ownership became so pivotal. Jesus could be black. Beethoven could be black. And maybe the founding fathers are black, too. Claims like these tend to make the empirically minded sputter, but the point was to call attention to the equal fiction that Beethoven was "white," as if he was white in the sense that twentieth-century America means being white.

This is where *Hamilton* offers an especially effective intervention, at a time when the Tea Party and constitutional originalism offer their own contemporary fantasies of eighteenth-century political culture. Miranda's performance of history is no less fictional than those of conservative movements or those of my family; but rather than retaining "history" as a source of privilege, Miranda makes its emotional intimacy potentially available to all. It's crucial, I believe, that the most powerful moments in *Hamilton* are not always the urgent calls to action but, rather, the more personal numbers. Almost always these moments have to do with children. Aaron Burr's major number "Wait for It" is addressed to his wife and his legacy, and the conflation of family and history is made explicit in the Hamilton and Burr duet "Dear Theodosia": "You will come of age with our young nation. . . . We'll pass it on to you, we'll give the world to you." And of course, the crushing "It's Quiet Uptown," in which the Hamilton family comes to terms with the death of their son Philip. In this last number, Miranda's verbal dexterity spills beyond the boundaries of its somewhat sentimental musical setting. Phillipa Soo as Eliza sings,

> There are moments that the words don't reach
> There is suffering too terrible to name
> You hold your child as tight as you can
> And push away the unimaginable.

The lyrics are too wordy, barely squeezing into the space allotted. That's a Miranda hallmark, a legacy of his particular hip-hop genealogy rooted in the late 1990s world of artists like Big Pun, and what the late Adam Krims calls "speech effusive" rapping.[9] Usually this style sounds clever and bombastic; paired here with a spare musical setting, it conveys numbness, and grief. It's a powerful move, and it conveys a feeling with which it is easy to identify.

That feeling of identification is precisely what identity politics hope to accomplish. Caricatures of identity politics, from the right and left, often figure them as divisive. From their earliest days, however, identity politics have always offered a model of solidarity and connectedness, a privileging, in the famous phrase, of the personal as the political. It's why it matters that the cast members are not white, but also that the story is told with such profound emotional intimacy. *Hamilton* does not rewrite history, but it does rewrite how it is felt and who gets to do the feeling.

The moral of these identity politics, however—and where socialist critics have a great deal to offer—is that it is not enough simply to achieve some sort of psychological self-actualization, solely on one's own, individual terms. Identity politics offer a chance to mobilize people, together, in a dizzying array of relationships often fraught with conflict that nevertheless extends to our current American society some of the best chances we have at creating change.

CHAPTER 1

1. Allen Churchill, "Tin Pan Alley's Git-tar Blues," *New York Times Sunday Magazine*, July 15, 1951, 5.
2. My source for chart information in this book comes from Joel Whitburn's authoritative compilations of data from the music industry magazine *Billboard*, particularly *Billboard Pop Hits Singles and Albums, 1940–1954* (Menomonee Falls, WI: Record Research, 2002) and *Top R&B/Hip-Hop Singles, 1942–2004* (Menomonee Falls, WI: Record Research, 2004). References to chart listings are to those in *Billboard* unless otherwise noted, as in the occasional use of *Cash Box* charts.
3. James M. Manheim, "B-Side Sentimentalizer: 'Tennessee Waltz' in the History of Popular Music," *Musical Quarterly* 76, no. 3 (Autumn 1992): 350.
4. Carl Perkins, "Rock 'n' Roll Explodes," in *The History of Rock 'n' Roll*, dir. Andrew Solt, Time-Life Video and Television, 1995, quoted in Michael T. Bertrand, *Race, Rock, and Elvis* (Urbana: University of Illinois Press, 2004), 41.
5. Timothy D. Taylor, *Beyond Exoticism: Western Music and the World* (Durham, NC: Duke University Press, 2007), 118–21.
6. Timothy D. Taylor, *Music and Capitalism: A History of the Present* (Chicago: University of Chicago Press, 2015), 67.
7. Geoffrey Nunberg, "Counting on Google Books," *Chronicle of Higher Education*, December 16, 2010, http://chronicle.com/article/Counting-on-Google-Books/125735/.
8. As I hope is clear through my citations, I am indebted to Timothy Taylor for originally bringing this failure of historicization to my attention, initially in personal conversation.
9. Thomson replied, "I do hope you will continue to bring to my notice interesting musical events in which colored people are involved." Letter from Virgil Thomson, May 23, 1941, A426, Folder 2, Library of Congress, NAACP Papers.
10. Eight years later, the collection was republished under a new title with some additional essays; this edition will be cited here. Daniel Bell, ed., *The Radical Right* (New York: Doubleday, 1963).

11. Bell, "Interpretations of American Politics," in *Radical Right*, 56.
12. Hofstadter, "The Pseudo-Conservative Revolt," in *Radical Right*, 89–90.
13. Ibid., 2.
14. See, for example, Alan Nadel, *Containment Culture: American Narratives, Post-modernism, and the Atomic Age* (Durham, NC: Duke University Press, 1995).
15. Ann Douglas, "Periodizing the American Century: Modernism, Postmodernism, and Postcolonialism in the Cold War Context," *Modernism/Modernity* 5, no. 3 (1998): 71–98.
16. Ibid., 75.
17. Peter Schmelz calls active musicological engagement with the Cold War "long over-due," but unlike in, say, musicology's engagement with feminist theory, I don't see our discipline as particularly slower than others in this regard. See Peter J. Schmelz, "Introduction: Music in the Cold War," *Journal of Musicology* 26, no. 1 (2009): 3.
18. Martin Brody, "'Music for the Masses': Milton Babbitt's Cold War Music Theory," *Musical Quarterly* 77, no. 2 (1993): 161–92.
19. Peter J. Schmelz, *Such Freedom, If Only Musical: Unofficial Soviet Music During the Thaw* (New York: Oxford University Press, 2009); Andrea Florence Bohlman, "Activism and Music in Poland, 1978–1989," Ph.D. dissertation, Harvard University, 2012; Danielle Fosler-Lussier, *Music Divided: Bartók's Legacy in Cold War Culture* (Berkeley, CA: University of California Press, 2007).
20. See, for example, Emily Abrams Ansari, "Aaron Copland and the Politics of Cultural Diplomacy," *Journal of the Society for American Music* 5, no. 3 (2011): 335–64.
21. Barry Seldes, *Leonard Bernstein: The Political Life of an American Musician* (Berkeley: University of California Press, 2009).
22. Tamara Levitz, "Introduction to 'Musicology Beyond Borders,'" *Journal of the American Musicological Society* 65, no. 3 (Fall 2012): 821–24.
23. Schmelz, "Music in the Cold War," 8.
24. Arjun Appadurai, *Modernity at Large: Cultural Dimensions of Globalization* (Minneapolis: University of Minnesota Press, 1996), 15.
25. Michael Omi and Howard Winant, *Racial Formation in the United States: From the 1960s to the 1990s*, 2nd ed. (New York and London: Routledge, 1994), 14.
26. Karen Brodkin, *How Jews Became White Folks and What That Says about Race in America* (Piscataway, NJ: Rutgers University Press, 1998), 144.
27. Omi and Winant, *Racial Formation in the United States*, 98.
28. Philip Gentry, "Leonard Bernstein's The Age of Anxiety: A Great American Symphony during McCarthyism," *American Music* 29, no. 3 (2011): 313.
29. Nathan G. Hale, *The Rise and Crisis of Psychoanalysis in United States: Freud and the Americans, 1917–1985* (New York: Oxford University Press, 1995), 245–46.
30. Timothy Rice, "Reflections on Music and Identity in Ethnomusicology," *Muzikologija/Musicology* 7 (2007): 17–37.
31. Lawrence Jacob Friedman, *Identity's Architect: A Biography of Erik H. Erikson* (Cambridge, MA: Harvard University Press, 2000).
32. Erik H. Erikson, *Childhood and Society* (New York: Norton, 1950), 17.
33. Ibid., 35.
34. Ibid., 34–36.

35. David Riesman, *The Lonely Crowd; a Study of the Changing American Character* (New Haven, CT: Yale University Press, 1950).

36. Christopher Shannon, *A World Made Safe for Differences: Cold War Intellectuals and the Politics of Identity* (Lanham, MD: Rowman & Littlefield, 2000), xiii.

37. Ibid., xv.

38. Taylor, *Beyond Exoticism*, 120.

39. "Identity, *n*.," *OED Online*, March 2015, www.oed.com/view/Entry/91004?redirect edFrom=identity.

40. Judith Halberstam, *In A Queer Time and Place: Transgender Bodies, Subcultural Lives* (New York: New York University Press, 2005), 20.

41. Manning Marable and Leith Mullings, *Let Nobody Turn Us Around: Voices of Resistance, Reform, and Renewal* (Lanham, MD: Rowman & Littlefield, 2003), 524–28.

42. Satya P. Mohanty and Paula M. L. Moya, *Identity Politics Reconsidered*, ed. Linda Martín Alcoff and Michael Hames-García (New York: Palgrave Macmillan, 2006).

43. Sara Ahmed, *Willful Subjects* (Durham, NC: Duke University Press, 2014), 171.

44. Ian Biddle, *Music and Identity Politics* (Farnham, UK: Ashgate, 2012).

45. Ibid., xiv.

46. Ibid., xvii.

47. Shannon, *A World Made Safe for Differences*, xi.

48. While citationality is critiqued in a great deal of Amed's work, see especially Sara Ahmed, "White Men," in *Feminist Killjoys*, April 11, 2014, http://feministkilljoys.com/2014/11/04/white-men/.

49. Gayle Rubin, *Deviations: A Gayle Rubin Reader* (Durham, NC: Duke University Press, 2011).

50. Barbara Kirshenblatt-Gimblett, "Performance Studies," in *The Performance Studies Reader*, ed. Henry Bial (New York: Routledge, 2004), 43.

51. For a useful critique of the present state of research on "music and politics" from a sociological perspective, see Rob Rosenthal, "Serving the Movement: The Role(s) of Music," *Popular Music and Society* 25, no. 3–4 (September 1, 2001): 11–24.

52. For examples, see Susan McClary, "Music, the Pythagoreans, and the Body," in Susan Leigh Foster, ed., *Choreographing History* (Bloomington, IN: Indiana University Press, 1995), 82–104; Carolyn Abbate, "Music—Drastic or Gnostic?" in *Critical Inquiry* 30 (2004): 505–36; Charles Keil, "Motion and Feeling Through Music," in *Music Grooves: Essays and Dialogues*, ed. Charles Keil and Steven Feld (Chicago: University of Chicago Press, 1994), 53–76.

53. Peggy Phelan, *Unmarked: The Politics of Performance* (New York: Routledge, 1993).

54. Ibid., 146.

55. Diana Taylor, *The Archive and the Repertoire: Performing Cultural Memory in the Americas* (Durham, NC: Duke University Press, 2003), xvi; Joseph Roach, *Cities of the Dead: Circum-Atlantic Performance* (New York: Columbia University Press, 1996).

56. Susan Leigh Foster, "Choreographies of Gender," *Signs* 24, no. 1 (1998): 5.

57. Ibid., 30.

58. Ibid., 30.

59. The relationship between text and performance is obviously complicated, and even within performance studies there is no unanimity of opinion. For a provocative overview of the debates, see W. B. Worthen, "Disciplines of the Text/Sites of Performance," *TDR (1988–)* 39, no. 1 (1995): 13–28.

CHAPTER 2

1. For a fascinating analysis of Robeson's statement, see Tony Perucci, *Paul Robeson and the Cold War Performance Complex: Race, Madness, Activism* (Ann Arbor: University of Michigan Press, 2012).

2. U.S. House of Representatives, Committee on Un-American Activities, *Hearings Regarding Communist Infiltration of Minority Groups—Part 1* (Washington, DC: Government Printing Office, 1949), 480.

3. Ibid., 427.

4. Steve Estes, *I Am a Man!: Race, Manhood, and the Civil Rights Movement* (Chapel Hill, NC: University of North Carolina Press, 2005), 2.

5. For more on this discourse, see the essays in Marcellus Blount and George P. Cunningham, eds., *Representing Black Men* (New York: Routledge, 1995).

6. Frazier's work was originally published in French as *Le bourgeoisie noir* (Paris: Librairie Plon, 1955); an English language version did not appear until two years later as Franklin Frazier, *The Black Bourgeoisie* (New York: Simon and Schuster, 1957).

7. Ibid., 220.

8. Jeffrey Melnick, "'Story Untold': The Black Men and White Sounds of Doo-Wop," in *Whiteness: A Critical Reader*, ed. Mike Hill (New York: New York University Press, 1997), 144.

9. Brian Ward, *Just My Soul Responding: Rhythm and Blues, Black Consciousness, and Race Relations* (Berkeley: University of California Press, 1998), 56–89.

10. Ibid., 74.

11. Wynonie Harris, "Why Women Won't Leave Me Alone," *Tan* magazine, October 1954, 28–31, 76–77, quoted in Ward, *Just My Soul Responding*, 77. An extract of Harris's essay has circulated more widely in David Brackett, *The Pop, Rock, and Soul Reader: Histories and Debates*, 3rd ed. (New York: Oxford University Press, 2013), 61–62. *Tan* magazine was a rebranding of *Tan Confessions*, a publication to be discussed shortly.

12. Ward, *Just My Soul Responding*, 83.

13. "Sonny Til and His Orioles," *Ebony*, September 1952, 25.

14. Jerry Wexler and David Ritz, *Rhythms and Blues: A Life in American Music* (New York: Knopf, 1993), 62; See also Russell Sanjek and David Sanjek, *American Popular Music Business in the 20th Century*, abridged edition (New York: Oxford University Press, 1991), 87.

15. Albin Zak, *I Don't Sound Like Nobody: Remaking Music in 1950s America* (Ann Arbor: University of Michigan Press, 2010), 7.

16. Greil Marcus, "The Deborah Chessler Story," originally published in *Rolling Stone*, June 24, 1993, reprinted in Greil Marcus, *The Dustbin of History* (Cambridge, MA: Harvard University Press, 1998), 236.

17. Gage Averill, *Four Parts, No Waiting: A Social History of American Barbershop Quartet* (New York: Oxford University Press, 2010), 11.
18. Susan Leigh Foster, "Choreographies of Gender," *Signs* 24, no. 1 (1998): 1–33.
19. Judith Butler, *Gender Trouble: Feminism and the Subversion of Identity* (New York: Routledge, 1990).
20. Sue-Ellen Case, *The Domain-Matrix: Performing Lesbian at the End of Print Culture* (Bloomington: Indiana University Press, 1996), 17.
21. Foster, "Choreographies of Gender," 4.
22. See Philip Gentry, "Doo-Wop," *Encyclopedia of African American Music* (Westport, CT: Greenwood Press, 2010), 297–303.
23. Stuart L. Goosman, *Group Harmony: The Black Urban Roots of Rhythm & Blues* (Philadelphia: University of Pennsylvania Press, 2005), 196. Goosman's work is informed by a series of interviews with former members of a number of early R&B vocal groups from Baltimore and Washington, D.C.
24. Philip Groia, *They All Sang on the Corner; New York City's Rhythm and Blues Vocal Groups of the 1950's* (Setauket, NY: Edmond Publishing, 1974), 32.
25. Goosman, *Group Harmony*, 207.
26. See also Zak, *I Don't Sound Like Nobody*, 90–91.
27. Charles Keil, "Participatory Discrepancies and the Power of Music," in *Music Grooves: Essays and Dialogues*, by Charles Keil and Steven Feld (Chicago: University of Chicago Press, 1994).
28. "Sonny Til and His Orioles," 24–28.
29. Goosman, *Group Harmony*, 199–200.
30. For a useful discussion of the role of dance in vocal harmony groups, see Jacqui Malone, "'Let the Punishment Fit the Crime': The Vocal Choreography of Cholly Atkins," *Dance Research Journal* 20, no. 1 (July 1, 1988): 11–18.
31. *Tan Confessions* magazine, February 1952, 29.
32. Ibid.
33. For a historical overview, see Ayana D Byrd and Lori L Tharps, *Hair Story: Untangling the Roots of Black Hair in America* (New York: St. Martin's Press, 2001), 42–49.
34. Maxine Leeds Craig, *Ain't I a Beauty Queen?: Black Women, Beauty, and the Politics of Race* (New York: Oxford University Press, 2002), 111.
35. "Sonny Til and His Orioles," 28.
36. Thorstein Veblen and Stuart Chase, *The Theory of the Leisure Class: An Economic Study of Institutions* (New York: Modern library, 1934).
37. Sonny Til, "Why Women Go For Me," *Tan Confessions*, September 1952, 26.
38. Ibid.
39. For a historical overview of the confession magazine, see George Gerbner, "The Social Role of the Confession Magazine," *Social Problems* 6, no. 1 (1958): 29–40.
40. "Passion Without a Purpose," *Time* magazine, September 22, 1952, 101.
41. Adelina Harriott, "Letter to the Editor," *Tan Confessions* magazine, November 1950, 52.
42. Joan Everett, Letter to the Editor, *Tan Confessions* magazine, November 1950, 5; J. B. Arnold, Letter to the Editor, *Tan Confessions* magazine, November 1950, 52.
43. "Passion With a Purpose," *Time* magazine, October 23, 1950, 57.

44. Lizabeth Cohen, *A Consumers' Republic: The Politics of Mass Consumption in Postwar America* (New York: Vintage Books, 2003), 114.
45. Ibid., 116.
46. The critique is famously laid out in John Kenneth Galbraith, *The Affluent Society* (New York: Houghton Mifflin, 1958).
47. This oft-cited quote originally appeared in *Fortune*, May 1956, of which Whyte was then editor.
48. See Cohen, *A Consumers' Republic*, 133–51; Elaine May, *Homeward Bound: American Families in the Cold War Era*, rev. and updated ed. (New York: Basic Books, 1999).
49. *Tan Confessions* magazine, November 1950, 44.
50. Roderick A. Ferguson, "African American Masculinity and the Study of Social Formations," *American Quarterly* 58, no. 1 (2006): 216.
51. "If You Married . . . Jimmy Edwards," *Tan Confessions* magazine, November 1952, 30.
52. *Tan Confessions* magazine, May 1951, 68; June 1951, 8; May 1951, 68; June 1952, 5; August 1951, 9. Not all reviews were signed, but columns tended to be written either by Jim Goodrich or later Dan Gurley.
53. Hazel V. Carby, "Policing the Black Woman's Body in an Urban Context," *Critical Inquiry* 18, no. 4 (July 1, 1992): 738–55.
54. Noliwe M. Rooks, *Ladies' Pages: African American Women's Magazines and the Culture That Made Them* (New Brunswick, NJ: Rutgers University Press, 2004).
55. For a consideration of musical smoothness in a different historical moment, see Charles D. Carson, "'Bridging the Gap': Creed Taylor, Grover Washington Jr., and the Crossover Roots of Smooth Jazz," *Black Music Research Journal* 28, no. 1 (April 1, 2008): 1–15.
56. Manfred Berg, *The Ticket to Freedom: The NAACP and the Struggle for Black Political Integration* (Gainesville: University Press of Florida, 2005); Steve Estes's book on the role of masculinity in the civil rights movement unfortunately neglects African American masculinity in this period, focusing on the threatened white masculinity of racist groups such as the Citizens' Council; see Estes, *I Am a Man!*, 39–60.
57. Jim Jones, "Modest Church Inspires Elvis Hit," *Gadsen Times*, March 15, 1998, C8.
58. Elvis Presley later also recorded a well-known version in 1960, although it was not released until 1965 as an "Easter Special." For many, this is now the most famous version of the song.
59. Peter Doyle, *Echo and Reverb: Fabricating Space in Popular Music Recording, 1900–1960* (Middletown, CT: Wesleyan University Press, 2005); Gayle Wald has examined the generic and ideological tension—as well as sympathies—between R&B and country; see Gayle Wald, "'Have a Little Talk': Listening to the B-Side of History," *Popular Music* 24, no. 3 (October 1, 2005): 323–37.
60. Gayle Wald, "From Spirituals to Swing: Sister Rosetta Tharpe and Gospel Crossover," *American Quarterly* 55, no. 3 (2003): 387–416; Gayle Wald, *Shout, Sister, Shout!: The Untold Story of Rock-and-Roll Trailblazer Sister Rosetta Tharpe* (Boston: Beacon Press, 2007).
61. Frazier, *Black Bourgeoisie*, 87.

62. Vance Packard, *The Status Seekers: An Exploration of Class Behavior in America and the Hidden Barriers That Affect You, Your Community, Your Future* (New York: D. McKay, 1959).

63. For a rather elaborate genealogy of Eisenhower's remark, see Patrick Henry, "'And I Don't Care What It Is': The Tradition-History of a Civil Religion Proof-Text," *Journal of the American Academy of Religion* 49, no. 1 (March 1, 1981): 35–49.

64. Ward, *Just My Soul Responding*, 83.

65. Ralph Ellison, *Invisible Man* (New York: Random House, 1952), 3.

CHAPTER 3

1. Wayne Koestenbaum, *Jackie Under My Skin: Interpreting an Icon* (New York: Macmillan, 2009), 79.

2. Dennis Bingham, "'Before She Was a Virgin...': Doris Day and the Decline of Female Film Comedy in the 1950s and 1960s," *Cinema Journal* 45, no. 3 (2006): 3–31.

3. Bruce Bawer, "Whatever Happened to Doris Day," in *Beyond the Boom: New Voices on American Life, Culture, and Politics*, ed. Terry Teachout (New York: Poseidon Press, 1990), 149–54.

4. Erica Jong, *Fear of Fifty: A Midlife Memoir* (New York: Penguin, 2006), xix.

5. Richard Dyer, *Heavenly Bodies: Film Stars and Society* (London: Macmillan, 1986).

6. Elijah Wald, *How the Beatles Destroyed Rock "N" Roll: An Alternative History of American Popular Music* (New York: Oxford University Press, 2011), 182.

7. Andrea Friedman, "The Smearing of Joe McCarthy: The Lavender Scare, Gossip, and Cold War Politics," *American Quarterly* 57 (2005): 1105–30.

8. *Edward R. Murrow: The McCarthy Years*, Walter Cronkite for CBS News, broadcast reissued as DVD, New Video Group, 2005.

9. Seymour Lipset, "Three Decades of the Radical Right," in *The Radical Right*, ed. Daniel Bell (Garden City, NY: Doubleday, 1963), 377.

10. The most famous such study is the collection of essays edited by Daniel Bell in 1955, *The New American Right* (New York: Criterion Books, 1955), later reprinted with additional essays as *The Radical Right*, cited in note 9 and discussed in more detail in chapter 1.

11. The original 1950 text was reprinted in "Four Statements on the Race Question" (Paris: United Nations Educational, Scientific and Cultural Organization, 1969), 32.

12. See, for example, Christopher Shannon, *A World Made Safe for Differences: Cold War Intellectuals and the Politics of Identity* (Lanham, MD: Rowman & Littlefield, 2000), 65–88.

13. Richard Alba, "The Twilight of Ethnicity Among Americans of European Ancestry: The Case of the Italians," in *Ethnicity and Race in the U.S.A.: Toward the Twenty-First Century*, ed. Richard Alba (New York: Routledge, 1988), 142; Josh Kun, *Audiotopia: Music, Race, and America* (Berkeley: University of California Press, 2005), 62.

14. Alba, "The Twilight of Ethnicity," 142.

15. Ibid., 141.

16. See appendix F of Stanley Lieberson, *Ethnic Patterns in American Cities* (Glencoe, IL: Free Press, 1963), 206.

17. See Cheryl Shanks, *Immigration and the Politics of American Sovereignty, 1890–1990* (Ann Arbor: University of Michigan Press, 2001), 96–143.

18. Will Herberg, *Protestant, Catholic, Jew: An Essay in American Religious Sociology* (Chicago: University of Chicago Press, 1955), 258.

19. Richard Dyer, *White* (London and New York: Routledge, 1997).

20. Krin Gabbard, *Black Magic: White Hollywood and African American Culture* (New Brunswick, NJ: Rutgers University Press, 2004).

21. Gwendolyn Audrey Foster, *Performing Whiteness: Postmodern Re/Constructions in the Cinema* (Albany: SUNY Press, 2003).

22. George Lipsitz, *The Possessive Investment in Whiteness: How White People Profit from Identity Politics, Revised and Expanded Edition* (Philadelphia, PA: Temple University Press, 2009).

23. Doris Day and A. E. Hotchner, *Doris Day: Her Own Story* (New York: Morrow, 1975), 27. The book is supposedly Day's autobiography as told to Hotchner, interspersed with episodic commentary from Day's friends and family. Its release in the 1970s was a revelation for many fans, in that it revealed the tragedies behind Day's sunny persona. The other Day biographies, such as George Morris's lightweight *Doris Day* (New York: Pyramid, 1976) and Eric Braun's somewhat more probing *Doris Day* (London: Orion Books, 1991) are largely based on *Her Own Story*, especially with regard to her early career.

24. Ben King, *Ben King's Southland Melodies* (Chicago: Forbes and Co., 1911), 11.

25. I am condensing here a widely reported narrative in the history of jazz. For examples, see Ira Gitler, *Swing to Bop: An Oral History of the Transition in Jazz in the 1940s* (New York: Oxford University Press, 1985); Lawrence McClellan Jr. *The Later Swing Era: 1942–1955* (Westport, CT: Greenwood Press, 2004); Bernie Woods, *When the Music Stopped: The Big Band Era Remembered* (New York: Barricade Books, 1994). For the recording ban, see David and Russell Sanjek, *American Popular Music Business in the 20th Century* (Oxford: Oxford University Press, 1991).

26. There were African American women on the pop charts, most importantly Ella Fitzgerald. Popular criticism, however, almost always referred to her as a jazz singer. Singers like Lena Horne and Billie Holiday were largely absent from the pop charts in this period. For more on pop crossover singers, see Elaine Hays, "To Bebop or to Be Pop: Sarah Vaughan and the Politics of Crossover," Ph.D. dissertation, University of Pennsylvania, 2004.

27. Day and Hotchner, *Doris Day*, 94–95.

28. Ibid., 98.

29. Patty Fox, *Star Style: Hollywood Legends as Fashion Icons*, rev. ed. (Santa Monica, CA: Angel City Press, 1999), 108.

30. Raymond Knapp, *The American Musical and the Formation of National Identity* (Princeton, NJ: Princeton University Press, 2005), 209–15.

31. Jane Clarke and Diana Simmonds, *Move Over Misconceptions: Doris Day Reappraised* (London: British Film Institute, 1980).

32. Eric Savoy, "'That Ain't All She Ain't': Doris Day and Queer Performativity," in *Out Takes: Essays on Queer Theory and Film*, ed. Ellis Hanson (Durham, NC: Duke University Press, 1999), 165.

33. Robert J. Corber, *Cold War Femme: Lesbianism, National Identity, and Hollywood Cinema* (Durham, NC: Duke University Press, 2011), 164.

34. Ibid., 211n29.

35. Dyer, *White*.

36. This discussion of lighting is heavily indebted to Dyer, in particular the chapter "The Light of the World," in *White*, 82–144.

37. Day and Hotchner, *Doris Day*, 131.

38. James Harvey, *Movie Love in the Fifties* (New York: Knopf, 2001), 47.

39. The politics of the villains are never made clear, but in notes on the screenplay Hitchcock and his collaborators explicitly referred to them as "commies." See Dan Auiler, *Hitchcock's Notebooks: An Authorized and Illustrated Look Inside the Creative Mind of Alfred Hitchcock* (New York: Spike, 1999), 176–202.

40. Elsie B. Michie, "Unveiling Maternal Desires: Hitchcock and American Domesticity," in *Hitchcock's America*, ed. Jonathan Freedman and Richard Millington (Oxford and New York: Oxford University Press, 1999), 29–54.

41. *The Man Who Knew Too Much*, directed by Alfred Hitchcock, 1956, Paramount Pictures.

42. Brian T. Edwards, *Morocco Bound: Disorienting America's Maghreb, from Casablanca to the Marrakech Express* (Durham, NC: Duke University Press, 2005), 19X.

43. Ibid., 183–97.

44. The authoritative account of the song's composition, based on interviews with the writers, is found in Murray Pomerance, "'The Future's Not Ours to See': Song, Singer, Labyrinth in Hitchcock's The Man Who Knew Too Much," in *Soundtrack Available: Essays on Film and Popular Music*, ed. Pamela Wojcik and Arthur Knight (Durham, NC: Duke University Press, 2001), 53. The agrammatical title phrase was supposedly inspired by a scene from *The Barefoot Comtessa* (1954). As a matter of trivia, the Academy Award for Best Song won by "Que Sera Sera" was the only Oscar a Hitchcock film ever received.

45. Pomerance, "The Future's," 68.

46. Michie, "Unveiling Maternal Desires," 43.

47. Rollo May, *The Meaning of Anxiety* (New York: Ronald Press, 1950), 355.

48. Ibid., 234.

49. Hughson F. Mooney, "Songs, Singers and Society, 1890–1954," *American Quarterly* 6, no. 3 (1954): 232.

50. Anne Helen Petersen, "Jennifer Lawrence and the History of Cool Girls," *BuzzFeed*, February 28, 2014, www.buzzfeed.com/annehelenpetersen/jennifer-lawrence-and-the-history-of-cool-girls.

51. Robin James, "Hello From the Same Side," *The New Inquiry*, http://thenewinquiry.com/essays/hello-from-the-same-side/.

CHAPTER 4

1. Jim Lovensheimer, *South Pacific: Paradise Rewritten* (New York: Oxford University Press, 2013), 82–107.

2. Terry Teachout, "The Importance of Not Being Earnest," *Wall Street Journal*, April 8, 2008.

3. Christina Klein, *Cold War Orientalism: Asia in the Middlebrow Imagination, 1945–1961* (Berkeley: University of California Press, 2003), 5.

4. Rustom Bharucha, *The Politics of Cultural Practice: Thinking through Theatre in an Age of Globalization* (Middletown, CT: Wesleyan University Press, 2000).

5. Jonathan Hay, "Toward a Theory of the Intercultural," *Res* 35 (Spring 1999): 5.

6. See the classic 1975 text by Paul Fussell, *The Great War and Modern Memory* (New York: Oxford University Press, 2000); see also Jay Winter, *Sites of Memory, Sites of Mourning: The Great War in European Cultural History* (Cambridge: Cambridge University Press, 1998).

7. David M. Oshinsky, *A Conspiracy so Immense: The World of Joe McCarthy* (New York: Free Press, 1983), 30.

8. Ibid., 32.

9. Peter C. Rollins, "Victory at Sea: Cold War Epic," in *Television Histories: Shaping Collective Memory in the Media Age*, ed. Gary R Edgerton and Peter C. Rollins (Lexington: University Press of Kentucky, 2001), 105.

10. George Ferencz, "'The World's Longest Symphony': Issues of Collaboration and Thematic Transformation in Richard Rodgers and Robert Russell Bennett's Victory at Sea," paper given at meeting of the American Musicological Society, Washington, D.C., October 28, 2005.

11. M. Clay Adams, "Malanesian Nightmare," *Victory at Sea*, NBC broadcast, 1953.

12. Ruth Benedict, *The Chrysanthemum and the Sword* (Boston: Houghton Mifflin, 1946).

13. Ibid., 36.

14. Ibid., 37.

15. Timothy D. Taylor, *Beyond Exoticism: Western Music and the World* (Durham, NC: Duke University Press, 2007), 119.

16. Christopher Shannon, *A World Made Safe for Differences: Cold War Intellectuals and the Politics of Identity* (Lanham, MD: Rowman & Littlefield, 2000), 4.

17. Benedict, *The Chrysanthemum and the Sword*, 295.

18. Shannon, *A World Made Safe for Differences*, 13.

19. Anthony B. Chan, *Perpetually Cool: The Many Lives of Anna May Wong (1905–1961)* (Lanham, MD: Scarecrow Press, 2007), 81.

20. Richard Condon, *The Manchurian Candidate* (New York: McGraw-Hill, 1959).

21. Michael Rogin, "Kiss Me Deadly: Communism, Motherhood, and Cold War Movies," *Representations*, 6 (Spring 1984): 17.

22. Klein, *Cold War Orientalism*.

23. Ibid., 99.

24. U.S. Census Bureau, "Characteristics of the Population," 1950 (Washington, DC: Government Printing Office, 1953), 1–87.

25. Charlotte Brooks, *Alien Neighbors, Foreign Friends: Asian Americans, Housing, and the Transformation of Urban California* (Chicago: University of Chicago Press, 2009), 13.

26. Ibid., 157.

27. Ibid., 160.

28. Charlotte Brooks, *Between Mao and McCarthy: Chinese American Politics in the Cold War Years* (Chicago: University of Chicago Press, 2015).

29. Ibid., 5.
30. Jennifer Y. Fang, "Negotiating Chinese American Middle-Class Identity in the Cold War Suburbs" Ph.D. dissertation, University of Delaware, 2015.
31. Ibid., 136.
32. See also Yong Chen, *Chop Suey, USA: The Story of Chinese Food in America* (New York: Columbia University Press, 2014).
33. Mina Yang, "Orientalism and the Music of Asian Immigrant Communities in California, 1924–1945," *American Music* 19, no. 4 (2001): 396.
34. David Henry Hwang, "Introduction," in *The Flower Drum Song*, by Chen Ye Lee (New York: Penguin, 2002), xv.
35. Ibid., xvii.
36. Ibid., xix.
37. Lisa Lowe, *Immigrant Acts: On Asian American Cultural Politics* (Durham, NC: Duke University Press, 1996), 63–64.
38. *The New Yorker*, December 13, 1958, p. 73, quoted in Robert G. Lee, *Orientals: Asian Americans in Popular Culture* (Philadelphia: Temple University Press, 1999), 173.
39. Ibid.
40. Graham Russell Gao Hodges, *Anna May Wong: From Laundryman's Daughter to Hollywood Legend* (Hong Kong: Hong Kong University Press, 2012), 114.
41. See BarBara Luna website, www.barbaraluna.com/. She was later also famous for the role of Marlenea Moreau in the "Mirror Mirror" episode of the original *Star Trek* series.
42. "Patrick Adiarte," Internet Broadway Database, http://ibdb.com/Person/View/92712.
43. Kathryn Edney, "Integration Through the Wide-Open Back Door": African Americans Respond to Flower Drum Song," *Studies in Musical Theater* 4, no. 3 (2010): 261–72.
44. Sam Baltimore, " 'Here Am I, Your Special Island': Racial Drag, the Black Exotic, and Juanita Hall's Asian Roles," paper presented at Feminist Theory and Music conference, University of Wisconsin-Madison, August 7, 2015. I am grateful to Sam for providing me with a copy of his paper.
45. Arthur Dong, *Forbidden City, USA: Chinese American Nightclubs, 1936–1970* (Los Angeles: DeepFocus Productions, 2014) IBT>
46. Ibid., 18.
47. Krystyn R. Moon, *Yellowface: Creating the Chinese in American Popular Music and Performance, 1850s–1920s* (New Brunswick, NJ: Rutgers University Press, 2005), 151.
48. *Forbidden City, USA.*
49. "America Begins Training Its First Conscript Army in Its Peacetime History," *Life*, December 9, 1940, 27–31.
50. "Secret Nazi Speech: Reich Minister Darré Discusses the World's Future Under German Rule," *Life*, December 9, 1940, 43–44.
51. Ernest Hauser, "Konoye of Japan," *Life*, December 9, 1940, 110–114.
52. "Life Goes to the 'Forbidden City,'" *Life*, December 9, 1940, 125.
53. Ibid., 127.
54. Reproduced in *Forbidden City, USA*, 128.

55. Lorraine Dong, "The Forbidden City Legacy and Its Chinese American Women," *Chinese America: History and Perspectives* 6 (1992): 128–48.
56. Ibid., 135.
57. Lee, *Orientals*, 176.
58. *Forbidden City, USA*, 125–31.
59. Ibid., 127.
60. Ibid., 130.
61. Four historic recordings from the 1940s are included on a CD released at the end of Ching's life, after the success of Dong's *Forbidden City USA* documentary. Larry Ching, *Till the End of Time*, B00009WO8U (San Francisco: Forbidden City Records, 2003), audio CD.
62. Anthony W. Lee, *Picturing Chinatown: Art and Orientalism in San Francisco* (Berkeley: University of California Press, 2001), 276.
63. Ibid., 281.

CHAPTER 5

1. Lydia Goehr, *The Imaginary Museum of Musical Works: An Essay in the Philosophy of Music* (New York and Oxford: Oxford University Press, 1992), 264.
2. A. M. Rosenthal, "Abstract Murals Are Being Painted With Secrecy in U.N. Assembly Hall," *New York Times*, August 29, 1952, 1.
3. The Woodstock Artists Association unfortunately kept no administrative or financial records of the concert, or indeed of the year 1952. The sole mementos in their archives are the postcard mentioned and a copy of the program. I am grateful to the WAA archivist, Emily Jones, for her assistance.
4. These four snippets of interviews, conducted respectively by John Kobler, Michael John White, and Ellsworth Snyder, were assembled in this form by Richard Kostelanetz in his collection of Cage interviews, *Conversing with Cage* (New York: Routledge, 2003), 70; I reproduce them with Kostelanetz's abbreviations and addendums intact. Cage was prone to repeating himself in interviews; the description in the first quote, for instance, nearly exactly mirrors Calvin Tomkin's description in *The Bride & the Bachelors: The Heretical Courtship in Modern Art* (New York: Viking Press, 1965), 119.
5. Letter from "Helene" to John Cage, April 9, 1954, John Cage Papers, Northwestern University, Evanston, IL (hereafter JCP), File C6.67. Kyle Gann assumes that this was Helene Wolff, mother of Christian; see Kyle Gann, *No Such Thing as Silence: John Cage's 4′33″* (New Haven, CT: Yale University Press, 2010), 191.
6. David Revill, *The Roaring Silence: John Cage: A Life* (New York: Arcade Publishing, 1993), 166; Revill gives no attribution to this remark. In her recently published memoirs, Carolyn Brown remembers one audience member who loudly stormed out, but does not give further detail; see Carolyn Brown, *Chance and Circumstance: Twenty Years with Cage and Cunningham* (New York: Knopf, 2007), 26.
7. J. B., "Look, No Hands! And It's 'Music,'" *New York Times*, April 15, 1954, 34. The *Herald-Tribune* review was similarly negative. For a comprehensive look at Cage's relationship with music critics in New York City during this period, see Suzanne

Robinson, "'A Ping, Qualified by a Thud': Music Criticism in Manhattan and the Case of Cage (1943–58)," *Journal of the Society for American Music* 1, no. 1 (2007): 79–139.

8. Cage's mother proudly preserved this certificate in one of the several scrapbooks she filled with his accomplishments. The certificate is signed by trustee Sidney Berkowitz, who later helped sponsor the 1952 concert; JCP, unsorted.

9. Letter from Lucretia Cage to Lucille Cage, January 5, 1955, JCP, unsorted.

10. Susan Sontag, "The Aesthetics of Silence," originally published in *Aspen* 5–6 (1967): unpaginated, and republished in *Styles of Radical Will* (New York: Farrar, Straus and Giroux, 1969), 5.

11. Ibid., 33.

12. Moira Roth, "The Aesthetic of Indifference," originally published in *Artforum* 16, no. 3 (1977): 46–53, republished and here cited in Moira Roth and Jonathan D. Katz, *Difference/Indifference: Musings on Postmodernism, Marcel Duchamp and John Cage* (Amsterdam: A+B Arts International, 1998), 35.

13. Serge Guilbaut, *How New York Stole the Idea of Modern Art*, trans. Arthur Goldhammer (Chicago: University of Chicago Press, 1985).

14. Roth, "Aesthetic of Indifference, 33."

15. Kostelanetz, *Conversing with Cage*, 183. Jonathan Katz quotes Morton Feldman giving more information about their relationship: "I don't want to exaggerate this point, because John was very sensitive to it. I remember there was a little gathering in a Chinese restaurant, and Jackson Pollock was taunting John"; Jonathan D. Katz, "John Cage's Queer Silence; Or, How to Avoid Making Matters Worse," *GLQ* 5, no. 2 (1999): 49.

16. Morton Feldman, *Give My Regards to Eighth Street* (Cambridge, MA: Exact Change, 2004), 5.

17. Letter from David Tudor to M. C. Richards, November 11, 1954, Box 26, M. C. Richards Papers, Getty Research Institute, Los Angeles, CA.

18. Richard Kostelanetz, *John Cage (ex)plain(ed)* (New York: Schirmer, 1996), 167.

19. U.S. Senate, 81st Cong., 2d sess., Committee on Expenditures in Executive Departments, *Employment of Homosexuals and Other Sex Perverts in Government* (Washington, DC: Government Printing Office, 1950), quoted in John D'Emilio, *Sexual Politics, Sexual Communities*, 2nd ed. (Chicago: University of Chicago Press, 1998), 42.

20. Lesbians were occasionally targeted in these persecutions, but the vast majority of public discourse on homosexuality was focused on men. Lillian Faderman has pointed out, however, that there were fewer women employed by the federal government in the first place, so there would be fewer overall dismissals. See Lillian Faderman, *Odd Girls and Twilight Lovers: A History of Lesbian Life in Twentieth-Century America* (New York: Columbia University Press, 1991), 142.

21. Catherine Parsons Smith, "Athena at the Manuscript Club: John Cage and Mary Carr Moore," *Musical Quarterly* 79, no. 2 (1995): 351–67. Carolyn Brown sees Lucretia's homophobia as part of her larger naiveté about much of Cage's adult life; see Brown, *Chance and Circumstance*, 57–58.

22. Katz, "John Cage's Queer Silence," 231–52.

23. There is a small body of literature that has also addressed this subject, although with less attention to issues of sexuality. See Caroline A. Jones, "Finishing School: John Cage and the Abstract Expressionist Ego," *Critical Inquiry* 19, no. 4 (July 1, 1993): 628–65; Marjorie Perloff, "Watchman, Spy, and Dead Man: Jasper Johns, Frank O'Hara, John Cage and the 'Aesthetic of Indifference,'" *Modernism/ modernity* 8, no. 2 (2001): 197–223; David W. Bernstein, "John Cage and the Aesthetic of Indifference," in *The New York School of Art and Music*, ed. Steven Johnson (New York: Routledge, 2002), 113–34.

24. Katz, "John Cage's Queer Silence," 56–57.

25. It should be duly noted that there are some errors of historical record in Katz's article. For instance, when Cage finally moved to New York City, it was still in the company of Xenia—the move, in other words, does not mark Cage's permanent break with heterosexuality quite so neatly. I find, however, that while these details do somewhat complicate Katz's argument, they do not substantially affect his points.

26. Richards records this process in a series of letters in the late 1950s. See in particular her ultimatum to Tudor in January 1958: Series II, Box 3, Folder 3, M. C. Richards Papers.

27. Stuart Timmons, *The Trouble with Harry Hay: Founder of the Modern Gay Movement* (Boston: Alyson, 1990), 58.

28. D'Emilio, *Sexual Politics, Sexual Communities*, 66.

29. These are the conclusions Chauncey has presented in talks prior to the publication of his long-awaited sequel to *Gay New York: Gender, Urban Culture, and the Making of the Gay Male World, 1890–1940* (New York: Basic Books, 1994). See, for instance, his talk, "Why Come Out of the Closet?" presented at Brandeis University, February 6, 2003.

30. Nadine Hubbs, *The Queer Composition of America's Sound: Gay Modernists, American Music, and National Identity* (Berkeley: University of California Press, 2004), 51. In an unpublished paper, Mitchell Morris has examined Cage in relation to these circles, see Mitchell Morris, "Music Re-Ciphered: John Cage and the Aesthetics of the Secret," n.d.

31. Raymond Williams, "Base and Superstructure in Marxist Theory," in his *Problems in Materialism and Culture* (London: Verso, 1980), 31–49.

32. Henry Abelove, "New York City Gay Liberation and the Queer Commuters," in his *Deep Gossip* (Minneapolis: University of Minnesota Press, 2003), 70–88.

33. Ibid., 88. The term "queer" here is not a post-Queer Nation anachronism; many of these artists referred to themselves as "queer," with basically the same intended meaning as later activists.

34. Published later in Paul Goodman, *Nature Heals: The Psychological Essays of Paul Goodman*, ed. Taylor Stoehr (New York: Free Life Editions, 1977).

35. Thomas Hines, "'Then Not Yet "Cage"': The Los Angeles Years, 1912–1938," in *John Cage: Composed in America*, ed. Marjorie Perloff and Charles Junkerman (Chicago: University of Chicago Press, 1994), 65–99.

36. Leta E Miller and Fredric Lieberman, *Lou Harrison: Composing a World* (New York: Oxford University Press, 1998).

37. Katz, "John Cage's Queer Silence," 5.

38. Letter from Merce Cunningham to John Cage, July 16, 1953, JCP C6 34, 35. Correspondence from Cage's mother, dating from the thirties up until Lucretia's death in the 1970s, does not mention Cunningham once.

39. Recounted in Kostelanetz, *Conversing with Cage*, 292.

40. For more on this subject, see Henry Abelove, "From Thoreau to Queer Politics," *Yale Journal of Criticism* 6 (1993): 17–27. For Cage's intellectual sympathies with Thoreau, see Christopher Shultis, *Silencing the Sounded Self: John Cage and the American Experimental Tradition* (Boston: Northeastern University Press, 1998).

41. This is from an informal interview conducted by R. Wood Massi and related to Jonathan Katz; see Katz, "John Cage's Queer Silence," 54 n40.

42. Klye Gann, "Introduction to the 50th Anniversary Edition," in *Silence: Lectures and Writings*, by John Cage, 2nd ed. (Middletown, CT: Wesleyan University Press, 2011), ix–xxviii.

43. Two such versions of *4'33"* are preserved in Tudor's papers at the Getty Research Institute, and C. F. Peters, Cage's publisher, has recently released a new edition of the work recreating it.

44. Patricia Carpenter, "The Musical Object," *Current Musicology* 5 (1967): 71.

45. James Pritchett, *The Music of John Cage* (Cambridge: Cambridge University Press, 1993), 5.

46. Carpenter, "The Musical Object," 71.

47. William Fetterman, *John Cage's Theatre Pieces: Notations and Performances* (Amsterdam: Harwood Academic Publishers, 1996).

48. John Cage, "Experimental Music," reprinted in John Cage, *Silence: Lectures and Writings*, 2nd ed. (Middletown, CT: Wesleyan University Press, 2011), 12.

49. Tamara Levitz, "Syvilla Fort's Africanist Modernism and John Cage's Gestic Music: The Story of Bacchanale," *South Atlantic Quarterly* 104 (2005): 123–49.

50. The most thorough account of the *Black Mountain Piece* can be found in David W. Patterson, "Appraising the Catchwords: John Cage's Asian-Derived Rhetoric and the Historical Reference of Black Mountain College," Ph.D. dissertation, Columbia University, 1996, 229–34.

51. In this discussion I am indebted to the comprehensive index of Cage's performance assembled by David Patterson, with some additional consultation of Cage's own collection of concert programs at JCP, Northwestern University.

52. This discussion is based upon James Pritchett's description of the piece's composition in *The Music of John Cage*, 78–88. His discussion is based upon Tudor's notes, interviews with Cage, and the description Cage himself published in his essay collection, *Silence*, 57–59.

53. David W. Bernstein, "'In Order to Thicken the Plot': Toward a Critical Reception of Cage's Music," in *Writings Through John Cage's Music, Poetry, and Art*, ed. David W. Bernstein and Christopher Hatch (Chicago: University of Chicago Press, 2001), 38. See also Mark David Nelson, "Quieting the Mind, Manifesting Mind: The Zen Buddhist Roots of John Cage's Early Chance-Determined and Indeterminate Compositions," Ph.D. dissertation, Princeton University, 1995.

54. Fetterman, *John Cage's Theatre Pieces*, 72.

55. Christopher Shultis, "No Ear for Music: Timbre in the Early Percussion Music of John Cage," in *John Cage: Music, Philosophy, and Intention, 1933–1950*, ed. David W. Patterson (New York: Routledge, 2001), 83–104.

56. Cage was always concerned about spreading his music to as large an audience as possible. In 1959, he wrote to the music librarian at the New York Public Library proposing a scheme to distribute his music for free to libraries across the country, saying "I feel strongly the obligation to get my own music out of my hands"; letter from John Cage to John Edmunds, December 31, 1959, JCP C6.136.

57. Richard Winslow, "The $100 Riot," *Wesleyan*, 74 (1993): 6–7.

58. Jill Dolan, "Performance, Utopia, and the 'Utopian Performative,'" *Theater Journal* 53 (2001): 2.

EPILOGUE

1. Matt Flegenheimer, "$2,700 for Hillary Clinton at 'Hamilton'? That Would Be Enough," *New York Times*, July 12, 2016, www.nytimes.com/2016/07/13/us/politics/hillary-clinton-hamilton.html?_r=0.

2. Amber A'Lee Frost, Twitter posting. May 18, 2016. 10:45 A.M. https://twitter.com/AmberALeeFrost/status/732990611108855808.

3. Sarah Jaffe, "Trickle-Down Feminism," *Dissent*, Winter 2013, www.dissentmagazine.org/article/trickle-down-feminism.

4. Raymond Williams, "Base and Superstructure in Marxist Theory," in his *Problems in Materialism and Culture* (London: Verso, 1980), 34.

5. Kendra James, "Race, Immigration, and Hamilton: The Relevance of Lin-Manuel Miranda's New Musical," http://the-toast.net/2015/10/01/race-immigration-and-hamilton/.

6. Saeed Jones, "Watching HAMILTON Was the First Time in My Life I Felt like the History of Our Founding Fathers Was Being Told with Me in Mind." Twitter posting, *@theferocity*, September 24, 2015, https://twitter.com/theferocity/status/647077687853477888.

7. Elisabeth Le Guin, *Boccherini's Body: An Essay in Carnal Musicology* (Berkeley: University of California Press, 2005).

8. Diana Taylor, "Performance And/As History," *TDR: The Drama Review* 50, no. 1 (2006): 67–86.

9. Adam Krims, *Rap Music and the Poetics of Identity* (Cambridge: Cambridge University Press, 2000).

BIBLIOGRAPHY

ARCHIVES

David Tudor Papers. Getty Research Institute, Los Angeles, CA.
John Cage Papers. Special Collections. Northwestern University, Evanston, IL.
Mary Caroline Richards Papers. Getty Research Institute, Los Angeles, CA.
National Association for the Advancement of Colored People Papers. Library of Congress, Washington, DC.

SECONDARY SOURCES

Abelove, Henry. "From Thoreau to Queer Politics." *Yale Journal of Criticism* 6 (1993): 17–27.
Abelove, Henry. "New York City Gay Liberation and the Queer Commuters." In his *Deep Gossip*, 70–88. Minneapolis: University of Minnesota Press, 2003.
Adams, M. Clay. "Malanesian Nightmare." *Victory at Sea*. Television series, NBC, 1953.
Ahmed, Sara. "White Men." *Feminist Killjoys*. November 4, 2014. http://feministkilljoys.com/2014/11/04/white-men/.
Ahmed, Sara. *Willful Subjects*. Durham, NC: Duke University Press, 2014.
Alba, Richard. "The Twilight of Ethnicity Among Americans of European Ancestry: The Case of the Italians." In *Ethnicity and Race in the U.S.A.: Toward the Twenty-First Century*, edited by Richard Alba, 134–48. New York: Routledge, 1988.
"America Begins Training Its First Conscript Army in Its Peacetime History." *Life* magazine, December 9, 1940.
Appadurai, Arjun. *Modernity at Large: Cultural Dimensions of Globalization*. Minneapolis: University of Minnesota Press, 1996.
Arnold, J. B. Letter to the Editor. *Tan Confessions*, November 1950.
Auiler, Dan. *Hitchcock's Notebooks: An Authorized and Illustrated Look Inside the Creative Mind of Alfred Hitchcock*. New York: Spike, 1999.

Averill, Gage. *Four Parts, No Waiting: A Social History of American Barbershop Quartet.* New York: Oxford University Press, 2010.

Baltimore, Sam. "'Here Am I, Your Special Island': Racial Drag, the Black Exotic, and Juanita Hall's Asian Roles." Talk presented at the Feminist Theory and Music, University of Wisconsin-Madison, August 7, 2015.

BarBara Luna Website. http://www.barbaraluna.com/.

Bawer, Bruce. "Whatever Happened to Doris Day." In *Beyond the Boom: New Voices on American Life, Culture, and Politics*, edited by Terry Teachout, 149–54. New York : Poseidon Press, 1990.

Bell, Daniel, ed. *The Radical Right.* New York: Doubleday, 1963.

Benedict, Ruth. *The Chrysanthemum and the Sword.* Boston: Houghton Mifflin, 1946.

Berg, Manfred. *The Ticket to Freedom: The NAACP and the Struggle for Black Political Integration.* Gainesville: University Press of Florida, 2005.

Bernstein, David W. "'In Order to Thicken the Plot': Toward a Critical Reception of Cage's Music." In *Writings Through John Cage's Music, Poetry, and Art*, edited by David W. Bernstein and Christopher Hatch, 7–40. Chicago: University of Chicago Press, 2001.

Bernstein, David W. "John Cage and the Aesthetic of Indifference." In *The New York School of Art and Music*, edited by Steven Johnson, 113–34. New York: Routledge, 2002.

Bernstein, Mary. "Identity Politics." *Annual Review of Sociology* 31 (2005): 47–74.

Bertrand, Michael T. *Race, Rock, and Elvis.* Urbana: University of Illinois Press, 2004.

Bharucha, Rustom. *The Politics of Cultural Practice: Thinking through Theatre in an Age of Globalization.* Middletown, CT: Wesleyan University Press, 2000.

Biddle, Ian. *Music and Identity Politics.* Farnham, UK: Ashgate, 2012.

Bingham, Dennis. "'Before She Was a Virgin . . .': Doris Day and the Decline of Female Film Comedy in the 1950s and 1960s." *Cinema Journal* 45, no. 3 (2006): 3–31.

Blount, Marcellus, and George P. Cunningham, eds. *Representing Black Men.* New York: Routledge, 1995.

Brackett, David. *The Pop, Rock, and Soul Reader: Histories and Debates.* 3rd ed. New York: Oxford University Press, 2013.

Brooks, Charlotte. *Alien Neighbors, Foreign Friends: Asian Americans, Housing, and the Transformation of Urban California.* Chicago: University of Chicago Press, 2009.

Brooks, Charlotte. *Between Mao and McCarthy: Chinese American Politics in the Cold War Years.* Chicago: University of Chicago Press, 2015.

Brown, Carolyn. *Chance and Circumstance: Twenty Years with Cage and Cunningham.* New York: Knopf, 2007.

Butler, Judith. *Gender Trouble: Feminism and the Subversion of Identity.* New York: Routledge, 1990.

Byrd, Ayana D., and Lori L. Tharps. *Hair Story: Untangling the Roots of Black Hair in America.* New York: St. Martin's Press, 2001.

Cage, John. *Silence: Lectures and Writings.* 2nd ed. Middletown, CT: Wesleyan University Press, 2011.

Carby, Hazel V. "Policing the Black Woman's Body in an Urban Context." *Critical Inquiry* 18, no. 4 (July 1, 1992): 738–55.

Carpenter, Patricia. "The Musical Object." *Current Musicology* 5 (1967): 56–87.

Carson, Charles D. "'Bridging the Gap': Creed Taylor, Grover Washington Jr., and the Crossover Roots of Smooth Jazz." *Black Music Research Journal* 28, no. 1 (April 1, 2008): 1–15.

Case, Sue-Ellen. *The Domain-Matrix: Performing Lesbian at the End of Print Culture*. Bloomington: Indiana University Press, 1996.

Chan, Anthony B. *Perpetually Cool: The Many Lives of Anna May Wong (1905-1961)*. Lanham, MD: Scarecrow Press, 2007.

Chen, Yong. *Chop Suey, USA: The Story of Chinese Food in America*. Reprint. New York: Columbia University Press, 2014.

Ching, Larry. *Till the End of Time*. Forbidden City Records, B00009W08U, 2003, CD.

Clarke, Jane and Diana Simmonds. *Move Over Misconceptions: Doris Day Reappraised*. London: British Film Institute, 1980.

Cohen, Lizabeth. *A Consumers' Republic: The Politics of Mass Consumption in Postwar America*. New York: Vintage Books, 2003.

Condon, Richard. *The Manchurian Candidate*. New York: McGraw-Hill, 1959.

Corber, Robert J. *Cold War Femme: Lesbianism, National Identity, and Hollywood Cinema*. Durham, NC: Duke University Press, 2011.

Craig, Maxine Leeds. *Ain't I a Beauty Queen?: Black Women, Beauty, and the Politics of Race*. Oxford and New York: Oxford University Press, 2002.

Day, Doris, and A. E. Hotchner. *Doris Day: Her Own Story*. New York: Morrow, 1975.

D'Emilio, John. *Sexual Politics, Sexual Communities*. 2nd ed. Chicago: University of Chicago Press, 1998.

Dolan, Jill. "Performance, Utopia, and the 'Utopian Performative.'" *Theater Journal* 53 (2001): 455–479.

Dong, Lorraine. "The Forbidden City Legacy and Its Chinese American Women." *Chinese America: History and Perspectives* 6 (1992): 128–48.

Doyle, Peter. *Echo and Reverb: Fabricating Space in Popular Music Recording, 1900-1960*. Middletown, CT: Wesleyan University Press, 2005.

Dyer, Richard. *Heavenly Bodies: Film Stars and Society*. London: Macmillan, 1986.

Dyer, Richard. *White*. London and New York: Routledge, 1997.

Edney, Kathryn. "'Integration Through the Wide-Open Back Door': African Americans Respond to Flower Drum Song." *Studies in Musical Theater* 4, no. 3 (2010): 261–72.

Edward R. Murrow: The McCarthy Years. Walter Cronkite, report for CBS News. Broadcast reissued as DVD, New Video Group, 2005.

Edwards, Brian T. *Morocco Bound: Disorienting America's Maghreb, from Casablanca to the Marrakech Express*. Durham, NC: Duke University Press, 2005.

Ellison, Ralph. *Invisible Man*. New York: Random House, 1952.

Erikson, Erik H. *Childhood and Society*. New York: Norton, 1950.

Estes, Steve. *I Am a Man!: Race, Manhood, and the Civil Rights Movement*. Chapel Hill: University of North Carolina Press, 2005.

Everett, Joan. Letter to the Editor. *Tan Confessions* magazine, November 1950.

Faderman, Lillian. *Odd Girls and Twilight Lovers: A History of Lesbian Life in Twentieth-Century America*. New York: Columbia University Press, 1991.

Fang, Jennifer Y. "Negotiating Chinese American Middle-Class Identity in the Cold War Suburbs." Wilmington: University of Delaware, 2015.

Feldman, Morton. *Give My Regards To Eighth Street*. Cambridge, MA: Exact Change, 2004.

Ferencz, George. "'The World's Longest Symphony': Issues of Collaboration and Thematic Transformation in Richard Rodgers and Robert Russell Bennett's Victory at Sea." Talk presented at meeting of the American Musicological Society, Washington, DC, October 28, 2005.

Ferguson, Roderick A. "African American Masculinity and the Study of Social Formations." *American Quarterly* 58, no. 1 (2006): 213–19.

Fetterman, William. *John Cage's Theatre Pieces: Notations and Performances*. Amsterdam: Harwood Academic Publishers, 1996.

Forbidden City, USA: Chinese American Nightclubs, 1936-1970. Directed by Arthur Dong. Film 1989, 16mm, color/black and white; digitally remastered Blu-Ray and DVD, DeepFocus Productions, 2014.

Foster, Gwendolyn Audrey. *Performing Whiteness: Postmodern Re/Constructions in the Cinema*. Albany: SUNY Press, 2003.

Foster, Susan Leigh. "Choreographies of Gender." *Signs* 24, no. 1 (1998): 1–33.

"Four Statements on the Race Question." Paris: United Nations Educational, Scientific and Cultural Organization, 1969.

Fox, Patty. *Star Style: Hollywood Legends as Fashion Icons*. Rev. ed. Santa Monica, CA: Angel City Press, 1999.

Frazier, Franklin. *The Black Bourgeoisie*. New York: Simon and Schuster, 1957.

Friedman, Andrea. "The Smearing of Joe McCarthy: The Lavender Scare, Gossip, and Cold War Politics." *American Quarterly* 57 (2005): 1105–30.

Friedman, Lawrence Jacob. *Identity's Architect: A Biography of Erik H. Erikson*. Cambridge, MA: Harvard University Press, 2000.

Foster, Susan Leigh. *Choreographing History*. Bloomington: Indiana University Press, 1995.

Fussell, Paul. *The Great War and Modern Memory*. New York: Oxford University Press, 2000.

Gabbard, Krin. *Black Magic: White Hollywood and African American Culture*. New Brunskwick, NJ: Rutgers University Press, 2004.

Galbraith, John Kenneth. *The Affluent Society*. New York: Houghton Mifflin, 1958.

Gann, Kyle. "Introduction to the 50th Anniversary Edition." In *Silence: Lectures and Writings*, by John Cage, ix–xxviii, 2nd ed. Middletown, CT: Wesleyan University Press, 2011.

Gann, Kyle. *No Such Thing as Silence: John Cage's 4′33″*. New Haven, CT: Yale University Press, 2010.

Gentry, Philip. "Doo-Wop." *Encyclopedia of African American Music*. Westport, CT: Greenwood Press, 2010.

Gentry, Philip. "Leonard Bernstein's The Age of Anxiety: A Great American Symphony during McCarthyism." *American Music* 29, no. 3 (2011): 308–31.

Gentry, Philip. "Whiteness and Sex in the Music of Rosemary Clooney." *American Music Review* 43, no. 2 (Spring 2014). www.brooklyn.cuny.edu/web/academics/centers/hitchcock/publications/amr/v43-2/gentry.php.

Gerbner, George. "The Social Role of the Confession Magazine." *Social Problems* 6, no. 1 (1958): 29–40.

Gitler, Ira. *Swing to Bop: An Oral History of the Transition in Jazz in the 1940s.* New York: Oxford University Press, 1985.

Goehr, Lydia. *The Imaginary Museum of Musical Works: An Essay in the Philosophy of Music.* New York and Oxford: Oxford University Press, 1992.

Goodman, Paul. *Nature Heals: The Psychological Essays of Paul Goodman.* Edited by Taylor Stoehr. New York: Free Life Editions, 1977.

Goosman, Stuart L. *Group Harmony: The Black Urban Roots of Rhythm & Blues.* Philadelphia: University of Pennsylvania Press, 2005.

Groia, Philip. *They All Sang on the Corner; New York City's Rhythm and Blues Vocal Groups of the 1950's.* Setauket, NY: Edmond Publishing, 1974.

Guilbaut, Serge. *How New York Stole the Idea of Modern Art.* Translated by Arthur Goldhammer. Chicago: University of Chicago Press, 1985.

Guin, Elisabeth Le. *Boccherini's Body: An Essay in Carnal Musicology.* Berkeley: University of California Press, 2005.

Halberstam, Judith. *In A Queer Time And Place: Transgender Bodies, Subcultural Lives.* New York: New York University Press, 2005.

Hale, Nathan G. *The Rise and Crisis of Psychoanalysis in United States: Freud and the Americans, 1917-1985.* New York: Oxford University Press, 1995.

Harriott, Adelina. Letter to the Editor. *Tan Confessions* magazine, November 1950.

Harris, Wynonie. "Why Women Won't Leave Me Alone." *Tan* magazine, October 1954.

Harvey, James. *Movie Love in the Fifties.* New York: Knopf, 2001.

Hauser, Ernest. "Konoye of Japan." *Life* magazine, December 9, 1940.

Hay, Jonathan. "Toward a Theory of the Intercultural." *Res* 35 (Spring 1999): 5–9.

Hays, Elaine. "To Bebop or to Be Pop: Sarah Vaughan and the Politics of Crossover." Philadelphia: University of Pennsylvania, 2004.

Henry, Patrick. "'And I Don't Care What It Is': The Tradition-History of a Civil Religion Proof-Text." *Journal of the American Academy of Religion* 49, no. 1 (March 1, 1981): 35–49.

Herberg, Will. *Protestant, Catholic, Jew: An Essay in American Religious Sociology.* Chicago: University of Chicago Press, 1955.

Hines, Thomas. "'Then Not Yet "Cage"': The Los Angeles Years, 1912–1938." In *John Cage: Composed in America*, edited by Marjorie Perloff and Charles Junkerman, 65–99. Chicago: University of Chicago Press, 1994.

Hodges, Graham Russell Gao. *Anna May Wong: From Laundryman's Daughter to Hollywood Legend.* Hong Kong: Hong Kong University Press, 2012.

Hubbs, Nadine. *The Queer Composition of America's Sound: Gay Modernists, American Music, and National Identity.* Berkeley: University of California Press, 2004.

Hwang, David Henry. "Introduction." In *The Flower Drum Song*, by Chen Ye Lee, . New York: Penguin, 2002, xiii–xxi.

"Identity, *n.*" *OED Online.* Oxford: Oxford University Press, March 2015. www.oed. com/view/Entry/91004?redirectedFrom=identity.

"If You Married . . . Jimmy Edwards." *Tan Confessions* magazine, November 1952.

James, Kendra. "Race, Immigration, and Hamilton: The Relevance of Lin-Manuel Miranda's New Musical." October 1, 2015. http://the-toast.net/2015/10/01/race-immigration-and-hamilton/.

James, Robin. "Hello From the Same Side." *The New Inquiry*. December 8, 2015. http://thenewinquiry.com/essays/hello-from-the-same-side/.

J.B. "Look, No Hands! And It's 'Music.'" *New York Times*, April 15, 1954, p. 34.

Jones, Caroline A. "Finishing School: John Cage and the Abstract Expressionist Ego." *Critical Inquiry* 19, no. 4 (July 1, 1993): 628–65.

Jones, Jim. "Modest Church Inspires Elvis Hit." *Gadsen Times*, March 15, 1998, p. C8.

Jones, Saeed. "Watching HAMILTON Was the First Time in My Life I Felt like the History of Our Founding Fathers Was Being Told with Me in Mind." Twitter posting. *@theferocity*, September 24, 2015. https://twitter.com/theferocity/status/647077687853477888.

Jong, Erica. *Fear of Fifty: A Midlife Memoir.* New York: Penguin, 2006.

Katz, Jonathan D. "John Cage's Queer Silence; Or, How to Avoid Making Matters Worse." *GLQ* 5, no. 2 (1999): 231–52.

Keil, Charles. "Participatory Discrepancies and the Power of Music." In *Music Grooves: Essays and Dialogues*, by Charles Keil and Steven Feld, 96–108. Chicago: University of Chicago Press, 1994.

King, Ben. *Ben King's Southland Melodies.* Chicago: Forbes and Co., 1911.

Kirshenblatt-Gimblett, Barbara. "Performance Studies." In *The Performance Studies Reader*, edited by Henry Bial, 43–56. New York: Routledge, 2004.

Klein, Christina. *Cold War Orientalism: Asia in the Middlebrow Imagination, 1945-1961.* Berkeley: University of California Press, 2003.

Knapp, Raymond. *The American Musical and the Formation of National Identity.* Princeton, NJ: Princeton University Press, 2005.

Koestenbaum, Wayne. *Jackie Under My Skin: Interpreting an Icon.* New York: Macmillan, 2009.

Kostelanetz, Richard. *Conversing with Cage.* New York: Routledge, 2003.

Kostelanetz, Richard. *John Cage (ex)plain(ed).* New York: Schirmer, 1996.

Krims, Adam. *Rap Music and the Poetics of Identity.* Cambridge: Cambridge University Press, 2000.

Kun, Josh. *Audiotopia: Music, Race, and America.* Berkeley: University of California Press, 2005.

Lee, Anthony W. *Picturing Chinatown: Art and Orientalism in San Francisco.* Berkeley: University of California Press, 2001.

Lee, Robert G. *Orientals: Asian Americans in Popular Culture.* Philadelphia: Temple University Press, 1999.

Levitz, Tamara. "Syvilla Fort's Africanist Modernism and John Cage's Gestic Music: The Story of Bacchanale." *South Atlantic Quarterly* 104 (2005): 123–49.

Lieberson, Stanley. *Ethnic Patterns in American Cities.* Glencoe, IL: Free Press, 1963.

"Life Goes to the 'Forbidden City.'" *Life* magazine, December 9, 1940.

Lipset, Seymour. "Three Decades of the Radical Right." In *The Radical Right*, edited by Daniel Bell, 313–377 Garden City, NY: Doubleday, 1963.

Lipsitz, George. *The Possessive Investment in Whiteness: How White People Profit from Identity Politics, Revised and Expanded Edition.* Philadelphia: Temple University Press, 2009.

Lovensheimer, Jim. *South Pacific: Paradise Rewritten*. New York: Oxford University Press, 2013.

Lowe, Lisa. *Immigrant Acts: On Asian American Cultural Politics*. Durham, NC: Duke University Press, 1996.

Malone, Jacqui. "'Let the Punishment Fit the Crime': The Vocal Choreography of Cholly Atkins." *Dance Research Journal* 20, no. 1 (July 1, 1988): 11–18.

Man Who Knew Too Much, The. Directed by Alfred Hitchcock, 1956, Paramount Pictures.

Manheim, James M. "B-Side Sentimentalizer: 'Tennessee Waltz' in the History of Popular Music." *Musical Quarterly* 76, no. 3 (Autumn 1992): 337–54.

Marable, Manning, and Leith Mullings. *Let Nobody Turn Us Around: Voices of Resistance, Reform, and Renewal*. Lanham, MD: Rowman & Littlefield, 2003.

Marcus, Greil. *The Dustbin of History*. Cambridge, MA: Harvard University Press, 1998.

May, Elaine. *Homeward Bound: American Families in the Cold War Era*. Rev. and updated ed. New York: Basic Books, 1999.

May, Rollo. *The Meaning of Anxiety*. New York: Ronald Press, 1950.

Melnick, Jeffrey. "'Story Untold': The Black Men and White Sounds of Doo-Wop." In *Whiteness: A Critical Reader*, edited by Mike Hill, 134–50. New York: New York University Press, 1997.

Michie, Elsie B. "Unveiling Maternal Desires: Hitchcock and American Domesticity." In *Hitchcock's America*, edited by Jonathan Freedman and Richard Millington, 29–54. Oxford and New York: Oxford University Press, 1999.

Miller, Leta E., and Fredric Lieberman. *Lou Harrison: Composing a World*. New York: Oxford University Press, 1998.

Mohanty, Satya P., and Paula M. L. Moya. *Identity Politics Reconsidered*. Edited by Linda Martín Alcoff and Michael Hames-García. New York: Palgrave Macmillan, 2006.

Moon, Krystyn R. *Yellowface: Creating the Chinese in American Popular Music and Performance, 1850s-1920s*. New Brunswick, NJ: Rutgers University Press, 2005.

Mooney, Hughson F. "Songs, Singers and Society, 1890–1954." *American Quarterly* 6, no. 3 (1954): 221–32.

Morris, Mitchell. "Music Re-Ciphered: John Cage and the Aesthetics of the Secret." Unpublished paper, n.d.

Nelson, Mark David. "Quieting the Mind, Manifesting Mind: The Zen Buddhist Roots of John Cage's Early Chance-Determined and Indeterminate Compositions." Ph.D. dissertation, Princeton University, 1995.

Nunberg, Geoffrey. "Counting on Google Books." *Chronicle of Higher Education*, December 16, 2010. http://chronicle.com/article/Counting-on-Google-Books/125735/.

Omi, Michael, and Howard Winant. *Racial Formation in the United States: From the 1960s to the 1990s*. 2nd ed. New York and London: Routledge, 1994.

Oshinsky, David M. *A Conspiracy so Immense: The World of Joe McCarthy*. New York: Free Press, 1983.

Packard, Vance. *The Status Seekers; an Exploration of Class Behavior in America and the Hidden Barriers That Affect You, Your Community, Your Future*. New York: D. McKay, 1959.

"Passion With a Purpose." *Time* magazine, October 23, 1950.

"Passion Without a Purpose." *Time* magazine, September 22, 1952.

Patterson, David W. "Appraising the Catchwords: John Cage's Asian-Derived Rhetoric and the Historical Reference of Black Mountain College," Ph.D. dissertation, Columbia University, 1996.

"Patrick Adiarte." Internet Broadway Database. http://ibdb.com/Person/View/92712.

Perloff, Marjorie. "Watchman, Spy, and Dead Man: Jasper Johns, Frank O'Hara, John Cage and the 'Aesthetic of Indifference.'" *Modernism/modernity* 8, no. 2 (2001): 197–223.

Perucci, Tony. *Paul Robeson and the Cold War Performance Complex: Race, Madness, Activism.* Ann Arbor: University of Michigan Press, 2012.

Petersen, Anne Helen. "Jennifer Lawrence and the History of Cool Girls." *BuzzFeed,* February 28, 2014. www.buzzfeed.com/annehelenpetersen/jennifer-lawrence-and-the-history-of-cool-girls.

Phelan, Peggy. *Unmarked: The Politics of Performance.* New York: Routledge, 1993.

Pomerance, Murray. "'The Future's Not Ours to See': Song, Singer, Labyrinth in Hitchcock's The Man Who Knew Too Much." In *Soundtrack Available: Essays on Film and Popular Music,* edited by Pamela Wojcik and Arthur Knight, 53–73. Durham, NC: Duke University Press, 2001.

Pritchett, John. *The Music of John Cage.* Cambridge: Cambridge University Press, 1993.

Revill, David. *The Roaring Silence: John Cage: A Life.* New York: Arcade Publishing, 1993.

Rice, Timothy. "Reflections on Music and Identity in Ethnomusicology." *Muzikologija/ Musicology* 7 (2007): 17–37.

Riesman, David. *The Lonely Crowd; a Study of the Changing American Character.* New Haven, CT: Yale University Press, 1950.

Roach, Joseph. *Cities of the Dead: Circum-Atlantic Performance.* New York: Columbia University Press, 1996.

Robinson, Suzanne. "'A Ping, Qualified by a Thud': Music Criticism in Manhattan and the Case of Cage (1943–58)." *Journal of the Society for American Music* 1, no. 1 (2007): 79–139.

Rogin, Michael. "Kiss Me Deadly: Communism, Motherhood, and Cold War Movies." *Representations,* 6 (Spring 1984): 1–36.

Rollins, Peter C. "Victory at Sea: Cold War Epic." In *Television Histories: Shaping Collective Memory in the Media Age,* edited by Gary R Edgerton and Peter C. Rollins, 103–22. Lexington: University Press of Kentucky, 2001.

Rooks, Noliwe M. *Ladies' Pages: African American Women's Magazines and the Culture That Made Them.* New Brunswick, NJ: Rutgers University Press, 2004.

Rosenthal, A. M. "Abstract Murals Are Being Painted with Secrecy in U.N. Assembly Hall." *New York Times,* August 29, 1952, 1.

Rosenthal, Rob. "Serving the Movement: The Role(s) of Music." *Popular Music and Society* 25, nos. 3–4 (September 1, 2001): 11–24.

Roth, Moira, and Jonathan D. Katz. *Difference/Indifference: Musings on Postmodernism, Marcel Duchamp and John Cage.* Amsterdam: A+B Arts International, 1998.

Rubin, Gayle. *Deviations: A Gayle Rubin Reader.* Durham, NC: Duke University Press, 2011.

Sanjek, Russell, and David Sanjek. *American Popular Music Business in the 20th Century*. Abridged ed. New York: Oxford University Press, 1991.

Savoy, Eric. "'That Ain't All She Ain't': Doris Day and Queer Performativity." In *Out Takes: Essays on Queer Theory and Film*, edited by Ellis Hanson, 151–82. Durham, NC: Duke University Press, 1999.

"Secret Nazi Speech: Reich Minister Darré Discusses the World's Future Under German Rule." *Life* magazine, December 9, 1940.

Shanks, Cheryl. *Immigration and the Politics of American Sovereignty, 1890-1990*. Ann Arbor: University of Michigan Press, 2001.

Shannon, Christopher. *A World Made Safe for Differences: Cold War Intellectuals and the Politics of Identity*. Lanham, MD: Rowman & Littlefield, 2000.

Shultis, Christopher. "No Ear for Music: Timbre in the Early Percussion Music of John Cage." In *John Cage: Music, Philosophy, and Intention, 1933–1950*, edited by David W. Patterson, 83–104. New York: Routledge, 2001.

Shultis, Christopher. *Silencing the Sounded Self: John Cage and the American Experimental Tradition*. Boston: Northeastern University Press, 1998.

Smith, Catherine Parsons. "Athena at the Manuscript Club: John Cage and Mary Carr Moore." *Musical Quarterly* 79, no. 2 (1995): 351–67.

"Sonny Til and His Orioles." *Ebony* magazine, September 1952.

Sontag, Susan. *Styles of Radical Will*. New York: Farrar, Straus and Giroux, 1969.

Tan Confessions, November 1950.

Taylor, Diana. "Performance And/as History." *TDR: The Drama Review* 50, no. 1 (2006): 67–86.

Taylor, Diana. *The Archive and the Repertoire: Performing Cultural Memory in the Americas*. Durham, NC: Duke University Press, 2003.

Taylor, Timothy D. *Beyond Exoticism: Western Music and the World*. Durham, NC: Duke University Press, 2007.

Taylor, Timothy D. *Music and Capitalism: A History of the Present*. Chicago: University of Chicago Press, 2015.

Teachout, Terry. "The Importance of Not Being Earnest." *Wall Street Journal*, April 8, 2008, W7.

Til, Sonny. "Why Women Go For Me." *Tan Confessions*, September 1952.

Timmons, Stuart. *The Trouble with Harry Hay: Founder of the Modern Gay Movement*. Boston: Alyson, 1990.

Tomkins, Calvin. *The Bride & the Bachelors: The Heretical Courtship in Modern Art*. New York: Viking Press, 1965.

U.S. Census. "Characteristics of the Population." *Census of the Population: 1950*. Washington, DC: Government Printing Office, 1953.

U.S. House of Representatives. Committee on Un-American Activities. *Hearings Regarding Communist Infiltration of Minority Groups—Part 1*. Washington, DC: Government Printing Office, 1949.

Veblen, Thorstein, and Stuart Chase. *The Theory of the Leisure Class; an Economic Study of Institutions*. New York: Modern library, 1934.

Wald, Elijah. *How the Beatles Destroyed Rock "N" Roll: An Alternative History of American Popular Music*. New York: Oxford University Press, 2011.

Wald, Gayle. "From Spirituals to Swing: Sister Rosetta Tharpe and Gospel Crossover."
    American Quarterly 55, no. 3 (2003): 387–416.

Wald, Gayle. "'Have a Little Talk': Listening to the B-Side of History." *Popular Music* 24,
    no. 3 (October 1, 2005): 323–37.

Wald, Gayle. *Shout, Sister, Shout!: The Untold Story of Rock-and-Roll Trailblazer Sister
    Rosetta Tharpe.* Boston: Beacon Press, 2007.

Ward, Brian. *Just My Soul Responding: Rhythm and Blues, Black Consciousness, and Race
    Relations.* Berkeley: University of California Press, 1998.

Wexler, Jerry, and David Ritz. *Rhythms and Blues: A Life in American Music.*
    New York: Knopf, 1993.

Whitburne, Joel, ed. *Billboard Pop Hits Singles and Albums, 1940-1954.* Menomonee
    Falls, WI: Record Research, 2002.

Williams, Raymond. "Base and Superstructure in Marxist Theory." In his *Problems in
    Materialism and Culture,* 31–49. London: Verso, 1980.

Winslow, Richard. "The $100 Riot." *Wesleyan,* vol 75, 1993.

Winter, Jay. *Sites of Memory, Sites of Mourning: The Great War in European Cultural
    History.* Cambridge: Cambridge University Press, 1998.

Worthen, W. B. "Disciplines of the Text/Sites of Performance." *TDR (1988-)* 39, no. 1
    (1995): 13–28.

Yang, Mina. "Orientalism and the Music of Asian Immigrant Communities in California,
    1924-1945." *American Music* 19, no. 4 (2001): 385–416.

Zak, Albin. *I Don't Sound Like Nobody: Remaking Music in 1950s America.* Ann
    Arbor: University of Michigan Press, 2010.

Žižek, Slavoj. "Grimaces of the Real, or When the Phallus Appears." *October* 58 (Fall
    1991): 44–68.

INDEX